First Light

BERKLEY BOOKS BY AMY E. DEAN

Caring for the Family Soul

First Light

First Light

Morning Meditations for Awakening to the Living Planet

AMY E. DEAN

BERKLEY BOOKS, NEW YORK

This book is an original publication of
The Berkley Publishing Group.

FIRST LIGHT: MORNING MEDITATIONS
FOR AWAKENING TO THE LIVING PLANET

A Berkley Book/published by arrangement with
the author

PRINTING HISTORY
Berkley trade paperback edition/November 1997

The Putnam Berkley World Wide Web site address is
http://www.berkley.com

ISBN: 0-425-16000-9

BERKLEY®
Berkley Books are published by The Berkley Publishing Group, a
member of Penguin Putnam Inc.,
200 Madison Avenue, New York, New York, 10016.
BERKLEY and the "B" design are trademarks belonging to Berkley
Publishing Corporation.

PRINTED IN THE UNITED STATES OF AMERICA

10 9 8 7 6 5 4 3 2 1

TO MARYANN,

for sharing nature with me

First Light

"It seems to me," Irish playwright, poet, and essayist Oscar Wilde observed shortly before the turn of the century, "that we all look at Nature too much, and live with her too little." Nearly a century later, those words still ring true. For what is it that you talk about in the morning with your coworkers? Surely not the beautiful sunrise you saw on your morning commute, the boisterous songs of the birds in the park, or the smell of a new season in the air. Rather, you discuss the bumper-to-bumper traffic or the crowded buses or subways, the television show you watched the night before, how you hate to get up in the morning, or how busy your day is going to be. Even though you may sense the nature that's around you—the trees in your yard or along your street, the birds that flutter about your door, the flowers in your garden, the rainbow that briefly reveals its magical arch in the sky, the smell of freshly mown grass that invades your nostrils, the crackling sounds of autumn leaves beneath your feet, the misty rain that caresses your cheeks, the moon and stars that shine in the night sky—what usually captures your attention is not the enjoyment and appreciation of such subtle, sensual, natural pleasures but what you've already done in your life, what you're doing in your life, or what you're about to do.

Decades before Wilde wrote the above-mentioned words, American writer and naturalist Henry David Thoreau penned, "If a man walks in the woods for love of them half of each day, he is in danger of being regarded as a loafer; but if he spends his whole day as a speculator, shearing off those woods and making earth bald before her time, he is esteemed an industrious and enterprising citizen. As if a town had no interest in its forests but to cut them down!" Turn back the hands of time even further, to the end of the seventeenth century, and heed English poet and artist William Blake's timely advice: "Great things are done when men and mountains meet;/This is not done by jostling in the street."

To understand your destiny, you need to understand your universe. To understand your universe, you have to learn the language of a different world. To learn the language of a different world, you need to let the trees and the stones and the wild animals and the babbling brooks and the crashing waves teach you what you can never learn from books. To receive these lessons, you need to consult with nature in everything you do. To consult with nature in everything you do, you have to live in agreement with nature. To live in agreement with nature, you must "Hold your hands out over the earth as over a flame," advised American nature writer Henry Beston. "To all who love her, who open to her the doors of their veins, she gives of her strength, sustaining them with her own measureless tremor of dark life. Touch the earth, love the earth, honour the earth, her plains, her valleys, her hills, and her seas; rest your spirit in her solitary places. For the gifts of life are the earth's and they are given to all, and they are the songs of birds at daybreak, Orion and the Bear, and dawn seen over the ocean from the beach."

FIRST LIGHT: Morning Meditations for Awakening to the Living Planet offers 366 different ways to forge a connection with nature or to strengthen an existing connection so you can celebrate nature, nurture it, protect it, meditate upon it, trust it, understand it, be intrigued by it, feel responsible toward it, heal it, love it. This is a book to keep on your nightstand so you can open it in the morning after you open your eyes, to read as you sip your coffee or eat your breakfast, to take with you on your commute, to pack with your lunch, or to tote along with you on your forays into nature. Use a discarded bird feather, pressed wildflower, autumn leaf, or twig to hold your place for each new day's reading, or turn the pages and skim through a variety of readings at your leisure. Read what so many other people have learned from nature and then reflect on what each of those lessons can teach you not only about your connection with the living planet, but also your responsibility in ensuring a vital, thriving planet for future generations.

First Light

"Hold your hands out over the earth as over a flame. To all who love her, who open to her the doors of their veins, she gives of her strength, sustaining them. . . . Touch the earth, love the earth, honour the earth, her plains, her valleys, her hills, and her seas; rest your spirit in her solitary places. For the gifts of life are the earth's and are given to all, and they are the songs of the birds at daybreak . . . and dawn seen over the ocean from the beach."

—AMERICAN NATURE WRITER HENRY BESTON

HONORING THE EARTH

The start of a new year can be a time of mixed emotions. On the one hand, a new year holds promise, offers a clean slate, rejuvenates, and provides a "second chance." On the other hand, it can be a time when you confront the many choices you've made thus far in your life, a time of intensely discomforting emotional reckoning, or a time when you begin to question your ability to achieve all your goals.

Yet you can make this new year different by resolving not to look *within* you at what you can or need to do for yourself, but *around* you, at the world in which you live. When was the last time you noticed the natural world? When did you last pay attention to the sights, the sounds, the smells, the feel, and the taste of nature? When did you last look to nature as a sustaining, strengthening support that could guide you through difficult times or trying moments?

Today, resolve to spend each morning awakening in peace and harmony to a living, lively planet. Open your eyes to the beauty that is quietly being offered to you each day. Spend time each day discovering or rediscovering your spirituality through a connection to nature. And have as your goal to give something back to nature that will preserve it and protect it for each new year.

I resolve to honor the earth and
protect the gifts she gives me.

"OUT-OF-DOORS, n. That part of one's environment upon which no government has been able to collect taxes. Chiefly useful to inspire poets."

—AMERICAN WRITER AMBROSE BIERCE

NATURE FOR FREE

To enjoy a new snowfall, you can spend a lot of money on the best equipment and fanciest outfit, drive a few hours, shell out a few bills for an all-day lift ticket, wait your turn in a long lift line, and then experience a brief adrenaline-pounding rush of shushing down the side of a mountain.

Or you can throw on a few layers of mismatched clothes, open your back door, step into a pair of used cross-country skiis, and break a few trails. You can strap on a pair of snowshoes and leave your mark next to the prints of rabbit, deer, and fox. You can join the hordes of youngsters on a hill in a city park and flop down on a cheap piece of plastic for a jouncing joyride. You can roll snow and fashion it into a snow character.

The true wonder of nature is that it's free. While national parks, white-water-rafting expeditions, climbs up Mt. Everest, and downhill skiing all have their price to experience nature, in reality there's a great deal more nature you can enjoy without paying anything. Nature can be just a short drive from home. Nature can be just a short walk away. Nature can be right out your back door. Nature can even be experienced as you sit in your home, watching the sun shine brightly over a night snowfall as the winter birds joyously breakfast at your feeders.

Today, enjoy nature for free. Whether you're in for a blustery, bundle-up experience; a sloshy, slushy experience; or a balmy, tropical vacation experience, enjoy being out-of-doors and in nature. It's worth it!

Nature is always affordable to me.

> *"All the world was before me and every day was a holiday, so it did not seem important to which one of the world's wildernesses I first should wander."*
>
> —SCOTTISH-BORN AMERICAN NATURALIST JOHN MUIR

ABOUT JOHN MUIR

John Muir, who lived from 1838 to 1914, was one of the most notable spokespeople for the wilderness. "When I was a boy in Scotland," he wrote, "I was fond of everything that was wild, and all my life I've been growing fonder and fonder of wild places." He worked eleven years on his family's frontier homestead in Wisconsin; studied geology, chemistry, and botany at the University of Wisconsin; tramped up the Mississippi and into the wilds of Canada; and walked a thousand miles from Indiana to the Gulf of Mexico.

While working in Yosemite as a sheepherder and mill hand, Muir was thrown into the national spotlight when he contradicted scientific belief that a sudden collapse of the earth's surface had created the spectacular Yosemite Valley. His discovery of sixty-five living glaciers in the Sierra supported the fact that the valleys had, in actuality, been sculpted by ice.

But Muir achieved his greatest recognition—and left his most indelible mark—when he devoted himself completely to conservation issues and for twenty-two years served as the first president of the Sierra Club. He successfully battled to make Yosemite a national park, although he was unsuccessful in preventing Yosemite's Hetch Hetchy Valley from being dammed and flooded into a municipal reservoir.

Today, thanks to the work of John Muir, you can experience your own "spiritual affinity" with mountains, trees, and glaciers. And you can return the favor by giving something of yourself today to protecting the world before you.

I support a cause or organization that protects nature.

"And it may have been that his only happy moments were these at dawn, when he went with his dog over the known ways, freeing his bronchial tubes of the catarrh that had oppressed his night, and watching as color gradually emerged from the indistinct gray among the field rows and the olive branches, and recognizing the song of the morning birds one by one."

—ITALIAN WRITER ITALO CALVINO

A DOG'S POINT OF VIEW

To own a dog means that you also own nature. For your relationship with your dog requires that the two of you share a relationship with nature that begins with the first light of day and ends as darkness falls. The runs, walks, and hikes you take with your pet carry you through city parks and quiet suburban tracts, across peaceful pastures and forest paths, and over rugged mountain trails. The tail-wagging glee your dog shows at the first hint that you'll soon be going outdoors or the impatient nudge of a cold, wet nose—which you may pretend not to notice as you snuggle under your bedcovers for a few more minutes of sleep—can be more incessant and arousing than any alarm clock.

It doesn't matter if it's raining, snowing, or sleeting; the morning chatter of squirrels and songbirds is the canine call of the wild. Each day comes to your dog new and fresh and full of promise; your dog is not bounded by days of the week, business meetings, deadlines, weekly shopping expeditions, or other obligations and commitments that prevent you from looking forward to the day.

Perhaps it's time to start today to adopt more of your canine's outlook on life. Each morning can be a new beginning—a time for joy and play, a time for fresh air and sunshine, a time for bounding around, a time of canine delight!

I learn how to enjoy this morning from my dog.

"If we lived on a planet with no cycle of seasons, we would miss the beauty and wonder of spring's renewal, of summer's bounty and fall's glowing moments. Winter's time of healing and sleep and preparation for regeneration is also necessary to the human heart, if in more subtle ways."

—WRITER JANE L. MICKELSON

ENERGY CYCLES

Cyclical patterns occur throughout nature: an orchard tree blossoms in springtime, bears fruit in the summer, drops its leaves in the fall, and remains dormant in the winter before springing forth with new life.

Like the seasons, you undergo daily cycles in your emotions as well as your physical energy. For example, you may be aware that there are times during the day when your energy flows the strongest. Maybe you're a morning person who arises feeling alert and ready to exercise or begin other activities but then find that your energy level ebbs in mid-afternoon or early evening. Or you may consider yourself to be the world's slowest-moving morning person but then find yourself awake and alert in the afternoon and long into the night.

As well, your body has its own cycles, which, as you age, change from year to year and decade to decade. Just as the fruit tree bears varying amounts and qualities of fruit from year to year, so, too, you may recognize previous years in which you accomplished a great deal and other years in which your achievements were relatively low-key.

Today, respect the energy cycles around you as well as the energy cycles within you, and you'll find that you'll be happier and more productive.

I accept and work with the energy cycles of my life.

"There is an art to wandering. If I have a destination, a plan—an objective—I've lost the ability to find serendipity. I've become too focused, too single-minded. I am on a quest, not a ramble. I search for the Holy Grail of particularity and miss the chalice freely offered, filled and overflowing."
—NATURALIST AND WRITER CATHY JOHNSON

THE SPIRITUALITY OF NATURE

Each day you may pay attention to your physical and intellectual goals—you eat, you exercise, you rest, you read the paper, you do your chores, you work, or take care of others. But do you also pay attention to your goals for daily spiritual renewal? If you neglect taking care of your body, it will eventually break down. So, too, can you become emotionally imbalanced and find your world filled with conflict if you avoid meeting your spiritual goals.

Setting aside time each day for moments of reflection is the best way to pay attention to your spiritual goals. This may seem like self-indulgence when you feel there are so many other things you need to do or that there are "better" uses of your time. Yet it's one of the most responsible things you can do for yourself.

When you wake up in the morning, say out loud the words of this Navaho song: "Walk on a rainbow trail; walk on a trail of song, and about you will be beauty." Then go outside and make contact with nature. Go for a walk in the still-dark early morning. Wander from your home without a set plan or destination. Take in deep breaths of fresh morning air. Notice how the sky changes colors. Watch the world wake up. Then return home at first light. Do this for one morning a week, and you'll soon begin all your days more spiritually centered.

I balance my intellectual and physical needs with spiritual ones.

"Then to my morning work. First I take an axe and pail and go in search of water, if that not be a dream. After a cold and snowy night I needed a divining rod to find it. Every winter the liquid and trembling surface of the pond . . . becomes solid to the depth of a foot or more . . ."
—NATURALIST AND WRITER HENRY DAVID THOREAU

FINDING THE PIONEER SPIRIT

Can you imagine a time when the piece of ground you lived on was occupied only by buffalo? Think of how difficult it must have been being hundreds of miles by horse and buggy from the nearest general store. What if your child got smallpox and you lived miles from a doctor? Or, worse, what if there was no doctor?

Today you live in a much different world. Your house or apartment may be sitting on landfill. Twenty-four-hour supermarkets and convenience stores are as close as a five-minute drive. Walk-in medical clinics and discount pharmacies keep your medicine cabinet stocked with a variety of supplies. And you're blessed with an endless supply of water regulated by the mere twist of your wrist.

Where has the true American pioneer spirit gone—the spirit of independence and pride a person felt from being able to live each day to the fullest without the benefit of material possessions and creature comforts but with a sharp mind, grit, and determination? Living centenarians are the last of the true pioneers in this country. They lived at a time when nature was their vital provider. Even though nature was sometimes cold and cruel, nature was also life-sustaining.

Rediscover this pioneer spirit today by talking to an older friend or family member. Find out what life was like for them. Learn what they persevered through so your life could be much easier today.

I recognize and learn about the pioneers in my life.

"In nature there are neither rewards nor punishments—there are consequences."

—AMERICAN ATTORNEY R. D. INGERSOLL

INTERCONNECTIONS

In the 1950s, the World Health Organization tried to eliminate malaria in northern Borneo by using the pesticide dieldrin to kill mosquitoes that were carrying the disease. Almost immediately, the project appeared to be a success. The mosquitoes disappeared; incidences of malaria dramatically decreased. But then something strange happened. The roofs of the villagers began falling in on them, and the people faced the threat of a typhoid epidemic. Why? The thatched roofs collapsed because the dieldrin also killed the wasps and insects that ate the caterpillars that fed on the roofs; hundreds of lizards died from eating the poisoned mosquitoes, the village cats died from eating the poisoned lizards, and rats began to run rampant through the village, carrying typhus-infested fleas with them.

The moral of the story is, everything in life is interconnected; eliminating even one living thing can have detrimental effects and even larger implications upon others. To maintain the delicate balance of life, every living thing must be respected and embraced.

Start today to see all of creation as one. Begin by experiencing the inherent connections between yourself and other people as well as other living things. Recognize that you need to love and accept every living person and every living thing in order to truly harmonize with yourself and the world. As French marine explorer Jacques Yves Cousteau has said, "We must love life in all its forms, even in those which we find least attractive."

I foster and embrace my interconnection with all living things.

"Yet it is a singular contradiction that in their outlines old mountains look young, and young mountains look old. . . . All the gauntness, leanness, angularity, and crumbling decrepitude are with the young mountains; all the smoothness, plumpness, graceful, flowing lines of youth are with the old mountains."

—AMERICAN WRITER AND NATURALIST JOHN BURROUGHS

AGING AS RENEWAL

Your beliefs about aging may be based on a simple rule that one first must grow progressively older, then one must grow progressively weaker and more decrepit, and finally one must eventually die. But what if, instead of growing weaker and more decrepit, you grew more youthful, more spry, more mature, more experienced, more joyous, more content? In nature, the oldest mountains, rivers, forests, gorges, and deserts are the most impressive. Garden perennials multiply and flourish with each succeeding year. Vines and ivy grow more lush with each decade. Rocks at the seashore and in mountain streams become more finely polished over time. And even though Old Faithful spouts less majestically and more unpredictably than in previous decades, it is still quite impressive.

In terms of chronological years you will grow progressively older, and in terms of mortality you will eventually die, but the true reality about aging is that your mind, body, and spirit can be in a continual state of renewal throughout your life. Start today to think about aging in a different way—a way that allows more time for beginnings rather than time for just an ending. Be willing to pursue new knowledge, develop new skills, and explore new ways of looking at the world to keep your mind and body growing. As well, strengthen or rekindle your spiritual faith through prayer, meditation, and connection with nature.

Every day I improve my mind, body, and spirit.

"Something will have gone out of us as a people if we ever let the remaining wilderness be destroyed; if we permit the last virgin forests to be turned into comic books and plastic cigarette cases; if we drive the few remaining members of the wild species into zoos or to extinction; if we pollute the last clean air and dirty the last clean streams and push our paved roads through the last of the silence. . . ."

—WRITER WALLACE STEGNER

EXERCISING NATURAL CONTROL

Just one generation ago, most people bought food in bulk in local stores. You probably remember being in the kitchen of your mother or grandmother and seeing on the countertop canisters filled with sugar, tea, rice, flour, coffee, and other dry goods that were purchased in reusable cotton bags. But today you live in a "paper-or-plastic?" choke-a-fish or kill-a-tree world. In fact, you live in a society that is so wasteful that it thinks nothing of destroying thousands of trees for the privilege of reading a single edition of the Sunday newspaper.

Can you learn to exercise natural control in your life—to learn how not to waste things in your home or business? Can you start to have an impact on controlling the amount of new construction that's being done in your neighborhood or the city or town in which you live by showing your opposition to the continued destruction of natural areas? Can you visit museums, local zoos, and nearby aquariums and observe the treatment of animals in captivity to ensure there's no abuse? Can you purchase less plastic and fewer packaged materials and buy in larger quantities or in bulk? Can you exert more control in your life by becoming aware of how much you crave and by starting to limit such excesses? Can you do all these things—and more? Your fate, and the fate of future generations, depends upon it.

I control wastefulness to preserve my world.

"*I like trees because they seem more resigned to the way they have to live than other things do.*"

—AMERICAN NOVELIST WILLA CATHER

ACCEPTING THIS SPACE AND TIME

If a tree's soil becomes dry or low in valuable minerals, the tree can't pull up its roots and move to a better place. Instead, the tree spreads its roots deeper and wider, seeking more fertile ground; as well, it makes the surrounding soil richer by dropping dead branches and leaves to mulch the ground below. The tree also remains firm in the wind, bends but doesn't break under the weight of ice and snow, and gives shade, shelter, and nourishment to the ground below.

Beginning today, if you can think of yourself as a tree firmly planted in your particular space and time, you can learn to be more accepting of what's going on in your life right now. You can learn to grow no matter how difficult or trying your situation or how unsupportive your environment. You can learn to move with the winds of change and bend with the weight of difficulties while still standing firm and tall. You can continue to change and grow, even at those times when it seems impossible.

You, too, can be as strong and enduring as a tree if you accept, rather than reject, your current space and time. Push down your roots deeply and hold on securely, and you'll see the truth in Sarah Orne Jewett's words: "There's sometimes a good hearty tree growin' right out of the bare rock, out o' some crack that just holds the roots; right on the pitch o' them bare stony hills where you can't seem to see a wheel-barrowful o' good earth in a place, but that tree'll keep a green top in the driest summer."

I accept where I am right now in my life.

*"No two turtles ever lunched together with the idea of promoting anything.
. . . Turtles do not work day and night to perfect explosive devices that
wipe out Pacific islands and eventually render turtles sterile. Turtles never
use the word 'implementation' or the phrases 'hard core' and 'in the last
analysis.' No turtle ever rang another turtle back on the phone. In the last
analysis, a turtle, although lacking know-how, knows how to live."*

—AMERICAN ESSAYIST E. B. WHITE

A "NO-COMPETITION" DAY

Imagine what it would be like if the animal kingdom was as
competitive as man. Beavers would push and shove at one
another as they strove to build the most striking den—one that
would be featured on the cover of *Den Beautiful*. Hyenas would
be giving each other "high fives" every time they killed a ga-
zelle. Owls would be excitedly hooting about their nightly
mouse maneuvers. Bees would be awarded blue ribbons for
their honey. Peacocks would stage beauty contests. Camels
would run marathons; cheetahs, 10Ks. Lions would have men's
heads stuffed and mounted on the walls of their dens.

Certainly animals compete over many things—territories,
nests, mates, and food. Certainly many of the strongest animals
survive and many of the weaker ones don't. But although animals must compete with one another—and, oftentimes, with
humanity—for their survival, animals don't think in terms of
"us versus them." They don't equate their gains with success
and their losses with failure. They don't feel ecstasy with victory
or agony with defeat. They set no goals. They live each day
without the need to win or lose.

Imagine what today could be like if you went at your own
pace and did what you wanted to do, simply for the fun of it.

I enjoy today as a "no-competition" day.

"Among all our good people, not one in a thousand sees the sun rise once in a year. They know nothing of the morning. Their idea of it is that it is that part of the day which comes along after a cup of coffee and a piece of toast."

—AMERICAN STATESMAN AND ORATOR DANIEL WEBSTER

WAKE UP WITH NATURE

What do you know of the morning? Make the wilderness your home, and you'll find that morning is always a time of joyful celebrations, wonderous awakenings, ever-changing landscapes, and resounding glories. Each morning the sky presents a new palette of colors, each morning the birds sing a new tune, each morning the air feels new, and each morning the earth begins anew.

But make a city or a place in suburbia your home, and morning most often is a time of unhappy rituals, rude awakenings, unappealing sights, and deafening noises. Morning is probably a time you dread, unless it's a Saturday or a Sunday morning. Yet even on those days, sleeping in or puttering around your home can prevent you from truly enjoying and appreciating the morning.

While it may be hard to see the natural wonder at the start of each new day, if you can begin your day before the pressures and stresses and endless rushing around begin, then you can awaken the way nature does—slowly, subtly, quietly, carefully. For the sunrise doesn't leap up each morning over the horizon; it gradually eases its way up, sending its rays like long limbs over the land in one great big morning stretch.

To truly know the morning, you must experience it. Just one morning a week, get up fifteen minutes earlier. Watch the natural world rouse itself out of slumber and slowly come to life.

I experience nature's enticing wake-up call.

"The touching appeal of nature, as I have called it therefore, the 'Do something kind for me,' is not so much a 'Live upon me and thrive by me' as 'Live with me, somehow, and let us make together what we may do for each other—something that is not merely estimable in greasy greenbacks.'"

—WRITER HENRY JAMES

MUTUAL PROTECTION

The relationship human beings ought to have with nature should not be, as some might preach, equal, for there can be no equity when one part of the relationship can't speak for itself, can't communicate its wants or needs, and can't make changes to ensure its health and growth. Instead, human beings' relationship with nature must be one of reciprocal protection.

But unless and until you can protect every living thing, nature can't protect you. Poisons spewed into the atmosphere poison the air you breathe. The fertilizers and pesticides that are sprayed over fields seep into the ground and pollute rivers, streams, and lakes, forcing you to drink bottled water. Fish fill with mercury. Your skin burns quickly and the rate of skin cancer soars because of the depletion of the ozone layer. Gulls and aquatic animals choke on refuse and leaking fuel. Acid rain burns the once-rich soil. Diverted water sources parch water-dependent living things and create deserts out of forests. Prey is eliminated or relocated, causing predator starvation and senseless slaughter. Moose and bear stroll down thoroughfares; hawks roost on the sills of city buildings.

But treat the land and every living creature as if they were your children, and you offer them ultimate protection. What the land and every living creature then return to you protects the quality of your life.

I protect nature so nature protects me.

"Once in his life a man ought to concentrate his mind upon the remembered earth. He ought to give himself up to a particular landscape in his experience; to look at it from as many angles as he can, to wonder upon it, to dwell upon it."

—WRITER N. SCOTT MOMADAY

CHILDHOOD MEMORIES

Imagine that this morning the clock turns back in time to when you were a child. It's January 15, and you're in the sixth grade. School is canceled for the day. What do you do? Close your eyes and let your mind take you back in time. Remember what you could have been doing on this day.

Perhaps you're outside playing with friends—throwing snowballs, building snow forts, jumping from snowbanks. Maybe you're fishing at a nearby pond or scanning a stream for tadpoles. Perhaps you're eating your breakfast high above the ground in your treehouse. Or maybe you're rock climbing, beachcombing, or hiking. As you allow such memories to filter through your mind, recall some of the other things you used to do outdoors when you were younger, in all of nature's seasons—camping, tracking wild animals, collecting rocks, sledding, climbing trees, swimming, or just lying on your back and looking up at the clouds as they drifted across the sky.

Even though the childhood home and cherished pond may no longer exist doesn't mean you can never revisit them. All you need to do is close your eyes and remember. They will always be there for you.

I go back in time whenever I wish to keep my childhood memories alive.

"We are here to witness the creation and to abet it. We are here to notice each thing so each thing gets noticed. . . . We are here to bring to consciousness the beauty and power that are around us and to praise the people who are here with us. We witness our generation and our times. We watch the weather. Otherwise, the creation would be playing to an empty house."

—ESSAYIST, POET, AND TEACHER ANNIE DILLARD

THE HERITAGE OF LIFE

Nature shows you that you have a place in the living heritage of life every time you look around you at the passion, the challenges, the grandeur, the beauty, the discipline, and the opportunities represented by all of nature's wonders. Each and every wonder is a part of you; you are as profound as the sea, as gentle as a snowflake, as beautiful as the side of a mountain, as soft as the warm sand, as active as the environment in which you live.

Your heritage of being a member of humanity, too, gives you justification and validation for being here on this planet each day. Your heritage encourages you to be strong. Your heritage helps you to trust and have faith in yourself. Your heritage implores you to act. Your heritage urges you sometimes to abandon the search for security and reach out to the risk of living. Your heritage tells you to accept living and dying equally. Your heritage stretches your mind and body. Your heritage pushes you to go out often in the world—both the natural world and the world in which you oftentimes live elbow to elbow with others—to go out into the Great Unknown as well as the Great Known in order to know more about yourself and the world around you.

You can make your time on earth most worthwhile by becoming more conscious of it—by noticing, every day, the wonder of creation in all living things.

I am here to witness the creation.

" 'You silly thing,' said Fritz, my eldest son, sharply, 'don't you know that we must not settle what God is to do for us? We must have patience and wait His time.' "

—WRITER JOHANN R. WYSS

SPIRITUAL RESCUE

Johann R. Wyss's classic story of the shipwrecked Robinson family, *The Swiss Family Robinson,* provides a lesson in patience that is unheard of today. It was years before their rescue. They didn't know what their fate would be on the unfamiliar island. Yet they survived every day by working together, making use of the natural resources that surrounded them, and keeping a strong faith in a Power greater than themselves.

Today individuals are rarely so stranded from rescue, so dependent upon natural resources for their survival, or so cut off from civilization for such a long period of time. Even travelers to some of the most remote locations on earth—Mt. Everest, for example—are linked by electronic technology to friends, authorities, and loved ones who, while they may not be able to reach them if they are in danger or distress to save their lives, are nonetheless afforded access.

Today a novel such as *The Swiss Family Robinson* might be seen as an antiquated fantasy. As Argentine-born English writer W. H. Hudson opines, "For we are no longer isolated, standing like starry visitors on a mountain-top, surveying life from the outside; but are on a level with and part and parcel of it; and if the mystery of life daily deepens, it is because we view it more closely and with clearer vision." Yet a clearer vision and less isolation still requires you to be patient and to trust all matters of your life and fate to the care of a spiritual Power that works in Its own time and in Its own way.

I trust that there is a guiding power and presence in my life.

> "*Tiny white crystalline flakes falling through the air, billions of them which when you take some in your hand and study them, no two are the same. You can't study them long because they melt in your hand, but no two are the same, that's what they say. But who said this? Who would do a study of billions of snowflakes to prove no repetition?*"
>
> —AMERICAN HUMORIST GARRISON KEILLOR

A WORLD OF WONDER

What is wonder? The oldest English prose ever written, around A.D. 720 in *Beowulf*, uses the word *wonder* for the first time, translated from Old English verse to mean "marvel" or "miracle." But today wonder, used as both a noun and a verb, has several different meanings, from "marvel" and "miracle" to "to be filled with curiosity."

To wonder at the world in which you live is to see beyond the mere existence of something or to move beyond taking that something for granted, such as a snowflake in the winter, and to look at it through different eyes—eyes that question, that seek to discover, and that desire to understand not in a textbook sense but in a creative sense, such as wondering why no two snowflakes are alike.

You can live in this world on a day-to-day basis without ever questioning the existence of even the most obvious things. You can get by in this world by taking pleasure from knowing the responses to one-answer questions, such as "What's the capital of South Dakota?" You can consult encyclopedias and other reference books to learn the answers you don't know.

Or you can live in this world on a day-to-day basis always questioning, always appreciating, always seeking to discover. Live with wonder, and your life will be wonder-filled!

I marvel at all the wonders of the world.

"I was born upon the prairie, where the wind blew free, and there was nothing to break the light of the sun. I was born where there were no enclosures, and where everything drew a free breath. . . . I know every stream and every wood between the Rio Grande and the Arkansas. I have hunted and lived over that country. I lived like my fathers before me, and like them, I lived happily."

—YAMPARETHKA COMANCHE CHIEF TEN BEARS

BEING TOLERANT

Although the many tribes that once lived and flourished in America centuries ago used symbols to express their beliefs about creation and were often thought to be godless savages because they believed that the Great Spirit spoke to the Indian through nature—through the howl of a wolf, through the sound of a brook, through the whispering of the wind, through the shape of the clouds—in reality all Indians believed in one God, one Creator, one Great Loving Spirit who watched over all living things. Despite spiritual differences and unique tribal prayers, for the most part tribes shared territories in peace, harmony, and tolerance. Artist George Catlin noted in his journals of 1830, "I love a people who have always made me welcome to the best they had . . . who are honest without laws . . . who never take the name of God in vain . . . who worship God without a Bible . . . and I believe God loves them too."

Today, remember that you share the world with a variety of different "tribes" of people who may worship differently from you, celebrate differently from you, and love differently from you. Their desire, as well as yours, is to live in this world they share with you in peace and harmony. Just as nature shows its tolerance by the variety of different species who share air space, ground space, ocean space, and even underground space, so, too, can you be tolerant of the differences of others.

I accept the differences of others by sharing the world with them.

"We went and sat in a certain beech-wood on a hill, a place of extraordinary beauty looking like an early Gothic cathedral, and with a glimpse of distant views in all directions. The morning was fresh and dewy, and I began to think that perhaps there might be happiness in human life."

—ENGLISH MATHEMATICIAN AND PHILOSOPHER
BERTRAND RUSSELL

FINDING HAPPINESS

Have you made happiness a goal? You can't find happiness by simply deciding, "Today I'll be happy" or "Today I'll be happier than I was yesterday." Happiness ought never to be a conditional aspect of your life; it's unrealistic to expect that you'll feel happiness once you get a raise or the coveted corner office. And happiness ought never to be an expected outcome for things that are sought after, worked hard for, or struggled over. There's much that you can expect to gain from such efforts—financial security, intellectual stimulation, or satisfaction of a physical or emotional need. But happiness ought not to be considered as a goal or a gain, for happiness just exists. Search for it, and you'll never find it. Yet pay no attention to it, and it will be there, right in front of you.

Nature brings you happiness through the lessons it teaches you, such as don't take yourself or life too seriously, laugh and play more, and focus less on answers and solutions and more on the things that bring you pleasure. Welcome happiness when it comes to you, for it is a wonderful gift—totally unexpected, yet never undesired. Happiness comes from being one with a moment, when you suddenly realize that the breeze through the trees, the bend of the branches, the mist rising from the top of a hill, and the sky brightening around you are all extensions of you.

I lose myself in a moment with nature and, in so doing, find happiness.

"One touch of nature makes the whole world kin."
—ENGLISH DRAMATIST AND POET WILLIAM SHAKESPEARE

MORNING *PRO MUSICA*

All of nature is song. Sometimes the song is a joyous burst of sheer ecstasy, full of bright, rich melodies and thrilling chords that inspire movement. Sometimes the song is an answering call, an echoed response of reassurance and companionship. Sometimes the song is deep and mournful, with steady, repeated refrains filled with sorrow and longing. Sometimes the song is a soothing lullaby, providing comfort and closure as darkness falls.

Do you pay attention to the songs of life that the birds serenade you with each day? Do you know what their songs mean? Do you know how to respond to them, to harmonize with them, to be touched by them?

The way you live your life may keep you too busy to listen to the morning melodies of the birds. As well, you may be so caught up each day in chipping away at lists of obligations, responsibilities, and countless other pursuits that you neglect to give yourself time to listen to nature's morning symphonies. You may get up each day taking for granted that the birds will sing or that they even are singing, without ever really hearing them. Or you may treat nature's solos as part of the normal background noise of life—a sort of natural elevator music.

But the song of the birds is the song of life; to experience it, you need to listen to it, appreciate it, harmonize with it—be touched by it in some small way. The song is an everlasting proclamation to life in all its glories; to hear it is to feel how wonderful it is to be alive.

I listen to the birds sing their songs of life.

"Go—not knowing where. Bring—not knowing what. The path is long, the way unknown."

—RUSSIAN FAIRY TALE

LIVING IN THE PRESENT

There's a Chinese parable in which a wise man journeys to a small village in the mountains, gathers all the villagers together, and tells them that if they care to join him, they can move a mountain together. He explains to them that moving the mountain will be a task to be accomplished over generations. "The truth that you must realize," the wise man tells the villagers, "is that for all the hard work you will do to move this mountain and the many, many hours of labor, in the end it will be as if you only moved a teaspoon of dirt and one small pebble. You will not live to see the finished product—the mountain moved—nor will you even be able to see, on a daily basis, the reward of your work—a mountain taking shape, a peak, a valley."

Rather than refuse to work or to try to devise ways to speed up the process of moving the mountain so the task could be finished and everyone could enjoy the fruits of their labors, the villagers who chose to participate in moving the mountain did so with a smile on their faces. They chose to live in the present moment and focused on the task of moving the mountain, bit by bit. In performing the task, time meant nothing to them, nor did reaching the actual goal of moving the mountain. Rather, it was the task itself, and the ability to focus on that task, that become most important to them.

Can you begin to live your life in such a way that you, too, can do something without the need of an outcome? Can you do something for the sheer pleasure of it, and live solely in the present moment and not in some past or future time?

I live in the present; and so, I love the present.

"If only nature is real and if, in nature, only desire and destruction are legitimate, then, in that all humanity does not suffice to assuage the thirst for blood, the path of destruction must lead to universal annihilation."
—FRENCH-ALGERIAN PHILOSOPHER ALBERT CAMUS

PURCHASING PRESERVATION

The depth charges and mines that exploded in the ocean during World War II may have sunk enemy vessels and gradually weakened Japanese forces, but they also annihilated hundreds of aquatic mammals and fish, many fragile coral reefs, and other natural life that happened to be in the vicinity. While oftentimes nature is mercilessly destroyed because of thoughtless actions—an unextinguished cigarette butt is tossed from a car window and rolls into a dry forest—or for lack of time or interest in pursuing a careful environmental-impact study before chemicals are sprayed indiscriminately or a valuable water source is diverted, what is most unforgivable in the destruction of nature is when living things are *knowingly* harmed. Poachers who slaughter, miners who strip, foresters who fell, fishermen who net, corporations who bury, and developers who level all know the environmental consequences of what they're doing. Yet they don't seem to care or pay heed to the fact that their thirst for whatever goal they want to achieve is quenched by the blood of senseless sacrifice. Over time, sacrifices mount up, the toll becomes greater, the impact more severe, and, eventually, like the atomic bomb that signaled victory over the Japanese empire, the destruction becomes so exorbitant that the annihilation of a valued species, an integral link in the chain of life, cannot be prevented.

What can you do about this? Become a mindful, careful consumer. Refuse to financially support the senseless destruction of any living thing.

I use my purchase power to protect and preserve nature.

"*Nature has no mercy at all. Nature says, 'I'm going to snow. If you have on a bikini and no snowshoes, that's tough. I am going to snow anyway.'*"

—AUTHOR MAYA ANGELOU

NATURE'S POWER

For as technologically advanced as the civilization in which you're living is, nature is still all-powerful. Rain can destroy a farmer's business as well as make it flourish. Snow can bring a metropolis to its knees as well as create recreational activities for millions. Wind can knock down power lines as well as effortlessly dry loads of laundry without the use of gas or electricity. Sunshine can scorch the earth as well as ripen fruits and vegetables. Storms can disrupt schedules, create foul tempers, and challenge many "indestructible" inventions of a civilization that considers it vital to categorize natural elements over which it has no control as either good or bad. Nature, however—like weather—just is; as well, nature's power just is.

One of the most important lessons to be learned from nature concerns its power. You might view this power as controlling, particularly when it's your weekend golf game that has been canceled because of rain or your bad back that aches after shoveling out from another record snowfall. Yet somewhere a garden is being watered while you're fretting and fuming about your missed golf game, and somewhere else a family is joyously building snow caves together in the high snowbanks while you're icing your back. Nature ministers to all equally; it's your interpretation of nature's ministry that determines how you view as well as how you accept nature's power. To honor nature's power, know that you can never possess it, control it, predict it, or prevent it. But know, too, that by honoring nature, you can attain infinite wisdom.

I honor nature's power today; I accept and appreciate this day I've been given.

"I believe in God, only I spell it Nature."
—U.S. ARCHITECT FRANK LLOYD WRIGHT

SPIRITUAL STRENGTH

There's a story of a religious teacher whose daily sermons were wonderful and inspiring, and he often spent hours preparing them. He thought that someday he might collect them into a book and seek a publisher or even appear on his own cable television show so his wonderful words could inspire more than just his small following. With such outcomes in the back of his mind, he was about to begin his sermon one day when a little bird came and sat on the windowsill. It began to sing, and sang away with a full heart. Then it stopped and flew away. The teacher thought for a moment, folded the pages to his prepared sermon, and announced, "The sermon for this morning is over."

While there's great strength you can attain from listening to wise spiritual leaders, great hope you can gain from reading spiritual words, great faith you can gather from prayer and spiritual meditation, and great comfort you can feel from the reassurance of a spiritual adviser, there's also great spiritual strength you can attain, gain, gather, and feel from the natural world. For the natural world is the visible presence of your spiritual source, living proof that a Great Hand sculpts beauty and joy and wonder for you each day. When you connect with the natural world in some way—from listening to the song of a morning bird to letting the soft morning breeze caress your face to tramping through the woods to collect pinecones and boughs for a dining-room centerpiece—you connect with your idea of a Higher Power or a Power Greater Than Yourself. Nature is your daily "direct line" to your spiritual power.

I am spiritually strengthened when I connect with nature.

"Peace of mind produces right values, right values produce right thoughts. Right thoughts produce right actions and right actions produce work which will be a material reflection for others to see of the serenity in the center of it all."

—WRITER ROBERT PIRSIG

GIVING AND RECEIVING

If you were boating on the ocean, accidentally fell overboard, and a stranger saved your life, how would you treat that person? The right thing to do would be to express gratitude for such a selfless act, offer a reward, or ask if you could do something in return. The act of giving and receiving inspires reciprocation; perhaps because of your experience, you might be more willing to extend a hand to another.

Certainly the wrong thing to do would be to hurt, injure, or even contribute to the death of your rescuer. Yet this is what happens every day to nature's ocean rescuers, the gentle dolphin. Off the Japanese island of Iki, thousands of dolphins are slaughtered every year by fishermen who are doing so in order to protect their fishing grounds from such "competitors." In other parts of the world, dolphins are routinely killed for human consumption or used for bait. In the United States, dolphins have been trained and then used to retrieve mines that are too dangerous for human divers; many dolphins have lost their lives as a result.

All living things participate in the process of giving and receiving. Yet humans are the only living creatures who seek to receive and then carefully dole out how much is given in return. Today, begin to do the right thing. Learn to accept and respect the delicate balance of giving and receiving that nature so willingly offers humankind. Treat all of nature's living things as you would want to be treated.

I give and receive with love and compassion.

"This moment, this being, is the thing. My life is all life in little. The moon, the planets, pass around my heart. The sun, now hidden by the round bulk of the earth, shines into me, and in me as well. The gods and angels both good and bad are like the hairs of my own head, seemingly numberless, and growing from within. I people the cosmos from myself, it seems, yet what am I? A puff of dust, or a brief coughing spell, with emptiness and silence to follow."

—WRITER ALEXANDER ELIOT

LIVING A FULL LIFE

Scientist and writer Barry Evans once penned, "Our lives last for two or three billion seconds. The universe is fifteen billion years old." What this means is that even though you have, by today's standards, the ability to live for several decades—perhaps even a century—you are really here on this planet for only a short time. The span of your life, when compared with the span of life itself, is a mere blip. Of course, to some living things, even a handful of seconds—which equates to about six years of your life—is a lifetime.

And yet the true wonder of it all is not how little time you really have, but how much you can learn, grow, experience, and contribute within this short period of time—or, on the other side of the coin, how much time you can potentially waste. For example, if you sit in front of the television each day, on average, for two hours, and you've done this every day from the time you were about seven or eight years old, then simple multiplication will give you a sum total that will reflect the total wasted hours of your life.

Today, take time to assess how you're living out each of the valuable seconds on earth you've been given. Strive to make the most of your life, your time, this moment. Create a full lifetime of living, loving, and learning.

Starting today, I make the most of my time.

"There have always been hard times. There have always been wars and troubles—famine, disease, and such-like—and some folks are born with money, some with none. In the end it is up to the man what he becomes, and none of those other things matters. It is character that counts."

—WRITER LOUIS L'AMOUR

ACCEPTING THE PAST

Have you ever thought, "If I only knew back then what I know now?" Perhaps you think about how you could've handled differently the difficult times you may have had in high school, college, during the first decade of your marriage, or during middle age. Or maybe you stop to think about where you might be in your life right now if you could've used today's knowledge to help you make your decisions years ago. You may question, "Would I still have married when I did? Would I have opted for a degree instead of a job? How might my life be different today?"

Yet nothing in nature besides a human being ever looks longingly back at the past or lives in sorrow or regret over yesterday's experiences or decisions. In nature's view, what has happened, has happened. The past is gone; the present is all that's important. Like a flowing river, no molecule of water ever stays in one place; to remain life-sustaining, the river must flow ever onward.

To live life meaningfully means to be able to live fully in the present. While the past can provide you with a valuable point of reference or may contribute to the maturity and experience you've gained today, ultimately it's how you utilize your learning rather than how you reflect on how or what you learned that makes each present moment count. Today, resolve to live as nature does, flowing ever onward with the current of life.

I live anew each day when I can look forward, not backward.

"My kids ask me, 'Where does the sun go at night?' and 'How come I can suck soda up through a straw?' Later in life they are trained not to ask questions of this kind. Not all of them. Some of them maintain this primordial quality of curiosity. Some of them become artists. Some become composers. Some become physicists. Some become astronomers. These people in a sense have kept the faith. They really want to know what's going on."

—SCIENTIST AND WRITER SHELDON GLASHOW

USING YOUR IMAGINATION

Imagination makes all things probable and, in many cases, possible. Each day, thousands of humanity's winged birds take flight, all because someone once saw birds soaring overhead and asked, "What if?" Walk down any city sidewalk, and you'll see examples of how the human mind has used imagination to translate what exists in nature for its own purposes. Threads of telephone wires drape from location to location—connecting strands in an intricate web that allows you to communicate with others and to receive communication, much as the delicate strands on a spiderweb signal the tiny weaver. Streams of people flow in and out of the ground like busy ants as they tunnel from one location to another on subway systems.

Imagination is the unending ability to wonder—to be continually curious about the world around you. To exercise your imagination every day, stop and notice phenomena in the natural world around you. Pick up a rock from the ground and feel its texture, the solidness of its form. Bend down next to your sleeping dog and feel the gentle rise and fall of each breath. Grow an avocado tree from the pit. Borrow a stethoscope and listen to the sound of your own heartbeat. Be curious, and the world will become an amazing place in which to live!

I exercise my imagination today and every day.

"The land . . . belongs to the first who sits down on his blanket . . . which he has thrown down on the ground, and till he leaves it, no other has a right."

—SHAWNEE INDIAN TECUMSEH

RESPECTING SPACE

Imagine that you spread a blanket in a field to picnic with your family. But then someone picks up your blanket and drags it to another spot. You go to this new location, but then someone else moves your blanket. This happens again and again, until finally your blanket is moved far away from the field.

Tecumseh never accepted the American claim that American freedom meant Indian freedom. He doubted Thomas Jefferson's words that the two races would peacefully merge and spread together across the continent. For he had had his blanket moved many times; he learned that the price of American freedom was the loss of Indian freedom, and that American prosperity would be built on Indian lands. So he stressed to his people Indian unity. He encouraged Indians to renounce drinking and their reliance on the white man's tools and technology. He called for religious renewal as well as recognition that the land belonged to all Indian peoples.

But soon after Tecumseh's failed attempt at Indian unity, American armies invaded Indian lands. At the Battle of the Thames, on October 18, 1813, Tecumseh was killed by the bullet of a white man. Less than ten years later, the Indians found themselves under increasing pressure to surrender their lands and move across the Mississippi. In May of 1830, President Andrew Jackson signed into law the Indian Removal Act. The Indians lost their sovereign rights to the soil of their homelands.

Today, remember that you share this planet with the blankets of many. Respect their blankets so that they, too, might respect yours.

I respect what belongs to others.

"Books on nature seldom mention wind; they are written behind stoves."
—AMERICAN CONSERVATIONIST AND WRITER ALDO LEOPOLD

NATURE'S INTENSITY

Nature has incredible power. Volcanoes erupt, and fiery lava cascades upon villages and people. Torrential rains rearrange hillside topography and wash away homes, cars, and livestock. Earthquakes split the earth and collapse seemingly indestructible buildings and highways like dominoes. Lightning strikes a powerful match to dry forests and ignites frightening bonfires as well as sends deadly currents into unlucky souls. Tornadoes twist like maniacal screws, boring unpredictable paths that leave death and destruction in their wake. No doubt about it—nature can be quite intense. As Will Rogers once opined, "It's the elements that make you great, or break you."

More often than not, nature is gentle with mankind. Winds breathe rhythmically through the trees, the rain sprinkles down upon the earth, the sunshine warms from the cloudless sky, brooks trickle harmlessly down hillsides. But because nature also has such incredible power—fearing nature is sometimes wise, as is staying indoors whenever nature displays its intensity, where you can be sheltered, safe, warm, and secure.

Yet remaining sheltered when conditions improve keeps you from growing; part of growth involves accepting challenges and taking risks. Whether you wish to scale a mountain peak few have scaled before or conquer a lifelong fear by learning how to swim, what's most important is that you sometimes confront nature's intensity. For it's when you strive against great odds that you make the greatest gains.

I conquer a fear and take a risk today.

"The book of nature is like a page written over or printed upon with different-sized characters and in many different languages, interlined and crosslined, and with a great variety of notes and references. There is coarse print and fine print; there are obscure signs and hieroglyphics. . . . It is a book which he reads best who goes most slowly or even tarries long by the way."

—AMERICAN WRITER AND NATURALIST JOHN BURROUGHS

ABOUT JOHN BURROUGHS

The richness of nature was well understood by John Burroughs, preeminent naturalist of the mid–Hudson River and Catskill regions of New York, who lived from 1837 to 1921. A teacher for a short time, as well as a government employee, he spent most of his life working—in his own words—as a "nature essayist." The twenty-seven volumes of Burroughs's work that provide a lasting legacy today were the product of a writing career that spanned half a century.

Although Burroughs camped in Yosemite with John Muir and in Yellowstone with Theodore Roosevelt, as well as traveled with Muir to the Grand Canyon and Alaska, he was less interested in the intensities of such wild, rough locales. Instead, he felt more in tune and in touch with intimate, calm, and more accessible natural places. It was in those places, he felt, that nature was more easily understood and far more fascinating. "One has only to sit in the woods or fields," Burroughs wrote, "or by the shore of the river or lake, and nearly everything of interest will come round to him, the birds, the animals, the insects."

Today, sit in nature for a short time—in the woods, in the fields, or even on a city park bench. Then wait and watch the nature that comes around to you.

I find nature in an intimate, accessible locale.

"Think of our life in nature,—daily to be shown matter, to come in contact with it,—rocks, trees, wind in our cheeks! the solid earth! the actual world! the common sense! contact! Contact! Who are we? where are we?"
—AMERICAN WRITER HENRY DAVID THOREAU

CONTACTING NATURE

When you want to make contact with a person who's important to you, you can make a telephone call. You can plan a visit or get-together. You can touch, embrace, kiss, caress. You can whisper sweet nothings or loudly proclaim outrage. You can give a gift. You can write a letter. You can fax or E-mail. Because making contact with another human being is important to you, you seek avenues through which you can do so. Should you try to make similar contacts with nature? Although there will always be a fundamental distinction between human beings and nature, nature does have a relationship with you; you, too, have a relationship with nature, and because of this, it's important that you make time to make contact with nature.

If you're like most people, you may find it hard—if not impossible—to make daily contact or even sporadic contact with nature. As one unknown source comments, "Everything goes so fast and makes so much noise, and men hurry by without heeding the grass by the roadside, its color, its smell, and the way it shimmers when the wind caresses it." Yet it is in the experience of nature that you can truly find yourself, for nature can teach you about your strengths, how to trust, what the answers are as well as what questions should be asked, how life and death must walk hand in hand, about silences and nothingness, about floundering and discovery, about patience and hope, about magic and wonder, about the differences between loneliness and solitude, and many other valuable lessons.

I learn about myself through my contact with nature.

"The awe one feels in an encounter with a polar bear is, in part, simple admiration for the mechanisms of survival it routinely employs to go on living in an environment that would defeat us in a few days."

—AMERICAN WRITER BARRY LOPEZ

SURVIVAL SKILLS

For all the technological marvels that have been created to make your life easier and more comfortable today—from home heating and cooling systems that keep you warm in the winter and cool in the summer to lightweight fabrics that repel water to tablets that contain all the essential vitamins and minerals you need—unless you've been trained, you could not survive for very long in some of the more common environments in which other human beings thrived years ago.

Long before there were furnaces and insulation, there were logs and mud, animal hides, and—even further back in time—caves. Long before the production of clothing or the manufacture of textiles, there were animal skins. Long before supermarkets and government nutrition guidelines, there was organic farming and an all-you-can-eat-if-you-can-catch-and-kill-it philosophy. This was the way of life for the early settlers; to survive, they had to live close to nature and sometimes even imitate nature—they wore the fur of the beast that could survive in the cold; they drank the fluid of the plant that thrived in the desert heat; they ate the foods other living things ate without getting sick. In those long-ago times, nature provided people with the necessary guidelines for living a better life; today, you get such guidelines from the owner's manual of each new life-enhancing device you purchase.

Today, make it a point to learn one survival skill. Grow with the knowledge of how not only to live with nature, but how to survive in it as well.

Today I learn how to live as well as how to survive.

"When you have seen one ant, one bird, one tree, you have not seen them all."

—AMERICAN ENTOMOLOGIST EDWARD O. WILSON

CHILDHOOD WONDER

A child often experiences great joy and wonder at the natural world—even at such simple things as a discarded bird's feather, a colorful autumn leaf, or a scurrying bug. But as this child grows older, natural awe is often supplanted by an interest in peers, in school, and in activities. Growing older, the young adult is rarely focused on the natural but on the material and the emotional world—love, relationships, career, finances, and living independently. With each succeeding year, the adult comes to believe that nature isn't "where it's at." Where it's at, instead, is in the city, in front of the computer, in the living room watching television, on the telephone, in the midst of a morning or evening commute, in the middle of a project, in the throes of balancing a full-time job with night school, in the day-to-day stresses of single parenthood—in sum, in countless other pursuits, problems, and pastimes.

Sometimes, to get back to nature after you've drifted so far away, you need to see the world more as you did when you were a child. Take time to notice the little things that you pass by each day without notice. Open your mouth during a snowfall; feel and taste the snowflakes on your tongue. Touch and smell the bark of a tree. Watch a pigeon skillfully negotiate its way through the morning crowds. See how the sunlight colors the world differently. Look up at the sky and imagine creatures in the shape of the clouds. Pay less attention to the hustle and bustle of everyday life and more attention to the ebb and flow of nature.

I experience the world today with childlike wonder.

"The duck spreads oil on its feathers with its beak from a small sac above the tail. The feathers then lie smooth and waterproof, reminding us that we too must take time to care for our bodies and equipment."

—AMERICAN POET MARIANNE MOORE

CARING FOR YOURSELF

Since 1900, the average American life span has increased by 50 pecent; Americans are living well into their seventies and eighties rather than their fifties or sixties. Yet there are some things that haven't changed. For example, modern medicine has still not been able to prevent cancers or heart disease or do more than ease the pain and slow the progression of degenerative disorders such as arthritis, diabetes, multiple sclerosis, and osteoporosis. Despite numerous studies, foods still contain inordinately high amounts of fats, and meals are often sporadic, high-caloric, and nutritionally unfulfilling. Timesaving devices still leave less leisure time and do little to alleviate stress. And mental functions, without "exercise," decline with age.

Even though everyone is different and some people are more physically capable, mentally alert, and emotionally capable of handling stress than others, it's up to you to take care of your own body as best as you can. The duck that doesn't take time to oil its feathers puts itself at risk; so, too, do you when you don't place taking care of yourself high on your list of priorities.

Starting today, make time to care for yourself. Resolve to begin to exercise on a regular basis, and then start with a twenty-minute workout. Decide to eat better from now on, and then prepare a meal that's fresh and rich with vitamins. Make up your mind to handle your stress more effectively, and then set aside time in which you can relax. Exercise your mind by learning something new every day.

I make time to take care of myself.

"My father considered a walk among the mountains as the equivalent of churchgoing."

—WRITER ALDOUS HUXLEY

THE CHALLENGE OF THE CLIMB

Where youth may have the stamina, guts, and the desire to take incredible risks, those who are older have the need to seek out challenges—to respond to the challenges in life with a dogged determination as well as a deep, spiritual understanding. While a young person may look at a mountain and think, "I'd like to climb that mountain someday," the youth may not know why that desire exists. Ask, "Why climb such a mountain?" and the youth may not know the reason why or even see the prospect of any gains.

But the older person looks at the mountain and sees it as a challenge to which he must respond. For the older person knows that there is much to be gained from having scaled the mountain—a rugged path filled with challenges and risks, a physically and emotionally stimulating journey, a majestic view, a grand spiritual connection from nearly reaching the heavens, and the personal satisfaction from having attained such a lofty goal.

Mountaineer George Leigh Mallory, who conquered Mt. Everest, once said, "If you cannot understand that there is something in man which responds to the challenge of the mountain and goes out to meet it, that the struggle is the struggle of life itself upward and forever upward, then you won't see why we go. What we get from this adventure is just sheer joy. And joy is, after all, the end of life."

I meet the mountainous challenges in my life for spiritual fulfillment.

"To be seventy years old is like climbing the Alps. You reach a snow-crowned summit, and see behind you the deep valley stretching miles and miles away, and before you other summits higher and whiter, which you may have strength to climb, or may not. Then you sit down and meditate which it will be."

—AMERICAN POET HENRY WADSWORTH LONGFELLOW

NATURAL MATURATION

It's truly remarkable that some of the greatest achievements have been accomplished by those in their mature years. Chaucer wrote *The Canterbury Tales* at quite an advanced age. Jomo Kenyatta was purported to be in his seventies when, in 1964, he became the first president of the republic of Kenya. Charles Darwin wrote *On the Origin of Species* when he was fifty; he completed *The Descent of Man* at the age of sixty-two and *The Power of Movement in Plants* at seventy-one. Charles de Gaulle was sixty-eight years old when he returned to power in France. Benjamin Franklin served on the committee that drafted the Declaration of Independence and was one of its original signers at the age of seventy; at eighty-one, he effected the compromise that made the Constitution of the United States a reality. Golda Meir resigned as Israel's prime minister at the age of seventy-five. George Bernard Shaw wrote his first play when he was thirty-six years old and his last produced play when he was in his late eighties. John Wayne won an Oscar at the age of sixty-two for his starring role in *True Grit*. Cecil B. DeMille produced and directed the Academy Award–winning *The Greatest Show on Earth* when he was seventy-one. And Duncan MacLean won a silver medal at the 1975 World Veterans' Olympics in Canada when he ran two hundred meters in forty-four seconds; he was ninety years old!

I view my age not as a quantity of time, but as a quality of life.

"From my stationary position the most reasonable explanation [for the snowstorm] seemed to be simply that winter had not quite liked the looks of the landscape as she first made it up. She was changing the sheets."

—AMERICAN WRITER JOSEPH WOOD KRUTCH

A NEW SNOWFALL

A snowy day has such charm, with the soft coloring it gives to the landscape and the insulating effect it has upon the usual sounds of the morning. The silent drift and fall of the snowflakes provides a gentle cover to the earth, a fresh cover that makes the world look clean and refreshed. Should the sun break through the clouds—even for a brief moment—the glittering effect of light on white is dazzling, a stunning display of sparkling delight.

A snowy day creates amazing transformations in the city as well as in the country. The city becomes a magnificent fairy-tale empire; the suburbs develop into picture-postcard-perfect winter portraits; the woods are transformed into nature's winter playground as evergreens playfully drop clumps of snow from their branches, squirrels cavort on the ground, and birds chirrup songs of glee.

A snowy day can be restful and relaxing in comparison with other mornings; sometimes when the sun is too bright and there are too many noises, restlessness can take over. But a snowy day guides you toward a more peaceful place in your heart and mind—a place where you can recall all the good memories of past snowfalls as well as participate in the magical miracle of cleansing transformation. A snowy day offers you and all of humanity a new outfit to wear—a change of clothing that gives you a new look, a new energy, and a new focus.

I see a snowy day as a time for rejoicing and renewal.

"Walking through the woods, you can never see far, either ahead or behind, so you move without much of a sense of getting anywhere or of moving at any certain speed. You burrow through the foliage in the air much as a mole burrows through the roots in the ground."

—AMERICAN POET AND WRITER WENDELL BERRY

NECESSARY WORK

For a long time property owners as well as foresters used to dismiss dead and dying trees as useless nuisances that needed to be cleared away as quickly as possible in order to make room for new young growth. But in recent years conservationists and forest ecologists have determined that dead trees—either still standing or fallen—are one of the most important components of a forest ecosystem. Botanists estimate that nearly one fifth of all the fauna on the planet would be lost if dead or dying trees were completely removed. Dozens of species of birds, mammals, and amphibians depend upon dead or decaying trees for food and shelter. Vigorous, productive trees gain valuable nourishment from the slow decomposition of the dead wood and leaf litter. And untold thousands of microorganisms, whose sole purpose is to break down dead wood into soluble cellulose compounds upon which the forest feeds, make a living from the dead and dying. With quiet determination, they chew and bore and grind and saw their way through dead and rotting wood. They feed on the wood and tunnel through it as well as deposit eggs in it so they can raise families of future decomposers.

Just as this constant and valuable labor goes on every day in the woods, so, too, does it go on in the human world, where each day you and millions of other people fulfill a necessary purpose in life—teaching, selling, creating, parenting, healing, enforcing, defending, installing, repairing, transporting, and so on. Each person you see this morning has necessary work to do.

I appreciate and value my work as well as the work of others.

> *"The sky is not less blue because the blind man does not see it."*
> —DANISH PROVERB

SENSUAL NATURE

Even though Helen Keller was blind, deaf, and mute, she knew what a mountain lion looked like. She could describe its color, the texture of its fur, the feel of its twitching tail, the ferocity that burned in its eyes, the sharpness of its teeth, the sound of its snarl and purr, the firmness of the pads on its feet, the sharp prick and tear its claws could inflict upon its prey. She knew all this from a mountain lion she had examined at the hands-on museum at the Perkins School for the Blind in Watertown, Massachusetts. The 163-year-old museum is not the only museum in the country with tactual displays to help those who are vision-impaired understand nature as well as man-made objects, but it is unique because of its expansive collection of items from the everyday world as well as more exotic species.

Because nature is a truly sensory experience, it's not enough to observe it, to study it, to discuss it. Truly to know nature, you must abandon the intellect and savor the effect it creates— that of pure sensation. Close your eyes and sense the colors of nature without seeing them. Open them, and watch the gait of a porcupine so you can sense the stiffness of its quills without touching them. Hold a seashell in your hand and sense the smell of the sea without inhaling it. See a flash of lightning and sense the rumble of thunder without hearing it. Peel an orange and sense its flavor without tasting it.

You can experience the full sensation of nature, even when you lack one of your senses. As Helen Keller once wrote, "Hold out your hands to feel the luxury of the sunbeams."

I feel nature in all of its sensual glory.

> "In beauty, I walk
> To the direction of the rising sun
> In beauty, I walk
> To the direction traveling with the sun
> In beauty, I walk
> To the direction of the setting sun
> In beauty, I walk . . .
> All around me my land is beauty
> In beauty, I walk."
>   —NAVAJO (YEBECHEI) CHANT

SOULFUL WALKING

Whether you go for a walk on a city sidewalk or on a trail through the woods, the desert, or into the mountains, it's always vital to consider many things: the path before you, the urban or rural features you see along your route, the temperature and the feel of the air on you, the items you're toting with you, the view before you as well as the distant view, the movements all around you, the sound of your breathing. For when you can take in everything on a walk, you participate in the walk in a way that allows you to become part of the walk, in tune with all that's around you, within you, beside you, ahead of you, and behind you.

Walk in the rhythms of nature not because you feel you have to, but because you want to. Walk as often as you can, and what you may rediscover is a rhythm that you've lost over the years—a rhythm that once kept you from feeling so pressured, so stressed, so tired at the end of the day, so unable to wake up feeling refreshed, so in need to get away from it all.

Walk in the rhythms of nature not just to exercise your body or to soothe your mind. Walk in the rhythms of nature to heal your soul.

I walk to restore my soul.

"I have never asked that nature open any doors to reveal the truth of spirit or mystery; I aspire to no shaman's path; I expect no vision, no miracles except the ones that fill every instant of ordinary life."

—AMERICAN ANTHROPOLOGIST RICHARD K. NELSON

TRUSTING IN NATURE

Sometimes there is just no way to explain, in reassuring or even comprehensible ways, some of the tragedies and difficulties you personally experience or learn about through the experiences of others. In the tapestry of life, the strands of right and wrong and good and bad are interwoven; there's no untangling them. The world contains starvation and abundance, violence and gentleness, injustice and equity, loss and gain, harmony and discord in its fabric. To trust that good will always triumph over evil isn't naive, but neither is it realistic. Still, it is not worthwhile to believe that catastrophe is inevitable.

Do you remember the story of the man who thought that God had deserted him during a most troubling time because, when he looked behind him, he only saw one set of footprints along the difficult path he had just walked? When he asked God why He wasn't with him when he needed Him the most, God told him that He had been, that the man had only seen one set of footprints because He had been carrying him through his difficult time.

Nature similarly carries you when you need to be carried, when you haven't developed trust through your experiences, faith in your world, or strength resulting from a spiritual connection. Nature provides you with a guiding voice that reminds you to trust that all things change, all wounds heal, and all pain is eased through the passage of time.

In connecting to nature, I make a trustworthy connection.

"The desert landscape is always at its best in the half-light of dawn or dusk. The sense of distance lacks: a ridge nearby can be a far-off mountain range, each small detail can take on the importance of a major variant on the countryside's repetitious theme. The coming of a day promises a change; it is only when the day has fully arrived that the watcher suspects it is the same day returned once again—the same day he has been living for a long time, over and over, still blindingly bright and untarnished by time."

—AMERICAN WRITER PAUL BOWLES

CREATING STABILITY

At times you may enjoy the sense of expectation, dependability, security, and familiarity that comes as a result of a nondisrupted daily schedule, from a usual way of doing things, from those sure things upon which you can depend. Other times you may crave variation, long for a change of pace, need to break out of a routine, yearn to be spontaneous and flexible. Knowing how to balance this need for a certain level of stability in your life with the need to break routines from time to time can be confusing.

Nature is based on a dependable routine. Day after day, the sun rises in the east and sets in the west. There are four seasons, migrations and returns, new growths and harvests, constant renewal and eventual death, endless evolutions, eternal cycles. Yet nature has a need to break out of routine, with unpredictable winds and storms, lightning and thunder, droughts and floods. Even nature's rain can be different each time, as described by English poet and nature writer Edward Thomas: ". . . the early momentous thunderdrops, the perpendicular cataract shining, or at night the little showers, the spongy mists, the tempestuous mountain rain."

Today, remember that nature teaches you to have some sort of order in your life, but to also have opportunities for change, risk, and new experiences.

I create a foundation of stability that will always be there.

"Like a great poet, Nature is capable of producing the most stunning effects with the smallest means. Nature possesses only the sun, trees, flowers, water and love. But for him who feels no love in his heart, none of these things has any poetic value. To such an individual the sun has a diameter of a certain number of miles, the trees are good for making fire, the flowers are divided into varieties, and the water is set."

—GERMAN POET AND CRITIC HEINRICH HEINE

LIVING AND LOVING

What makes life not only worth living, but also special to you? Your work? Your home? Your personal possessions? Your hobbies? While such things may rate highly with you, they may not have as profound an influence in your life as you may think. For if you should lose any one of them, the void created would certainly be devastating but could eventually be refilled—by a new job or home, a new purchase, a new interest, or pastime.

But if life is worth living to you because of the people you love—a life partner, your children, friends, neighbors, co-workers, and family members—then you've identified irreplaceable treasures. Loving relationships can make a profound influence in your life. They can take you outside yourself, encouraging you to think about and give to others. They can make the less enjoyable aspects of life more enjoyable by providing companionship and communication. They can bring you shared experiences and laughter. They can offer romance and passion. They can provide stability and security. They can strengthen and deepen love.

This Valentine's Day, romance someone you already love or show your affection to a new, special friend. Together share in the joys of life. Make someone your irreplaceable treasure.

I bring joy into my life by living and loving today.

*"The sea possesses a power over one's moods that has the effect of a will.
The sea can hypnotize. Nature in general can do so."*

—NORWEGIAN POET AND PLAYWRIGHT HENRIK IBSEN

AN EMOTIONAL COMFORTER

Have you ever despised a sunset? When was the last time you yelled at a tree? Do you need to apologize today to a clump of earth for your behavior toward it last night? Are you ashamed to face the birds this morning? Do you blame the sunshine for a recent loss? Have you decided that you're not speaking to the cactus until you get an apology?

Besides the annoying squirrel that robs your bird feeder or the raccoon that habitually tips over your garbage can at night, nature rarely causes you to feel angry or enraged, ashamed or guilty, abandoned or hurt. Nature never belittles you, confronts you, or threatens to leave you. Nature doesn't cause such emotions, but nature can certainly help cure them. For whenever you need an emotional resource, a wise therapist, a spiritual adviser, or a comforter, nature can be there.

Sometimes there's no better way to vent anger or frustration than to select a few smooth stones from the seashore and skip them on the ocean's waves. The sea gently absorbs the power in each rock you throw and allows you to do this until you're tired. Sometimes there's no better comforter for grief or loss than the ocean. Sit by the shore, wrap your arms around your legs, close your eyes, and let your tears of grief spill down into the thirsty sand; the rhythmic sound of the waves rocks you gently as they whisper a soothing *ssshhh-ssshhh* in your ears. Sometimes there's no better listener than the ocean. Without even speaking, the ocean seems to understand how you feel and reassures you that you're never alone, that it will always be there for you. Nature helps you to weather any emotional storm.

Today, I let nature provide me with emotional comfort.

"Being taken by camera into the deepest African jungle, across the Arctic wastes, thirty fathoms deep in the sea, may seem a 'miracle of modern technology,' but it will no more bring the viewer nearer the reality of nature . . . than merely reading novels is likely to teach the writing of them."

—ENGLISH WRITER JOHN FOWLES

KNOWING NATURE

What if the surgeon who was about to operate on you said, "Now don't worry about a thing. I've never done this before, but I've read about this type of procedure so often that I know what I'm doing." Or what if a contractor you had hired to build an addition to your home told you, "I've never worked with wood and power tools before, but I bought a series of books on home renovations and I'll just use those as a guide."

Mere accumulation of data doesn't necessarily build knowledge or impart experience. A picture of a whale in a book teaches you what the whale looks like; the writing in the book provides you with information on the whale. Yet you have not really *seen* the whale nor do you truly *understand* the whale. But go on a whale-watching expedition, come across the whale in its environment, watch its movements, feel it gently nudge the boat as it swims beneath it. Then you *know* the whale. For knowledge is not simply a mental process, but an experiential one. What this means is that when you can mix what you know with what you learn through an experience, then you have gained valuable insights that go far beyond words and photographs.

While there will be much in this world that you will never truly know, there's much that you can experience. Whenever you can, ignore the book; choose to see something with your own eyes.

I gain true knowledge of nature by experiencing it myself.

"Some parents are taking their children on trips both farther and more elaborate than in the past, hoping for educational fallout. But what will offspring actually reap from trekking up Kilimanjaro or floating down the Amazon?"

—WRITER JEAN SHRIVER IN *WESTWAYS*

SIMPLE, MEMORABLE VACATIONS

Ask any parent how his or her children responded to what may have seemed to have been an exciting family trip— a trip for children to learn about history or another country, a chance to experience different cultures, or a time to get closer to nature, and more often than not what the children take away from the trip is far different than the intended impact. "Not one of our kids remembers anything about Athens except the heat," remarks one father. "Williamsburg? The Tower of London?" asks one mother. "Ask the kids what they remember about each place, and all you'll get are blank stares." Two parents discovered that a long holiday weekend trip to Baja, Mexico, left a lasting memory on the whole family. For hours the children disappeared as the sound of firecrackers punctuated the night air. The frantic parents didn't know what to do until the children finally ran up to them. "We set off firecrackers!" they yelled gleefully. Fully pleased to see the children, the parents bought them dinner, with all the soft drinks they wanted. Years later, whenever anyone asked about their trip to Mexico, the kids remembered it was a place where they could set off firecrackers and drink a lot of soda.

Before you put too much thought and expense into planning what you think will be a unique experience for your children during the upcoming school vacation, consider staying close to home and discovering great natural places together.

I plan a simple vacation or fun activities to share with my children.

"If you seek, how is that different from pursuing sound and form? If you don't seek, how are you different from earth, wood or stone? You must seek without seeking."

—EASTERN SPIRITUALIST WU-MEN

NOT FINDING, NOT SEEKING

When was the last time you found peace of mind? Contentment? Fulfillment? Stillness? Patience? Resolution? Harmony? You may believe that you can find such things if you look for them—by getting away from it all, by purchasing meditation tapes and candles, by writing in your journal, by rearranging your schedule.

Some things in life, however, can't be found. Some things simply come to you with very little effort on your part, even when you desperately want them—answers, solutions, relaxation, a new job or relationship, a talkative teenager, an obedient dog. As Ralph Waldo Emerson once observed about naturalist Henry David Thoreau: "Thoreau knew how to sit immovable, a part of the rock he rested on, until the bird, the reptile, the fish, which had retired from him should come back and resume its habits—nay, moved by curiosity, should come back to him and watch him." Thoreau himself even remarked about a time in which he was hoeing in his garden and a bird alighted upon his shoulder, keeping him company as he labored. While it was always Thoreau's desire to leave society so he could find stillness in and connection with nature, he never set out crumbs to attract the bird to his shoulder or enticed curious creatures back to him. Without effort or pursuit, Thoreau received what he desired.

Today remember to "seek without seeking"—desire without desperation, wait without impatience, search without pursuit—and what you want will come to you.

Rather than play hide-and-seek today, I let myself be found.

"There on the flat stone, on which we so often have sat to weep and pray, we look down, and see it covered with the fossil footprints of great birds and the beautiful skeleton of a fish. We have so often tried to picture in our mind what the fossilized remains of creatures must be like, and all the while we sat on them. We have been so blinded by thinking and feeling that we have never seen the world."

—SOUTH AFRICAN WRITER AND FEMINIST OLIVE SCHREINER

OPENING YOUR SENSES

Imagine that you travel to a remote jungle village. The locals gather around you, peering at you and touching you, for they've never seen anything like you. They're curious, too, about what's in your backpack. One native pulls out your radio. You turn the radio on. Music suddenly blasts from the speaker, startling the natives, who turn the radio in every direction to find the musicians. In sign language, you explain to them that the music comes from the air, through radio waves. One native makes the sign for *cuckoo* to the others, who all nod in agreement.

Later that day, the natives guide you through the jungle to their village. Along the way, they sign for you to look at a snake. You stop and look, but can't see it. Then a native grabs you from behind and pushes you off the path, saving you from falling into a trap you hadn't seen. Before you reach the village, the natives cup their hands around their ears and nod to one another, but you hear nothing.

Everyone has limited detection abilities, limited awarenesses, limited sensitivities. Sometimes such limitations are good, as when you can block out the sounds of a jackhammer. But other times such limitations deprive you of unique experiences, interesting sightings, curious sounds, or sometimes even the most obvious things. Today strive to open all of your senses so you can truly see the world around you.

I experience the world in a way I never have before.

"I know no subject more elevating, more amazing, more ready to the poetical enthusiasm, the philosophical reflection, and the moral sentiment than the works of nature. Where can we meet such variety, such beauty, such magnificence?"

—SCOTTISH POET JAMES THOMSON

NATURE'S MAGNIFICENCE

You may feel that you live in a day-to-day world that's too ugly, too violent, too disgusting, too filthy, too vulgar, and too brutal to support natural beauty. You may think, then, that the only natural beauty that could possibly matter is in "the great outdoors"—far away from your back door, apartment balcony, or work location.

And yet the beauty of nature exists right alongside you. On the high, rocky ledges near the highway on which you commute every day, nature proudly displays "drip ice" sculptures that are diligently worked upon each day. Tall, stately trees line city streets filled with run-down buildings. Squirrels scamper and play near park benches occupied by the sick, drunk, and homeless. Hawks roost and raise families on massive bridges where the hopeless end their lives. On gritty city sidewalks, in the shadows of massive buildings, vendors display cheap plastic buckets filled with fragrant fresh flowers.

It has been said that even on the road to hell, flowers grow. Although fragile and easily destroyed, they can also be hardy and persistent. Pull one out, and another will grow in its place. Pave the earth, and they'll find a way to poke through a tiny crack. They're delicate, but determined. Grow them in your home, and you're rewarded for your efforts by their beautiful display. But come across them unexpectedly, out of their element and in a constant struggle against the elements, and they're truly magnificent.

I especially appreciate the nature that exists outside of nature.

"No snowflake falls in an inappropriate place."

—ZEN SAYING

NATURE'S SIGNIFICANCE

When a second-year nursing student took her seat in class one morning, her professor surprised the class with a pop quiz. Since the student had kept up with her studies, she was pleased that the questions proved to be easy. The last question, however, stumped her: "What is the first name of the woman who cleans the school?" At first she thought the question was a joke. She shrugged her shoulders, left the question blank, and handed her paper in. She was not the only student who was thrown by the final question. As the future nurses filed out of class after the lecture, one asked the professor if the last question on the quiz would count toward the grade.

"Absolutely," the professor replied. "In your careers you will meet many people. All are significant. They deserve your attention and care, even if all you do is smile and say hello."

So, too, is it in nature. Every living thing is significant—from the elephant to the rat to the gnat. Every natural act is important—from birth to growth to decline to death. Every cause has an effect that's appropriate. When nature adds another foot of snow to a seven-foot pile, for example, there's meaning to the additional snow as well as a purpose. Perhaps it won't be until a long dry spell in August that you'll understand the importance of today's snowfall. Perhaps you'll never know how many trees owe their lives to those extra drops of moisture they'll use in the spring. Perhaps you'll never see the vernal pool several miles away that's fed in the spring by the melting snow. All of nature's actions, just like all the people you'll meet in your life—including the cleaning woman named Dorothy—are significant.

I trust that everything in nature is significant.

"Among the great things which are to be found among us, the Being of Nothingness is the greatest."
— FLORENTINE ARTIST AND ENGINEER LEONARDO DA VINCI

TIMES OF NOTHINGNESS

In 1983, zoologist Alan Rabinowitz ventured into the rain forest of Belize, Central America, to study the jaguar in its natural habitat and to establish the world's first jaguar preserve. As he began his research, he discovered that the hours flew by, but he had few results to show for the amount of time he had spent hard at work. Equipment often took months to arrive or to be repaired. But what most dismayed him was the pace at which the villagers worked—much slower than his own. Sometimes he even came across them doing nothing when he knew they had lists of tasks he needed them to accomplish. As time plodded along, Rabinowitz started to lose faith in his mission. "It no big ting man," the villagers would tell him as they listened to him complain. "Saafly, saafly [softly, softly], tiger ketch monkey" was their advice to him—meaning that Rabinowitz would get what he wanted eventually, but he had to accept those times in which he could do nothing. After a while, Rabinowitz discovered that he had very little luck tracking the elusive jaguar when he was caught up in his tight schedule or pressuring himself for something to show for his efforts. But some of his best sightings came when he was "saafly, saafly" doing very little or nothing.

In nature, every living thing exists through its cycles of activity and inactivity. After the hunt, there's always the time of nonhunt, or rest. Today, learn to adopt the cycles of nature. Expend energy as well as preserve it. Do something, but always be sure to do nothing.

I let myself experience times in which I do nothing today.

"The spiritual eyesight improves as the physical eyesight declines."
—GREEK PHILOSOPHER PLATO

FINDING YOUR CENTER

While modern life emphasizes the surface of things—how things look and what they are—spirituality teaches you that without a center, a deep-rooted belief, and an inner sense of peace and calm, the surface really means nothing. For it's not what you look like, how old you are, what you do, how much money you have in the bank, or where you live that matters but what you think, feel, and believe in your heart. Externals are fleeting; what is internal becomes eternal.

To find this spiritual place inside your heart requires that you let go of the externals that rule your life. Perhaps you struggle to please others. Maybe you work hard for social causes. Perhaps your calendar is cluttered with commitments and obligations. Maybe your focus is more on your possessions than on your blessings. Or perhaps you've become overly concerned with your health or the health of someone close to you.

Now imagine that you're an ocean. On your surface are all the externals of your life. Sometimes they sway in gentle swells, sometimes they swirl about in turbulent motion. Yet below the surface are the quiet depths; herein lies your deep source of peace and spiritual inspiration. To get below the surface, think of the externals as things that flow through you; they are part of you, but they're really separate from you. Enjoy these externals, be committed to them, but keep them from ruling your life. What really matters is finding your center so you feel peaceful and harmonious no matter what is happening outside you.

I am centered, whole, and complete.

"Youth is happy because it has the ability to see beauty. Anyone who keeps the ability to see beauty never grows old.

—WRITER FRANZ KAFKA

BEAUTIFUL WONDERS OF LIFE

How often do you take time to notice the beauty of the natural world—the way the snow clings to trees after a snowfall, the glorious colors of the birds that frolic around your bird feeder, or the silvery brilliance of a full moon? How often do you pay attention to the softness of your cat's fur, the shine of your dog's coat after you brush it, and the melodiousness of your caged bird's songs? How often do you take time to look at friends or loved ones and appreciate their beauty—what you see on the outside as well as what you know is on the inside? How often do you look in the mirror and see the beauty of your own eyes, face, and smile?

When you're caught up in the web of grief, defeat, despair, dejection, or depression over things you can't control, you can easily forget that there's a world around you that's teeming with beauty. But those beautiful wonders won't come to you; you have to take time to notice them.

At this moment, no matter how you feel, take time to notice the beauty that surrounds you. As Maya Angelou once wrote, "I'm looking out a large window and I see about forty dogwood and maple and oak and locust trees and the light is on some of the leaves and it's so beautiful. Sometimes I'm overcome with gratitude at such sights and feel that each of us has a responsibility for being alive. . . ." Today, open your eyes to the world, look out on all of its beauty, and thank God that you're alive to experience this beauty for another day.

I notice the beauty around me and within me.

"Few city dwellers, however, realize that they are surrounded by a rich and secret wildlife. Ask which animals now share their habitat, and most people will name the stray dogs and lost cats they occasionally leave food for on their back porches. They know about rats . . . and, of course, pigeons. But they probably are unaware that high above them, on the ledges of skyscrapers and bridges, endangered falcons now make their home."

—ENVIRONMENTAL WRITER ADRIENNE ROSS

CITIFIED CREATURES

In late winter of 1994, two peregrine falcons began courting in downtown Seattle. Nicknamed Stewart and Virginia after two city streets, they were observed diving and perching, giving each other courtly mating bows. Although falcons usually inhabit craggy cliffs, shrinking habitats have led them into urban areas, where skyscrapers and bridges replicate their aerial homes. Yet Stewart and Virginia are not the only falcon city dwellers; some cities are working with bird-watchers, biologists, and urban planners to "stock" falcons not only to assist in increasing the species' number, but also to decrease the city scavenger population that the falcons would hunt.

What this means is that the line between country and city, natural and man-made is rapidly becoming blurred. Take away the wild and untouched places where living creatures make their year-round homes or to which these creatures return to for breeding or migration, and these same creatures are going to gravitate toward the city, making it their new home. Many city-dwelling naturalists are noticing that it's not just birds making moves to metropolises, but also animals, insects, and flora.

All this has led Seattleite Adrienne Ross to suggest, "Perhaps in cities lies the preservation of the wild." Volunteer to help your city's nature preservation effort.

I make nature's creatures feel welcome in their urban world.

"During your life, everything you do and everyone you meet rubs off in some way. Some bit of everything you experience stays with everyone you've ever known, and nothing is lost. That's what's eternal, these little specks of experience in a great, enormous river that has no end."
—AMERICAN WRITER HARRIET DOERR

SATORI

Have you ever experienced a time in your life when you suddenly felt the world was clear to you—a time when you somehow knew or could see deeply into the universe, into something that was much bigger than you, when you could see how all your past experiences, learning, and knowledge made sense, how circumstances in your life happened for a particular reason, and how many of the things that once confused or mystified you were now as clear and comprehensible to you as the answer to the simplest math problem?

Spiritualists refer to this state of mindfulness as *satori,* which describes a sudden experience of clarification—almost like a darkened room suddenly becoming illuminated—usually after a period of contemplation. One spiritualist describes satori this way: "You are sitting on the earth and you realize that this earth deserves you and you deserve this earth. You are there—fully, personally, genuinely." Others describe satori as the doors of perception being opened, an "Aha!"-like lightning bolt of sudden realization that forces arousal from a deep sleep.

You can experience a similarly profound state of enlightenment when you give yourself the opportunity to reflect on how you got to where you are today, based on all you've gone through to get there. Open your mind and senses to the paths you've already walked on, and you'll see that the course of your life is understandable and meaningful.

I seek to realize; I seek satori.

"Nay, in some sense, a person who has never seen the rose color of the rays of dawn crossing a blue mountain twelve or fifteen miles away, can hardly be said to know what tenderness in colour means at all. . . ."

—ENGLISH CRITIC AND ESSAYIST JOHN RUSKIN

KNOWING TENDERNESS

The subtlety of nature is sometimes greater than the subtlety of the senses. You can see a sunrise, feel a gentle breeze on your face, hear the ocean's motions, taste rain, dip your hands in a cold mountain stream. But to be able to distinguish nature's even more mysterious subtleties—the delicacies of color hidden away in the chalice of a flower; the orchestrallike movement of a sea of grass as it shifts and bends in response to the wind, its invisible conductor; the lively sounds of waves rolling pebbles, grains of sand, and shells on the shore as they drone on in incessant "wavespeak" to anyone who will listen; the fresh wood-burning smells that invade the nostrils on a cold February morning—requires you to make the transition from sensory awareness to sensual abandonment.

Too, the subtlety of human expressions is sometimes greater than the subtlety of the senses. You can feel love for another human being in your heart, you can say "I love you," make daily telephone calls, write loving notes, plan romantic times together, be passionate, and share laughter as well as tears. But can you know and show love's tenderness—that special feeling that comes not from your head or your heart, but from deep within your soul? To know such tenderness is to know the howl of the wolf, the path of the mountain stream, the flight of the eagle. To know such tenderness is to be able to feel the life force that pulses within all living things and to understand that this force exists because of all living things.

I know and show tenderness today.

"The time in our own life when we came closest to being convinced by silence was one time at sea in a light fall of snow. We heard nothing—no gravel, no wind, no waves, no wolves, no bell buoy. It was convincing and it was beautiful."

—AMERICAN ESSAYIST E. B. WHITE

EXPERIENCING SILENCE

Imagine that every time you're assailed by unwanted noise—from planes, trains, automobiles, and tractor-trailer trucks; from chain saws, snowplows, and snowmobiles; from honking horns, screeching brakes, and angry people; from slamming doors, barking dogs, and radio commercials; and from countless other sources, whether you live in the city or the country—a fine red dust settles on you. The Eastern religion of Taoism uses this symbol of red dust to refer to those things in the world that are hard to brush away and that keep your mind from becoming still.

Sometimes it may seem as if there's no escape from any sort of invasive noise. Too much red dust coats you and clogs your ears outside as well as inside your home. As long as the aural stimulations of the world continue to swirl around you and blow through your mind, true stillness—silence—will evade you.

"Silence," says naturalist Robert Kimber, "is not just quiet, which is the absence of noise. It is the voice of the living earth, unmuddied by aural clutter." Indian spiritual leader Mahatma Gandhi sought out periods of silence by setting aside a day of silence a week. No matter what happened on that day or who came to visit, he would spend the day quietly, communicating to others only in writing. Could you maintain an entire day in such silence? A few hours? A few minutes?

I am silent so I can know silence.

"The spider on its web was an engineer who spanned his delicate reaches in terms of a discipline and order that were beyond my grasp."

—AMERICAN NATURE WRITER JOHN HAY

LIFE'S IMPERMANENCE

To call where you live a home implies a sense of permanence. You dwell in the house you own, your rented apartment, your dormitory room, or your space in your childhood home, and in so dwelling, you put down roots. You belong. You belong not only to the space in which you reside, but also to the community that surrounds it—the neighborhood, the stores in the center of town, the church you attend, the nearby health club, the library.

But what would happen if your space were suddenly destroyed, leveled by a missile, ravaged by fire, crumbled by an earthquake, condemned in order to rebuild, or sold for development? The loss of personal landmarks, possessions, connections, and communal patterns and routines would cause terrible suffering and disorientation as well as impact upon your identity. For who are you, if you no longer have your home? Where are you, if your roots are torn up?

Yet each time the landscape is changed in nature, all the living things that have made that landscape their home are similarly disrupted and violated. The main difference, however, between man and nature is that nature accepts and lives with such impermanence. The spider that weaves its web across a forest path may have its web destroyed countless times. But it simply moves on to a new location or rebuilds. Its new web is as good as its last one, even though it's still temporary. The spider knows this and accepts this. For change is an inevitable part of life. Change gives new space and a new sense of place.

I accept change as part of life.

"North America is also embellished with thousands of . . . names, although many are opaque to the land itself, as if the earth were shaped into mountains and rivers as a way to commemorate the famous and the dead. There is no better example than Mt. McKinley, our continent's highest peak, named for a little-known politician who would later—coincidentally—become president. McKinley never laid eyes on the mountain, which Koyukon people know as Deenaalee, 'The High One.'"

—CULTURAL ANTHROPOLOGIST RICHARD K. NELSON

THE HERITAGE OF NAMES

Long before Lincoln, Nebraska; Washington, D.C.; or Madison, Wisconsin, these places had names that symbolized what the land meant to the people living there. When North America was taken away from its original dwellers, more than property was lost. The continent was plundered of its names, thereby losing the heritage of emotional attachments that had been formed between the land and its communal dwellers. For those who had known such places had named them with their hearts and minds; today, those who live in those same places have no idea of the incredible heritage lost in the name. Renaming means the loss of a description—a memento from a trapper or homesteader that reflects a relationship with a place (New Hope Land, Many Sorrows River), useful information (Hell Roaring Creek, Half Mile Creek), warnings to travelers (No Thoroughfare Bay, Boiling Pinnacles), events or personal experiences (Strangle Woman Creek, Sore Finger Cove), and insights into past life (*Nannugvik*, "Place to Hunt Polar Bears," *Qayaiqsigvik*, "Place Where a Kayak Was Accidentally Lost").

Today, find out the original name of the town or city in which you live. Learn what it means. Embrace the names that tell of the nation's history.

I learn the true meaning of a place name.

"Life is not living, but living in health."
—POET MARCUS VALERIUS MARTIALIS (MARTIAL)

LIVING IN HEALTH

Ancient Indian sages define healthy life energy as *prana;* the Chinese know it as *chi.* Other cultures and religions have different names for this life energy. But no matter what name it goes by, what it encompasses are the ways of attaining and maintaining a level of physical, emotional, and spiritual balance that results in physical vitality, enthusiasm, strong disease immunity, mental alertness, balanced body rhythms, a strong spiritual connection, and a sense of exhilaration.

A healthy life demands that you eat well, a diet that includes lots of fresh fruits and vegetables, complex carbohydrates, easily digestible proteins, plenty of water, and few processed or fried foods is the best. Physical exercise is also important because such activity helps bring energy to the body; the best exercise takes place outdoors, where large quantities of fresh air and an interesting and ever-changing landscape combine to promote high interest and motivation. Regular meditation clears the mind of negative emotions and eases stress; meditating for at least twenty minutes each day prompts the development of slow, deep-breathing techniques as well as restores balance of the senses. Conscious contact with a Higher Power through meditation, prayer, or connecting with nature releases negative emotions and restores faith, hope, and trust. And participating in an action or activity that benefits the planet—feeding birds and other wild animals during times of scarcity, planting a tree, starting a garden club, serving on your city or town's conservation board, or maintaining a nature trail—can help increase your physical, emotional, and spiritual vitality.

Today I live in health so I strengthen my life energy.

"When a man does a piece of work which is admired by all we say that it is wonderful; but when we see the changes of day and night, the sun, the moon, and the stars in the sky, and the changing seasons upon the earth, with their ripening fruits, anyone must realize that it is the work of someone more powerful than man."

—CHASED-BY-BEARS, SANTEE-YANKTONAI SIOUX

A WORLD OF WONDERS

Think of all the energy you must exert in order to accomplish something. Whether your goal is to run a marathon, to get your master's degree, to write a book, to wallpaper or paint a room in your home, or simply to transport your kids on time to the variety of after-school activities in which they participate, the time as well as the physical, mental, and emotional preparation and stamina you need to accomplish such things makes the reward of eventual achievement that much richer.

Yet so many of nature's marvels make even your most difficult accomplishment seem minor because they result from little exertion. Every day the sun rises and sets; each day brings a new weather pattern. Gravity is a constant force that keeps all things grounded. Air miraculously links every living thing. Seasons change on cue, constellations revolve around the sky, tides ebb and flow.

While each day you may need to set and achieve goals, and while the majority of these goals may be significant and meaningful, it's still important to realize the greatness that lies in the natural wonders that are accomplished each day. Nature opens doors of wonder every day; each day you live out your life against a wonderful tapestry of astonishing phenomena. Recognize your achievements for what they are; recognize, too, the achievements of all living things around you.

I marvel at the wonders I achieve as well as the world of wonders already being achieved.

"If we drive by an eroded field, we sneer at that farmer for not knowing that by losing his soil he is losing his farm. Yet we have watched the natural riches of our home bleed away and have said nothing, except to attack those who try to tell us that what is good for a large corporation is not necessarily good for us."

—SEASONAL FIREFIGHTER, SHEEP FARMER, AND
ENVIRONMENTAL WRITER LOUIS WAGENKNECHT

SAVING YOUR TREES

Passing a development in your area, observing from the road a section of leveled trees and bulldozed dirt, you may not realize the effect the changes can have. It may seem to be such a small section and, you may think, when all the houses are finally built, the access road paved, and the sidewalks poured, new trees will be planted, and eventually the community will look as if it is simply a natural part of the land.

But the reality of any development is that drastic cutting rarely allows for any restoration that will attain the quality of tree growth, ground vegetation, and soil richness that originally existed. The full impact of clearing and leveling fields, woods, forests, and timberlands can only be realized from an aerial view—from looking down upon what it really means to create a profitable cul-de-sac or to carve a mall out of the side of a mountain.

In Happy Camp, California, for instance, mining, logging, and milling, as well as the stores, homes, and businesses that were erected to support the blossoming community radically altered the darkly forested canyon area. An aerial photograph shows the big clear-cuts from the 1960s, some of them re-planted six or seven times, which have still not regenerated sufficiently, as well as large areas of fields that have resisted all efforts at reforestation. Today, be conscious of the development in your neighborhood. Resist man-made growth that will deplete the natural growth.

I will protect the natural riches of my home.

"Evolution did not intend trees to grow singly. Far more than ourselves they are social creatures, and no more natural as isolated specimens than man is as a marooned sailor or hermit."

—ENGLISH WRITER JOHN FOWLES

SUPPORTING OTHERS

Nature supports all of its living things; no one thing could ever live successfully on its own without the support of other living things. Every living thing, for example, needs the earth, needs water, and needs the air. As well, most every living thing needs other living things for sustenance and to ensure its continued growth.

Because of this supportive network of living things, all of creation can be seen as interdependent. What this means is that you may often find yourself in the position—not always by chance and sometimes by design—to involve yourself in many different ways in the world around you. Within the context of your home, your job, your partner, your family, your friends, your environment, and others with whom you have contact, there are hundreds of experiences that create opportunities for you to reach out to others—to support them in some way, to make yourself necessary to them.

How can you be necessary? Think of how a tree is necessary to you. On a hot day, its cooling shade gives you relief from the sun. So, too, can you provide relief and comfort to others who share your journey through life. A tree is essential to control the erosion of topsoil; its root systems not only help hold the soil in place, but also absorb runoff that would wash the soil away. So, too, can you support others during times of stress and strife, help hold them in place, give them strength so they can get through their difficult times.

Nature teaches me to extend myself to others.

"Hereafter, when I call up memories of the glorious, the view from this camping ground will come up. Looking east, gorges opened to the distant Plains, then fading into purple grey. Mountains with pine-clothed skirts rose in ranges, or, solitary, uplifted their grey summits, while close behind, but nearly 3,000 feet above us, towered the bald white crest of Long's Peak, its huge precipices red with the light of a sun long lost to our eyes."

—NATURALIST AND HUMANITARIAN ISABELLA BIRD

ABOUT ISABELLA BIRD

Just five years after John Wesley Powell led the first ascent to the summit of Long's Peak in Colorado in 1868, Isabella Bird (1831–1904) climbed to the summit. Despite being afflicted by a chronic spinal complaint since childhood, Bird was a tireless traveler who preferred to avoid the beaten path as she carved new ones for herself or followed in the footsteps of pioneers. She traveled to and lived in Japan and the Malay peninsula for short periods of time; covered eight thousand miles in fifteen months on a second trip to China; journeyed through India, Persia, Kurdistan, and Tibet; and established hospitals in Kashmir and Punjab as well as in China and Korea. Although she claimed to travel for recreation and interest, she was the first woman to be elected a fellow of the Royal Geographical Society.

In 1873, she traveled from the Hawaiian Islands to the Rocky Mountains, a place she once described as "no region for tourists and women." She rejected the commonly acceptable "female way" of riding a horse—sidesaddle—as she rode up to ten hours a day in the Rockies. She appreciated new places as they were intended—on their own terms—and wrote extensively about her travels, detailing precise geographical and botanical information. *A Lady's Life in the Rocky Mountains* records her ascent of the 14,700-high Long's Peak, or the "American Matterhorn."

I record my observations of nature in a journal or diary.

"There is one God looking down on us all. We are all children of one God. God is listening to me. The sun, the darkness, the winds are all listening to what we now say."

—GERONIMO

MORNING PRAYER

O God, there are many special places in my life that live on forever. Even though I may never be able to go back to those places—the fields of my childhood where I picked blueberries ripened in the warm afternoon sun, the rushing river stream where I cooled my feet, the summer camp in the pines where I learned to shoot an arrow or tie a secure knot, the tree I climbed so I could know what the leaves in the trees and the birds in the sky already knew, the rock that became a supportive shoulder that absorbed my sorrows and helped me to regain my solid footing—just entering them in memory makes them live again.

Dear Lord, there are too many reasons now for me to lose touch with some parts of me that were then—too many diversions, too many imbalances, too many stresses, too many other things that prevent me from seeing and feeling as I once did. Yet today I need to set aside time to follow my own path, think my own thoughts, feel my own feelings. I need to be able to remember that I am who I am today because of the many, many experiences I had in the past.

Today, please help me to remember that yesterday was the foundation for the house I live in today. While I need to spend time today keeping my house in order, help me to relive again some of the memories that once gave me strength, hope, security, pride, and faith in myself and in my future.

I pray today to not lose touch with yesterday.

"I saw that nothing was permanent. You don't want to possess anything that is dear to you because you might lose it."

—SINGER AND ARTIST YOKO ONO

LIFE'S UNPREDICTABILITIES

Change abounds in life; without change, life wouldn't be an ongoing process of birth, death, and renewal. Change keeps you from staying in dead-end jobs and unhappy relationships. Change helps you to improve hopeless situations. Change encourages you to trust the unknown. Change conquers fear and develops courage. Change releases your need to control everything and everybody. Change urges you to take positive action. Change supports you in doing your best. Change teaches you about limitations and how to challenge them. Change helps you to come face-to-face with yourself. Change alters your vision of life.

Sometimes the unpredictability of life catches you off guard and changes your life in marvelous ways; sometimes the unpredictability throws you an incredible challenge; sometimes the unpredictability forces you to give up something or someone you cherish. About the only thing you can count on in life is its unpredictability.

Rather than yearning to live in a predictable space in which everything stays the same and nothing becomes so meaningful to you that you can't let go of it if or when you have to, relish the experience of change that nature—and life—provides for you. As an unknown soul once observed, "There is more to be learned in one day of discomfort, poverty, and anxiety than in a lifetime of apparent happiness, security, riches, and power."

I welcome all of the surprises in life as natural parts of life.

"Old age is an island surrounded by death."
—SPANISH WRITER JUAN MONTALVO

HOPEFUL GRIEF

Visitors to the Fiji Islands learn about a strange custom among its native people known as "Calling to the Dead." A mourner climbs high up into a tree or scales a cliff and, after calling out the name of the deceased, cries out, "Come back! Come back!" The cry is made even more heartrending by the echoes that reverberate in "reply."

When you're filled with grief over the loss of another beloved person in your life, you may feel as if you're on an island that's surrounded by death. Your grief over yet another loss may make your present so unbearable that you lose sight of the future. You may feel hopeless and despairing. You may even blame God or your understanding of a god for your losses and cry out, "Why did You do this to me?" or "Why don't You help me? Can't You see I'm in pain?"

Deep grief, combined with estrangement from a Higher Power, can leave you with an intense spiritual emptiness. But even though you may feel as if you stand alone and are exposed to the elements of a cruel, heartless world that has been personally directed at you by some all-powerful unkind Being, that's just not the case. Every event in your life has been experienced by millions of others. You're not the victim of a vengeful act that has been inflicted upon you from above.

Rather than dwell in hopelessness and despair, reach out hopefully. Cry out your pain, let your tears fall, get on your knees, or simply close your eyes and silently ask for spiritual guidance. You will get an answer.

I pray in my grief and know my prayers are heard.

"Never does Nature say one thing and wisdom another."
—ROMAN SATIRIST JUVENAL

SAVING NATURE

While few would deny nature's profound importance and impact in their lives, people often regard such importance in diametrically opposed ways. Where one person may look at a towering tree and see it as a beautiful part of the landscape, another looks at the tree and sees it as a source of raw materials for the construction of a beautiful piece of furniture. Where one person may marvel at the chance sighting of a deer or moose while walking through the woods, another may marvel at the sighting of the same woodland creature through a rifle scope. Where one person may be awed by the power of a great creature like an elephant or a rhinoceros, another may be awed by the money that can be earned by obtaining an elephant's ivory tusks and a rhinoceros's horn through illegal poaching. Where one person may touch the coat of a mink or a fox and thrill at its soft texture, another may pay top dollar to thrill at the soft texture of a mink coat or a fox stole. Where one person may become excited at the sighting of a coyote near a suburban area, another may incite armed citizens to kill the wild beast.

Today, it may be quite difficult to imagine what this country was like just a few centuries ago, with its primeval forest, drinkable mountain streams well stocked with fish, abundant wildlife, and wild herbs and flowers. Many decisions have been made by mankind that have resulted in pollution, overdevelopment, endangered species, and vanishing resources.

To be an asset to the earth while you are on the earth, it's vital to make wise decisions, for both you and nature need one another for the planet to survive.

I step in when one of nature's living things is threatened.

"The raindrops patter on the basho leaf, but these are not tears of grief; this is only the anguish of him who is listening to them."

—ZEN SAYING

WORKING THROUGH THE BLUES

Here are some simple ways to let nature help you to work through a difficult time, a dark mood, sadness, or grief.

Notice the weather today and discover at least one positive thing about it. Sunshine is a warming and encouraging sign for the end of winter; wind promotes the movement of air and precedes change and renewal; rain nourishes the seeds, bulbs, and roots and washes away winter's grit and grime; snow is winter's "last word"—a final outburst before months of silence—as well as the assurance of a good, long drink for flowers that will soon burst out of the earth and for buds that will break open on the trees.

Observe the wild animals as they go about their daily activities, scurrying to and fro or flitting about, as if they had some great business deals to close or a meeting to attend, when, in reality, they are simply overjoyed at the dawning of a new day.

Go outdoors. Close your eyes and listen to the songs of the birds. Feel the rush of the wind or the wetness of nature's shower on your face. Open your mouth and taste the air. Be aware of how your feet feel planted on the earth.

Get active. Take your dog for a walk. Play with your cat. Exercise. Spend time with your children. Clean out a closet and recycle what you no longer need. Feel your existence. Know your value.

I use nature to lift my spirits.

"If the doors of perception were cleansed everything would appear to man as it is, infinite."

—ENGLISH POET AND ENGRAVER WILLIAM BLAKE

PERCEPTIONS

The Chinese gardener uses things wisely so nothing is overlooked, and lives by the philosophy that nothing is wasted. A good example of this has been exhibited by landscaper Peter Chan, whose beautiful gardens have won awards and been featured in magazines and on national television. When Chan moved his family to a new home in Oregon, the yard was filled with hard clay soil and large stones, enough to daunt even the most skilled gardener. But Chan saw the yard not as a problem, but as an opportunity. He enriched the clay soil with compost and used the stones to form neat pathways between the raised beds of his vegetable garden.

Your happiness and satisfaction, like Chan's view of his new property, depend upon your perceptions. If you perceive that you're standing in the middle of a hot, airless desert, then that's where you are. If you believe you're in the middle of a stagnant, smelly bog, then that's where you are. If you believe you're in the middle of a deep arctic freeze from which you'll never thaw, then that's where you are. But if you believe you're standing in the middle of an acre of rich potential and possibilities, then *that's* where you are.

When you're flexible, resourceful, and open to new possibilities, you can see the value, beauty, and potential in any situation. As the Tao teaches: "Wise people seek solutions; the ignorant only cast blame."

I perceive my life to be rich with possibilities and potential.

"The thing that makes the flowers open and the snowflakes fall must contain a wisdom and a final secret as intricate and beautiful as the blooming camellia or the clouds gathering above, so white and pure in the blackness."
—AMERICAN WRITER ANNE RICE

PATIENT GROWTH

You're part of a universal pattern of growth that renews itself in cycles. Night to day, spring to summer, youth to middle age—all give birth to something new within you. You're not the same person at this moment that you were yesterday; you're not even the same person you were when you read the quotation above. If you can trust in this process of change and renewal, then you'll find that your moods and outlook stay pretty consistent from day to day. You trust that your periods of darkness will be followed by light, that solutions to problems will eventually be found, and that injury will heal and illness be cured. But when you're impatient, your moods bounce up enthusiastically with each cycle of growth and renewal and fall down with each cycle of dormancy and sameness.

Working in a garden can teach you how to become familiar with such cycles. The seeds that need to be planted in the spring for summer growth can't be planted until the ground thaws. Now is the time to prepare the earth rather than to look ahead to the crop you'll be picking.

You and the projects you undertake, like the seeds you plant, have different seasons. Some spring up quickly. Others take longer to germinate, even longer to bear fruit. All the impatience in the world won't change this process. For as the Chinese proverb advises, "Patience is power; with time and patience the mulberry leaf becomes silk."

I allow time for patient growth in myself.

"Of all the things I have ever seen, only the sea is like a human being; the sky is not, nor the earth. But the sea is always moving, always something deep in itself is stirring it. It never rests; it is always wanting, wanting, wanting. It hurries on; and then it creeps back slowly, without having reached, moaning. It is always asking a question, and it never gets the answer."

—SOUTH AFRICAN WRITER AND FEMINIST OLIVE SCHREINER

CENTERING YOURSELF

Have you ever seen the ocean in a storm? The water is in constant, frightening motion, capable of sinking boats, eroding shorelines, and sweeping away entire homes. Yet below the surface is a stillness where even the tiniest fish gracefully darts to and fro.

Within you is a similar "center" of stillness—a part of you that's capable of achieving calmness in the midst of the most trying of circumstances. Being centered in the midst of chaos is like being a tree in a storm: while wind, rain, lightning, and other elements may affect you on the outside, your roots still hold you fast and firm in the ground.

Aikido masters who teach their students to maintain their centers claim that centering can generate such incredible personal force that one can withstand the power of many. While life is meant to be lived in motion, for all living things are in motion, beneath the restless strivings on the surface lives peace and serenity deep within. All living things go through periods of stillness, resting in order to return to the motion of living refreshed and renewed. All living things take time to center themselves so they can regain their footing. So, too, can you.

I center myself to feel safe, secure, and serene.

"It means nothing to strike up a friendship with a sea lion or dolphin if, at the same time, we are destroying their last refuges along our coasts and our islands. It is an exercise in vanity and absurdity to try to communicate with a killer whale and then to put it on exhibition in an aquatic zoo as a circus freak."

—FRENCH MARINE EXPLORER JACQUES YVES COUSTEAU

THE BEAUTY OF THE WHALES

In two Mexican lagoons off Baja, gray whales mate and give birth as well as interact with humans, earning them the title of "friendly whales." When people explore their cetacean nurseries, the whales lift their enormous heads out of the water and study the humans with a curiosity and trust that forgives a past in which such a birth sanctuary was turned into a slaughterhouse. Calves were killed to entrap protective mothers; the waters turned red as the gray whale population fell from twenty-five thousand to near-extinction levels, until 1946, when the gray whales were finally protected.

Today, thanks to the Endangered Species Act, the gray-whale population has rebounded to eighteen thousand. Such cooperation between man and mammal has restored balance between the species, although many whales are inadvertently killed from injuries caused by huge boat propellers.

Now, when someone yells, "Thar she blows!" it is to observe the grace and gentleness of such massive creatures, marvel at the majestic twenty-foot geyser that shoots out of the water, and hear the heartfelt whale singing that "is like," according to naturalist Brenda Peterson, "a combination of Tibetan overtoning, Gregorian chant, cello arpeggios, haunting moans and a low lute that suddenly lilts up into astonishing trills."

Saving the whale has saved a friend and a song for future generations.

I support the Endangered Species Act for all creatures in need.

"This grand show is eternal. . . . Eternal sunrise, eternal sunset, eternal dawn and gloaming, on sea and continents and islands, each in its turn, as the round earth rolls."

—SCOTTISH-BORN AMERICAN NATURALIST JOHN MUIR

CREATING PATTERNS OF STABILITY

Do you have rituals that help you start each day clear and focused so you can then move through the events of the day without making hurried decisions, "going with the flow," and ending each day with a sense of personal satisfaction, balance, and peace? Maybe you start your day with meditation or exercise. Perhaps you take your dog for a walk. Maybe you take a bath or write in a journal.

Peace and harmony are the benefits of a balanced life—one that's free from chaos, stress, and agitation. But living with balance means creating balance, and that takes discipline. Such discipline includes using rituals to create patterns of stability that help you to clear your vision, to leave you free to meet your needs and pursue your desires, to simplify the overload in your life, to guide you on the path to happiness and contentment, and to encourage you to see great beauty in your life.

It's time now to add a ritual to your life. Think about something that leaves you feeling calm, relaxed, and at peace with yourself. Maybe it's running through the neighborhood at sunrise or listening to classical music as you dress for work. Name this as your ritual, then resolve to do it every day at the same time. Then, no matter what happens, you'll have created one enduring pattern of stability in your life.

I create a ritual that brings stability in my life.

"As I look over my life, I find no disappointment and no sorrow I could afford to lose; the cloudy morning turned out the fairer day; the wounds of my enemies have done me good. So wondrous is this human life, not ruled by Fate, but Providence, which is Wisdom married unto Love, each infinite! What has been, may be. If I recover wholly, or but in part, I see new sources of power beside these waters of affliction I have stooped at."

—AMERICAN THEOLOGIAN AND ESSAYIST THEODORE PARKER

SEEING THE GOOD

Do you tend to remember old hurts? It may be hard to see the good in your life when grudges stand in your way, when you remember more cloudy days than sunny ones, when past sorrows are as painful today as they were yesterday, and when you see only failure and defeat rather than success and victory.

According to American Indian tradition, "enemies" such as disappointment, sorrow, failure, and hurt are sacred because they can make you strong. The unfortunate things that have happened in your past can teach you how to become stronger in the present and how to succeed in the future, but only when you can let them go, release the negative hold they have on you, and forgive them. Then, and only then, can you move on with your life. For it's then that you can see the good you've gained from such things.

Naturalist Henry David Thoreau learned how to see such good one rainy day at Walden Pond. He wrote: "The gentle rain which waters my beans and keeps me in the house today is not drear and melancholy, but good for me too. Though it prevents my hoeing them, it is of far more worth than my hoeing. If it should continue so long as to cause the seeds to rot in the ground . . . it would still be good for the grass in the uplands, and being good for the grass, it would be good for me."

When I see the good in my life, I see my life as good.

"If we didn't live venturously, plucking the wild goat by the beard, and trembling over precipices, we should never be depressed, I've no doubt; but already should be faded, fatalistic and aged."
—ENGLISH WRITER VIRGINIA WOOLF

LIVING ADVENTUROUSLY

Imagine the fear and anxiety Christopher Columbus and his crew felt as they set sail from the safe shores of their homeland, knowing that they might fall off the edge of the world and never return home. This didn't stop them from beginning their voyage. Nor have similar feelings of trepidation and unease stopped countless other pioneers from exploring, mountaineers from climbing, oceanographers from diving, aviators from flying, naturalists from journeying, spelunkers from caving, astronauts from rocketing—even when they may have slowly starved to death in the process, become hopelessly lost, succumbed to severe temperatures, or fell to the earth in a fiery explosion, dying in their quest to discover new lands, to gain more knowledge, or to simply understand more clearly those things that so many others took for granted or chose not to question.

Risk-taking means attempting something new, different, or unknown, without the comfort of knowing what the outcome will be. But no matter what the outcome, it's important to take the risk. Fear is a natural reaction to the unknown. But fearing and still taking the risk are what risk-taking is all about. The best risk-takers are those people who ask, "What do I have to lose?" They have the attitude that even if they don't succeed, they are at least willing to try. As French writer André Gide once said, "One doesn't discover new lands without consenting to lose sight of the shore for a very long time."

I focus on the gains in risk-taking, then take the risk.

"We are the offspring of history, and must establish our own paths in this most diverse and interesting of conceivable universes—one indifferent to our suffering, and therefore offering us maximal freedom to thrive, or to fail, in our own chosen way."

—BIOLOGIST AND HISTORIAN STEPHEN JAY GOULD

NO BOUNDARIES, NO LIMITS

In 1982, mountain climber Hugh Herr and his partner Jeffrey Batzer reached the top of Odell's Gully on Mt. Washington and decided to push for the summit. They immediately stumbled into a blinding blizzard. Herr and Batzer survived three nights in gale-force winds and below-freezing temperatures. Although they came out of the ordeal alive, Batzer ended up losing one leg; Herr lost both.

Doctors warned Herr about the limitations he would have to accept. Instead, Herr designed artificial limbs that enabled him to continue climbing. He invented a more comfortable socket for leg prostheses. And he became an advocate of technical solutions to physical disabilities, with the goal of designing legs to enable those who are physically challenged to run marathons.

Do you refuse to be as intimidated by limits or boundaries? Do you work with your own limitations in ways that foster a positive, determined attitude? Do you challenge and inspire yourself in ways that enable you to find out what you can do rather than what you can't?

Today, whether you realize it or not, there are no real boundaries—only those manifested in your imagination. For boundaries are walls you erect where walls have never existed. It's up to you to define in your mind how you'll conquer your limitations so you can treat any boundary you've erected as an illusion.

I tear down walls so I live without boundaries or limits.

"*Lost, yesterday, somewhere between sunrise and sunset, two golden hours, each set with sixty diamond minutes. No reward is offered for they are gone forever.*"

—AMERICAN NEWSPAPER PUBLISHER HORACE MANN

OUTWITTING THE TIME BANDITS

Do you see time as an enemy—a heartless bandit that steals your valuable jewels of seconds, minutes, and hours and hides them so well that you can never retrieve them? "Where did the time go?" you may frantically question. "I can't believe the day's nearly over!"

And, when time bandits band together in a gang, are you horrified to realize that days, weeks, months—even years—have been swiped from you? "I can't believe it's March already!" you may exclaim, and then realize you're yet another year older.

"Time bandits" have existed since the beginning of life. But their thefts may have only recently become more evident to you because you see the large accumulation of yesterdays and realize how quickly your todays are flying by. With each passing moment, time has become more precious to you. But trying to hold on to time, wishing there were more hours in a day, pushing yourself to do everything faster, or lamenting the things you can no longer do because of the passage of time can never get you more time or restore the time you once had. Time can't be protected, set aside for later, watched over, or hoarded.

But you can outwit the time bandits. From now on, cease agonizing over the passage of time; time's going to move on, and there's nothing you can do about it. Instead, make the most of the time you have. Spend time enjoying your time!

I get the most out of time as it passes by.

"The abundant wildlife provided almost constant excitement during the trip. Bear, caribou, otter, moose, and eagles were plentiful, and once, while I was fishing under an overhanging bluff, a light-gray wolf came across the tundra, lay down on the cliff above me to watch for a while, and then quietly loped away."

—FORMER U.S. PRESIDENT AND HUMANITARIAN JIMMY CARTER

KNOW YOUR POLITICIANS

One of former President Jimmy Carter's major legislative battles concerned a controversy about the disposition of millions of acres of land in Alaska. For more than twenty years a bitter debate had raged in Alaska and in Congress. How much Alaskan land should be in private hands and how much should be owned by the state? How much should be opened for mining and oil and gas exploration? How much should be retained by the native Eskimos, Indians, and Aleuts? How much should be set aside for public use?

On December 2, 1980, in one of his last legislative decisions as president, Carter signed a landmark bill into law that set aside for conservation an area larger than the state of California, doubled the size of the National Park and Wildlife Refuge System, and designated twenty-five free-flowing Alaskan streams as wild and scenic rivers. Years later, when Carter was invited by friends to go on a fishing trip on Alaska's Copper River, he asked his then–nine-year-old grandson Jason to accompany him and discovered, through his grandchild's eyes, what a great gift he had given to the American people.

How supportive are your local and state politicians of legislation that protects the wilderness and wildlife in your area? Find out how your politicians vote so you can decide if they deserve your vote.

I vote for politicians who support preservation of the environment.

"It was spring here, and juices were getting up in the stalks; leaves, terribly folded in husks, had begun to let loose and open to the light; stuff was stirring in the rot, water bubbled with the froth of sperm and ova, and the whole bog lay rank and eggy, vaporous and thick with the scent of procreation. Things once squeezed close, pinched shut, things waiting to become something else, something greater, were about ready."

—AMERICAN WRITER WILLIAM LEAST HEAT MOON

NATURE'S SEXUALITY

Are you amazed at the current of sexuality that runs through everyday life? There's often little difference between nature and humankind when it comes to sexual behavior. Both animals and people primp and preen, emit enticing aromas to attract potential partners, play coy games with one another, engage in ritualistic courting behaviors, seek a desirable as well as an appealing partner, communicate attraction, and act on their attractions. But it's not just the animal kingdom that flaunts its sexuality. Naturalist Diane Ackerman writes, "A flower's fragrance declares to all the world that it is fertile, available, and desirable, its sex organs oozing with nectar. Its smell reminds us in vestigial ways of fertility, vigor, life-force, all the optimism, expectancy, and passionate bloom of youth. We inhale its ardent aroma and, no matter what our ages, we feel young and nubile in a world aflame with desire."

Sex is a natural part of living, shared with every living thing. As such, it should always be respected—never based on manipulation, selfishness, or abuse. It should be part of a conscious and considered decision between two people. It should be safe and secure, filled with passion as well as honesty and trust. It should be treated as the most mysterious, sacred, and profound interaction two people can share with one another.

Being sexual feels natural and comfortable when it's mutual.

"I have noticed in my life that all men have a liking for some special animal, tree, plant, or spot of earth. If men would pay more attention to these preferences and seek what is best to do in order to make themselves worthy of that toward which they are so attracted, they might have dreams which would purify their lives. Let a man decide upon his favorite animal and make a study of it, learning its innocent ways. Let him learn to understand its sounds and motions."

—TETON SIOUX MEDICINE MAN BRAVE BUFFALO

ADOPTING AN ANIMAL

Native-American spirituality has always relied upon the enlightenment that can be gained from knowing the ways of animals. If a Native-American child was lost, the child could call upon the power of a particular animal and be guided home, protected through a storm, or led toward temporary shelter. In South America, children today are often taught that when they are born an animal is born with them that will be their lifelong guardian and guide.

How do you wish to teach your own children about their relationship with wild animals? If you could teach your child to adopt just one other species—to learn as much as possible about that species, to be concerned for its welfare, to learn the way of that species, and in so doing, learn more about him or herself, how would this impact upon the relationship between human and animal in the next generation? When you can teach the power, wisdom, inspiration, and connection that exists between humanity and nature, then you can create a relationship in which a creature's essence can become a child's essence—a relationship of harmony, of understanding, of beauty. You are passing on a classic expression of ancient and eternal genius of life, that animals are as much a child's teachers as parents.

I teach my child to adopt an animal to learn from as well as to care for that animal.

"Nobody, living upon the remotest, most barren crag in the ocean, could complain of a dull landscape so long as he would lift his eyes. In the sky there was a new landscape every minute, in every pool of the sea rocks, a new world."

—ENGLISH WRITER T. H. WHITE

TUNING INTO THE GOOD

Face it—the world no longer feels safe and secure; maybe it never did. Terrorism, dictatorships, shady political maneuverings, and unspeakable suffering dominate headlines. Government officials and those in positions of authority abuse trust. Random acts of violence defy explanation. Justice rarely seems to be served; people get away with murder. Children are kidnapped. Sweatshop reform seems all but forgotten. Crime is on the rise. Even your neighbors are not whom they appear to be.

Is it any wonder, then, that the strength you need to live on a day-to-day basis is so depleted by terrible news and rising fears that your spirit often feels broken, you feel physically drained and exhausted, and your mental outlook on the world you live in is often dominated by depression and anxiety about the future?

Yet you can restore your appreciation for the good in life by turning your attention away from newspapers, radio, and television. Focus instead on activities that can take you away from this world and transport you into another—a new world in which you can be a saner, healthier, more contented person. Follow the spiritually healing advice of naturalist Henry David Thoreau, who wrote, "I think I cannot preserve my health and spirits, unless I spend four hours a day at least,—and it is commonly more than that,—sauntering through the woods and over the hills and fields, absolutely free from all worldly engagements."

Today I change my landscape and, in so doing, change my outlook.

"To all the rest, given [Nature] hath sufficient to clad them everyone according to their kind: as namely, shells, cods, hard hides, pricks, shags, bristles, hair, down feathers, quills, scales, and fleeces of wool. The very trunks and stems of trees and plants, she hath defended with bark and rind . . . against the injuries both of heat and cold: man alone, poor wretch, she hath laid all naked upon the bare earth. . . ."

—ROMAN SCHOLAR PLINY THE ELDER

MAKING A DIFFERENCE

Does it sometimes seem as if you go through life totally unprotected—unshielded against verbal barbs, at the mercy of great tidal waves of emotion, helplessly caught in the sharp steel traps of stressful living, greatly affected by the unpredictable moods and attitudes of others?

A story is told of an old man who was walking along the beach at dawn. His joints were stiff and sore, his heart heavy with the recent loss of his wife, his view of the future hopeless. He noticed a little boy ahead of him picking up starfish and flinging them into the sea. Catching up to the youth, he asked why he was doing this. The answer was that the stranded starfish would die if left until the morning sun came up.

"But the beach goes on for miles and there are thousands of starfish," the old man grumbled. "How can your effort make any difference?"

The boy looked down at the starfish he held in his hand, then threw it to safety in the waves. "It makes a difference to this one."

So, too, had the interaction made a difference to the old man. As he bent down and joined the boy in his task, he realized that the only way to work through his sorrow, pain, and hopelessness was to instill joy, relief, and hope in others.

I resolve to make a difference to another.

"Dare. Go toward life. Take chances. Reach out to what you most fear. Develop the habit of daring life so that you will not look back with regret at what you have not done."

—AMERICAN WRITER DONALD M. MURRAY

LIVING ON THE EDGE

There may come a time in your life when interesting, exciting, unique, challenging, and stimulating activities will be well out of your reach. Then you'll have no choice but to sit back and let others participate. Right now, you can be a participant in all the adventures that life has to offer. There's so much to see, to do, to experience, to savor. Are you up to the challenge?

There are adrenaline-rushing thrills like jumping out of a helicopter with a snowboard strapped to your feet and landing on a steep Colorado mountain peak for the downhill challenge of your life. There are exotic, faraway locales that can teach you much about the world you share with other cultures and give you an opportunity to view many living things in their natural habitats rather than in a zoo. There are physically demanding activities you can train for—a marathon, a triathalon, a cross-country bike ride, a climb to a mountain peak—or intellectually stimulating activities you can set personal goals in—bird-watching, butterfly collecting, and botanical identification. There are unique, once-in-a-lifetime experiences you can have—paddling down the swift Susitna River in Alaska, the land of the midnight sun at one o'clock in the morning, or going on a cattle drive.

Today is the day to think about daring to do something different, something out of the ordinary, something that you'll look back on years from now with pride and happiness. Seek adventure rather than retreat from it.

I plan to sample one of life's thrilling adventures.

"In the skin of our fingers we can see the trail of the wind; it shows us where the wind blew when our ancestors were created."

—NAVAJO LEGEND

BAD WIND, GOOD WIND

How often do you think about the wind? You may pay little attention unless you want to go sailing, fly a kite, or need the wind to generate power or operate machinery. Most often the wind is ignored until it declares itself in emphatic ways—in a tornado, cyclone, thunderstorm, nor'easter, or sandstorm. Because of this, you may fear the wind and the havoc it can create. Naturalist W. H. Hudson writes about the *pampero* wind that tears across southern Argentina in his memoir, *Idle Days in Patagonia:* "The winds are hissing, whimpering, whistling, muttering and murmuring, whining, wailing, howling, shrieking. . . ." Mark Twain describes, "Hats, chickens and parasols sailing in the remote heavens; blankets, tin signs, sagebrush, and shingles . . . glass doors, cats and little children. . . ." And Raymond Chandler describes the Santa Ana season in his famous short story, "Red Wind" as a time when "Meek little wives feel the edge of the carving knife and study their husbands' necks. Anything can happen."

Yet the wind is not always a force of destruction. The wind carries beautiful scents in the air. The wind dries clothing and sheets. The wind cools. The wind whispers and soothes. The wind increases fertility. The wind guides. The wind powers. The wind airs out and cleanses.

If you listen closely today, the wind will tell you stories of where it has come from and where it is going. And if you close your eyes and breathe deeply, the wind will tell you of all its wanderings by the scents it carries along.

I see the wind as good and learn from it.

". . . such is the ignorance of Nature in large Citys that are nothing less than overgrown prisons that shut out the world and all its beautys."

—ENGLISH POET JOHN CLARE

SLOWING DOWN YOUR PACE

How do you accelerate through each day? From the moment your alarm rings, you may taxi down the runway of your life and then become airborne at Mach-2 speeds like the Concorde jet.

You jump into your car, screech into traffic, hug tightly to the bumpers of the cars ahead of you, and frantically cut in and out of travel lanes trying to better yesterday's drive-time record. You roar into the parking lot, jump out of the car, greet others with a rushed "goodmorninghihowareyouhaveaniceday," and leap into your desk chair as the telephone rings and piles of work multiply before your eyes. At lunch you may dash to an express-style restaurant, load up piles of food on a plastic plate, and sprint back to the office to take hurried bites in between meetings and the rest-of-the-day madness until it's time to get back in your car and begin the ride home.

After going through day after day at this frantic pace, stop for a moment and ask, "What am I really accomplishing by functioning at such a superhuman pace? What will all this mean years from now? Will I look back on this experience and think I really achieved something, or will I wonder, 'Why, oh why, didn't I take time out every once in a while to notice how nature goes on existing, without my even noticing, in the very heart of the city—but not in my own heart?'"

I want to do more today than move at a faster pace; I want to slow my pace and notice nature.

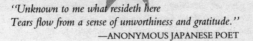

*"Unknown to me what resideth here
Tears flow from a sense of unworthiness and gratitude."*
—ANONYMOUS JAPANESE POET

FEELING WORTHY

Can you imagine any living thing in nature feeling unworthy or inferior? One daffodil doesn't look around at the garden of daffodils it's in and think, "You know, I'm just not as pretty as the others." One skunk doesn't look at another skunk and think, "Wow! Look at that big grub he just pulled out of the ground! I'll never be as lucky as he is finding grubs." One bird doesn't perch on the limb of a tree, listening to the melodious song of another, and then sigh, "I might as well give up singing—my song will never measure up to that one!"

Nature teaches you that every living thing is valuable and has its important place and vital contribution to make. As Ralph Waldo Emerson once commented, "What is a weed? A plant whose virtues have not yet been discovered." Each daffodil, each skunk, each songbird—even each weed—manifests its potential differently, yet beautifully. Each living thing has its own expression, its own fragrance, its own capabilities, its own skills, its own song. Only human beings suffer from a low sense of self-esteem.

Today, choose not to let personal criticisms, put-downs, or negative comments create or contribute to your feelings of unworthiness. You have a place in this world and a contribution to make. Focus on who you are and what you can do. Know that you are great because you're another living thing—another miracle of nature.

I feel worthwhile, valuable, and vital.

"The gaps are the thing. The gaps are the spirit's one home. . . . The gaps are the clefts in the rock where you cower to see the back parts of God; they are the fissures between mountains and cells the wind lances through, the icy narrowing fiords splitting the cliffs of mystery. Go up into the gaps. If you can find them; they shift and vanish too. Stalk the gaps."
—AMERICAN WRITER AND NATURALIST ANNIE DILLARD

SEEKING SPIRITUAL COMFORT

It has been said that in order to feel that you're truly one with your spirituality, you need to study a dozen years under the guidance of a good spiritual teacher. But when you're in the midst of a time of evaluation or reevaluation—of taking a good, long look at yourself and your life—you may not want to take such a large amount of time. So you make yourself a promise to "work on" your spirituality one day and then continue on with your life, taking care of your emotional, physical, and intellectual needs.

But then the urge to feel like you spiritually "belong"— that you're connected with a Higher Power, nature, or the universe—may suddenly develop into an obsession. So you may run off to spiritual workshops or retreats, carry a religious book with you at all times, restructure your life in order to accommodate a rigorous meditation schedule, or purchase numerous books, tapes, and guidance tools for fostering a relationship with a Higher Power. You may look for your spirituality everywhere—sometimes frantically—as if it were a lost set of car keys and you were already late for an appointment.

But sometimes you don't need to do anything to "find" your spirituality. It already exists within you. Sometimes it just slips away from time to time, falling between the cracks and gaps in your daily life.

I am always spiritually connected.

"Make it a rule of life never to regret and never to look back. Regret is an appalling waste of energy; you can't build on it; it's only good for wallowing in."
—NEW ZEALAND–BORN BRITISH AUTHOR KATHERINE MANSFIELD

JOURNEYING ON THE RIVER OF LIFE

Life is dynamic. Like a river it constantly flows, its currents forming new patterns based on change. If you live your life as a dynamic person, then you're unafraid to travel on that river. You go where it takes you. You remain becalmed when its waters run calm; you race along when its waters rush; you make twists and turns as the water forges its path. As the river of life changes, so does the way you move through it.

But when you live your life holding on to the past—by wishing you could relive the carefree days of your childhood or by reminiscing over "glory days" gone by—then you're not able to flow with the river. Instead, you watch the river go by or fight wherever the river wants to take you. Your longings for long ago keep you from enjoying your travels down the river today.

Do you resist enjoying the river journey of life? Or do you look forward with excited anticipation to where the waters of life have yet to take you? There's an old Chinese adage that says, "Flowing water does not decay." When you go with the flow, you move. When you don't, you stagnate.

Life is a flow of energy. Each day, you can let the energy carry you with its strong, determined current. From now on, get into motion. Move your mind, body, and spirit. Do something new, different, exciting, and challenging. Be like Huck Finn. Build your raft and journey to wherever the river of life takes you.

I flow easily with the river of life.

"The last fling of winter is over. . . . The earth, the soil itself has a dreaming quality about it. It is warm now to the touch; it has come alive; it hides secrets that in a moment, in a little while, it will tell."
—AMERICAN NATURALIST DONALD CULROSS PEATTIE

PRESPRING GROWTH

Spring is never far away in your life when you can live through each winter. The same is true for nature. The sugar-maple trees provide a good example of this. At a time when the weather achieves a perilous balance between winter and spring—when it's cold at night and warm during the day—the trees begin to activate for spring. As the weather warms up, the sap in the trees expels carbon dioxide, which forms bubbles. The bubbling, expanding carbon dioxide puts pressure on the vessels that conduct the sap; the pressure drives the sap upward and downward, flowing within the tree. If the weather stays warm for a while, the sap stops running. But if the cold weather returns, the tree recharges itself and reenters a sap-producing cycle. So the sugar maples, rather than depending upon the warmth of spring and summer, actually need the waning times of winter and autumn to grow. Then severing the vessels with a tap hole diverts the flow of sap into the waiting sap bucket, where it will take about forty gallons of sap to make just one gallon of syrup.

You, too, can begin to prepare for the new growth of spring that awaits you. Use this time of "season between season" to strengthen your muscles through exercise in the warming air and planting in the softening ground, to awaken your senses to the subtle greening that's beginning to show, to witness eternal miracles of mating and birth, and to sharpen your mental faculties through learning and thinking.

I witness the growth within me and around me.

"A sense of mortality should make us smarter. Life is short, so you do your work. You spend more time attending to music and art and literature, less time arguing politics. You plant trees. You cook spaghetti sauce. You talk to children. You don't let your life get eaten by salesmen and evangelists and the circuses of the media."

—HUMORIST AND WRITER GARRISON KEILLOR

BEING MORE CHILDLIKE

No one has to teach a child how to relax, have fun, sing, dance, laugh, and play. They come into this world prepared to participate in everything as if it were new. Can you imagine a child thinking, "I haven't taken time off from my schoolwork this week to go to the playground. Maybe I should set aside some time to have some fun."

As an adult, you may think play is too frivolous. Or that choosing to do something you like to do—rather than something you feel you ought to do—is a waste of time. But how much time have you already wasted in your life doing all those serious, focused, goal-oriented, achievement-centered tasks? You may now be so caught up in ambitious career endeavors, in taking care of your family, in working on your intimate relationship, in attending to the priorities in your life—in short, doing all the "adult" things—that you've forgotten what it's like to be a child.

When was the last time you felt like a kid? Flying a kite, riding a bicycle, tossing a ball, or playing on the equipment on a playground are a few of the ways kids have fun. What can you do? Today, decide to do something playful, spontaneous, and unadultlike. Read a children's book. Play a board game. Sing a silly song to yourself. Skip. Jump rope. Rediscover the fun in life by being a child.

I look at the world through a child's eyes.

"If spring came but once in a century, instead of once a year, or burst forth with the sound of an earthquake, and not in silence, what wonder and expectation there would be in all hearts to behold the miraculous change! But now the silent succession suggests nothing but necessity. To most men only the cessation of the miracle would be miraculous, and the perpetual exercise of God's power seems less wonderful than its withdrawal would be."

—AMERICAN POET HENRY WADSWORTH LONGFELLOW

THE MIRACLES OF NATURE

Some of nature's incredible, astounding events occur at great intervals. Comets, solar and lunar eclipses, or the appearance of a new species of plant, insect, or animal are once-in-a-lifetime happenings that you feel blessed to witness.

But the great majority of nature's incredible, astounding events occur so regularly and frequently that you may forget to pay attention to them. The first day of spring, like the first day of summer, autumn, and winter, is probably just a printed notation on your page-a-day calendar or a passing news item. The reappearance of the most famous "snowbird"—the robin—often goes unnoticed as does the tiny pale green shoot of a crocus or daffodil that tentatively pushes its way through the last remaining layer of snow you walk by each day.

If the world were the same every day, then it might not be unusual to pay little attention to it. Yet the world you live in is constantly changing. It's seasonal. It ebbs and flows. It waxes and wanes. It migrates and returns. Sometimes it trickles; sometimes it gushes. Sometimes it blows; sometimes it grows still.

Notice the world today. Pay attention to how the natural world is silently yet wondrously shifting its gears to advance into spring.

I witness the wondrous ways the natural world is moving into spring.

*"There is something infinitely healing in the repeated refrains of nature—
the assurance that dawn comes after night, and spring after the winter."*
—NATURALIST AND WRITER RACHEL CARSON

THE PASSAGE OF TIME

Time brings summer to a close, and winter as well. Time ages the brilliant petals of flowers and also prepares new buds. Time signals the end of a life, as well as the beginning of another. Because of this continuum, you can trust that time always brings new experiences.

As you age, you may become aware of this passage of time on a more personal level. Perhaps you find that you're more serious now, focused more on tasks and duties than on things that bring you pleasure—puttering around your garden, taking a weekly hike in the mountains, or designing and building bird-houses. Maybe it's been a long time since you played a friendly but rousing game of tackle football or even played catch without feeling the after effects of sore muscles. Perhaps you can't remember the last time you spent a night on the town with your friends, happily wasting time together.

You may wish you could slam shut the doors on each day to prevent time from moving on. Yet you can make today a time for new beginnings, for fresh starts, for doing things in your life differently—and more pleasurably. Start now to think of ways to create more balance in your life so you can offset work and duties with hobbies and recreation. Stretch and strengthen underused muscles through progressively more challenging workouts. And remember that the point of life is not to make the most in the time you have, but to make the most out of the time you've been given. Enjoy yourself!

I move forward with the passage of time in pleasurable, life-enhancing ways.

"We others, who have long lost the more subtle of the physical senses, have not even proper terms to express an animal's intercommunications with his surroundings, living or otherwise, and have only the word 'smell,' for instance, to include the whole range of delicate thrills which murmur in the nose of the animal night and day, summoning, warning, inciting, repelling."

—ENGLISH WRITER KENNETH GRAHAME

SENSUAL COMMUNICATION

Communication between human beings can oftentimes be so confusing and particular that even a dozen witnesses to the same event can't agree on a single account; each sees and hears something different, based on his or her own interpretation.

Yet in the natural world there's no room for such ambiguity or unclarity; clear communication is so essential that it can mean the difference between life and death. In the world of predator and prey as well as in the daily world of survival, all of an animal's senses need to remain open so appropriate action can be taken; animals use smell, sight, sound, taste, and touch to distinguish odors, spot movement, determine what should be ingested, and feel vibrations.

If you could similarly open up your senses to the natural world, you would discover that nature communicates clearly with you. The sound the rain makes on your roof communicates to you the type of rain it is—a gentle sprinkle, a steady shower, or a downpour. Rustling in the leaves communicates the presence of a living creature moving about on the ground. The surge of waves against the shore communicates a calm or stormy sea. The first warble of a bird communicates daybreak. Nature's communication teaches you that words are often imperfect; it is the subtle, sensual communication that's always distinct and clear.

I open my senses to pay attention to nature's communications.

"The morning dawns with an unwonted crimson; the flowers more odorous seem; the garden birds sing louder, and the laughing sun ascends the gaudy earth with an unusual brightness: all nature smiles, and the whole world is pleased."

—AMERICAN THEOLOGIAN DAY KELLOGG LEE

THE BEST PART OF THE MORNING

What's the best part of the morning to you? Maybe it's the brisk run you take before dawn on the deserted city, town, or country streets, with the sound of your breathing and the gentle slap of your feet as they greet the pavement your only companions. Perhaps it's the steamy shower you take that helps you to slowly open your eyes and rouse your sleepy muscles. Maybe it's the walk you make from the subway or bus stop to your favorite coffee shop, where you're greeted by the enticing smells of baked goods and freshly ground coffee. Perhaps it's the time you share with your excited, energetic dog as you toss a ball or Frisbee around a grassy field.

Even if you're not a "morning person," there's much you can enjoy in the morning. You're part of a still-sleepy world that yawns and stretches and needs its time to slowly and gently awaken much as you do. The first song of the morning birds is tentative, the first light in the sky is muted, the first rays of the sun are cool, the first tilt of the flower is toward the east. But as the morning progresses and the world lifts itself out of its bed, the birds' songs grow more confident, the colors in the sky more vibrant, the sun's rays warmer, and the flower buds more open and fragrant.

Start your day with song, with brightness, with warmth, and with joy, and the rest of your day will be pleasurable.

I start my day with a smile; I am pleased with the world.

"*I don't know whether a passionate love of the natural world can be transmitted or not, but like the love of beauty it is a thing one likes to associate with the scheme of inheritance.*"

—AMERICAN WRITER E. B. WHITE

ACTIVE LOVE

Love is an active process that requires you to do something, or you will receive nothing in return. You need to reach out, to act, to speak, and to give of yourself in order to love and be loved. Expressing love in this way takes you out of the usual course of life and into exciting, uncharted territories. Then love is like the waters of a mountain stream that rush down the mountainside each spring, fresh and clean and pure, to replenish ponds that have filled with dead leaves and rotted tree branches over the winter.

Giving love in this way to another living thing—a human being or a member of the natural world—transcends ego, materialism, anger, self-defeating situations, and the hustle and bustle of daily living. Such love brings compassion, tolerance, strength, and harmony with nature into your life. But this love happens only when you actively give of yourself by taking time to be tender, attentive, kind, thoughtful, considerate, and focused on the needs of other living things.

Today, believe that you have not given enough love to others in your life; now you must take the time to be loving. Offer help to a stranger. Listen to a friend. Reestablish contact with a family member who lives far away. Plant seeds and bulbs. Provide some of the funding to offer a pet partner to someone in need. Make a donation. Smile. Give a hug.

I actively give my love today.

"Give me the roughest of spring days rather than the loveliest of autumn days for there is death in the air."

—ENGLISH NOVELIST AND POET THOMAS HARDY

REPLACEMENT AND RENEWAL

Any loss of life is tragic. Even when death is expected, loss can be extremely painful. Part of this pain comes out of the process of grieving, which, while natural and quite necessary, can sometimes be prolonged. Focusing for too long on what has been lost can severely impair your ability to move on in life.

In the animal kingdom, creatures who have experienced the loss of their mate or an offspring have been observed to exhibit signs of grieving—refusal of food, inactivity, remaining in the nest, den, or other "home" even when their own lives are threatened, or staying near the deceased. But such grief behavior stops after a certain period of time; the creature then begins to resume normal activities, although some may not mate again.

While you need to allow time to mourn the loss of a loved one, you also need to keep in mind that sometimes the best way to work through your grief is to gradually force your way back into the normal routines of your daily life. You can still write about your sad and angry feelings in a journal, discuss how you feel in a self-help group, meditate, pray, seek spiritual counsel from a member of the clergy, or ask for help from a bereavement counselor. But you need to keep in mind the ongoing, natural process of renewal and replacement. As American physician and writer Lewis Thomas comments, "If it were not for the constant renewal and replacement going on before your eyes, the whole place would turn to stone and sand under your feet."

I accept the losses in my life as part of the necessary process of renewal.

"The sea is a noisy place. Just swim near the parrot fish on a coral reef. You can hear them chewing, crunch, crunch. *All through the water world, there are grunts, deep moans, snaps, drummings, squeaks, roars, clatters, bangs, and from time to time through the corridors of water, the calling of great whales."*

—AMERICAN WRITER MARY LEE SETTLE

THE SOUNDS OF NATURE

When you think about nature's sounds, more often than not you probably imagine hushed sounds—the gentle *swhoosh* of the wind filtering through the pine trees; the almost imperceptible *plink, plink, plink* of water dripping rhythmically onto a moss-covered rock in the middle of a forest; the whispered rustlings in the leaves—*shitch-shitch, shitch-shitch-shitch*— of a chipmunk foraging for food. Or you may think that the true sounds of nature are those long silences, when the sun sets or rises, when the clouds drift across the blue sky, when the flower and tree buds gradually open, when the fog embraces the surface of a lake, when bare rock absorbs the rays and colors of a brilliant sun, when apple blossoms bloom, when fresh, earthy smells drift through the air.

And yet, on this fine spring morning, you can be in the middle of a field or on a path deep in the forest, far away from civilization, and discover that daybreak can be deafening. Nature screams out to you, "Notice me! Notice me! Hear this!" Birds burst forth into song like competing street-corner musicians; squirrels chatter nonstop like neighbors conversing from backyard to backyard; gulls screech at one another like angry drivers caught in morning gridlock. Nature, like humanity, is hard not to hear.

I wake up to the rousing sounds of nature.

"Is it not possible that mammals look after their young with bumbling consciousness rather than with the expertness of instinct because nature has, in some way, been interested not merely in the survival of the fittest, but in 'the fittest' for something more than mere survival?"

—AMERICAN WRITER JOSEPH WOOD KRUTCH

ANIMAL PARENTING BEHAVIOR

There's much that you do for your children that you don't even think about. You feed them when they're hungry, protect them from extremes in temperature, and hire sitters or use day-care facilities you feel you can trust. But did you know that animal parents behave similarly with their young?

While some argue whether parenting behavior in the animal kingdom is instinctive or learned behaviors combined with instinct, for the most part parenting awards could be given out to those species who continue to care for their young after birth. These parents provide food and protect their young from hot and cold as well as teach them how to survive by showing them which plants to eat, where to go for water, how to avoid danger, how to hunt, and even how to choose a place to sleep. Too, they will discipline their young when they see them doing something dangerous. They will encourage their young to explore the world around them and to play with one another. And they will leave their young in the care of other adults in communal "day-care" units. This communal-care arrangement solidifies communities that have already been formed and allows for reciprocity; for example, the immature females in an elephant herd that care for the calves have this favor returned when they have their young, thereby building long-term relationships and enhancing the stability of the group.

I appreciate the parenting skills exhibited by the animal kingdom.

"I consider myself to have been the bridge between the shotgun and the binoculars in bird watching. Before I came along, the primary way to observe birds was to shoot them and stuff them."

—ARTIST, WRITER, AND BIRD-WATCHER
RICHARD TORY PETERSON

ABOUT "THE KING PENGUIN"

Many years ago, when a Ross's gull, a breed that lives in Siberia and migrates over western Alaska, made a totally unexpected appearance in the tiny New England seacoast town of Newburyport, Massachusetts, over five thousand birders rushed from all over the United States and Western Europe in the hope of adding this rare sighting to their "life list" of sightings. As the birders waited anxiously, a hushed announcement was suddenly passed through the crowd. "He's here," was the whisper, but the excitement was not about the Ross's gull. Rather, it was about the arrival of famed birder Richard Tory Peterson—the six-foot-tall, ruddy-faced, white-haired man known as "the King Penguin" to bird-watchers everywhere.

From the age of eleven, Peterson (1908–1996) devoted himself to caring for birds. In the seventh grade, he began drawing birds, applying his talent for meticulous detail. Soon he was drawing and photographing every bird in sight; when no models were available, he would draw birds from memory. He compiled his drawings and sought a publisher; when *A Field Guide to the Birds Including All Species Found in Eastern North America* was initially published, its press run was two thousand copies. They sold out in three weeks.

Today, four million copies of Peterson's *Field Guide* and three subsequent editions are in print; the simplicity of the Peterson system of identification has been credited as making bird-watching accessible to millions.

I identify at least three different birds today.

"I have enjoyed greatly the second blooming that comes when you finish the life of the emotions and of personal relations; and suddenly find . . . that a whole new life has opened before you, filled with things you can think about, study, or read about. . . . It is as if a fresh sap of ideas and thoughts was rising in you."

—BRITISH MYSTERY WRITER DAME AGATHA CHRISTIE

THE NATURE OF YOUTH

Nature can be discovered or rediscovered at any age; in fact, a great many programs that involve the natural world are specifically geared toward middle-aged and older men and women. For example, the University of Pittsburgh's floating campus, the *S.S. Universe,* takes students of all ages on cruises to such places as India and the Middle East, where they can participate in natural as well as cultural learning.

Combining learning with travel is becoming popular, for an innovative atmosphere of learning can take place on journeys to exotic locales. The excitement of discovery is often enhanced by interaction with anthropologists, ornithologists, historians, and naturalists. Society Expeditions, for example, takes more than 2,500 people on such exotic learning journeys a year. According to Aaltje E. van Zoelen, the majority of the passengers who are "jumping into the rubber Zodiac boats to examine the plant life on some obscure atoll or to learn about the ecology of a river on these vigorous expeditions are over fifty." As well, regular cruise lines are including lectures and workshops on everything from marine and bird life to financial planning.

The new experiences and understandings you can gain from participating in such programs can make your life exciting and challenging.

The nature of youth is contagious at any age.

"I cannot forever keep out the woodpecker that mistakes my house for a dead tree. For that matter, why should I object to a flicker banging away on the roof when what it is doing is proclaiming the triumph of spring?"
—AMERICAN NATURE WRITER JOHN HAY

THE LOVE OF THE INDOORS

While you may consider yourself to be a nature lover, you may be adamant about keeping the outdoors out of your house. Spiders and their webs, ladybugs, and other insects may have a low survival rate in your home or apartment; you may, however, choose to return them to the "wild" by guiding them outdoors on a piece of paper. Pigeons that roost on your roof may be frightened away by a plastic owl or discouraged from alighting with metal stakes or pieces of flashing. Eliminating bees and the hives they build against roof overhangs or inside overhangs is most often done by extermination. Squirrels that gnaw a hole under your attic eaves and mice that scurry about in the spaces between walls may be captured in traps and released miles from your home.

Yet such things never bothered naturalist Henry David Thoreau. He would often fling open his door and windows to admit not only light, but birds and squirrels as well. Wanting to live intimately with nature made him so willing to let the outdoors in that he refused even to chase wasps away at night.

While you may welcome nature to your home by erecting birdhouses and feeders and refuse to use chemicals to treat garden pests even when they ravage your prize tomatoes, you may draw the line at the nature that works its way through your windows and front door. Keeping your home comfortable for you means that sometimes you may have to be intolerant of even the smallest, least harmful creatures.

I love the outdoors yet wish to preserve my indoor sanctuary.

"Civilized people depend too much on man-made printed pages. I turn to the Great Spirit's book which is the whole of his creation."
—CHEROKEE INDIAN TATANGA MANI

GAINING WISDOM FROM NATURE

Who is wiser—the person who knows that Shakespeare wrote the play *Romeo and Juliet,* or someone who wonders who wrote the songs the birds sing? The person who knows the scientific names of herbs, or someone who dries and then blends them into a unique, aromatic combination? The person who can name all the oceans of the world, or someone who questions whether the sea—and not just all of the creatures in it—is alive? The person who relies upon maps to plan the route for a wilderness trek, or someone who uses the map as a guide in order to create a new trail?

Who is wiser—the person who has knowledge about most things and how they work, or the one who questions everything in the environment, seeking understanding through the wisdom that can be gained from contact and connection with the natural world? Writer and amateur stargazer Barry Evans writes that wisdom is "about awareness: noticing, stopping, looking, heeding, remarking, observing, beholding, discerning, perceiving, asking, examining, probing, considering, pondering, weighing, appraising, studying . . . right now. It's about wonder. . . . It's about stopping and noticing phenomena in the world around us—air, water, light, gravity, breath, dolphins, rocks, wind, and heartbeats—and appreciating them more for understanding them a little."

To gain true wisdom, you can learn more from consulting with nature than you can by consulting books. For nature has infinite teachings that are greater than any book or collection of books can ever contain.

I consult with nature to expand my wisdom.

"Poet William Stafford once said that we are defined more by the detours and distractions in life than by the narrow road toward goals. I like this image . . . it is the crazy asides in a day that lead me to fruitful territory."
—WRITER NANCY H. BLAKEY

TAKING A DETOUR

Imagine that you are planning a road trip. You can go anywhere you want and take as much time as you'd like. Would you choose the fastest, shortest, easiest route, make as few stops as possible, and be happy if you reached your destination ahead of schedule? Or would you take back roads and stop at farm stands and obscure points of interest, unconcerned about whether the trip took you three hours or three days?

When a lamb, Banner, "was rejected by his mother days before a planned trip to Boise," writes Nancy H. Blakey, "I had two choices: I could leave the lamb with my husband, who would have to take him to the office, feed him every two hours, and remember to change his diapers. Or I could take Banner to Boise with me." She opted to take Banner, her four kids, and baggage and bikes on the five-hundred-mile, nine-hour trip. She had to take back roads so she could stop every hour and let Banner shake out his legs. Her kids reveled in the stops, running around in fields by the sides of the roads and returning to the car laughing and breathless. They explored side roads, surrendered to whims, stopped at interesting locales, saw sights they had never seen before, and arrived at their destination days later, "fresh and full of stories."

On the way home, they discovered a new route. They visited a relative they hadn't seen in years. They stopped and rested by a field of flowers. "We discovered," Blakey writes, "that we *can* stop at a river just because our toes are hot and the water is cold . . . it took a tiny black lamb to make me realize that a detour may uncover the best part of a journey—and the best part of yourself."

I take a detour in my life today.

"How strange and wonderful is our home, our earth, with its swirling vaporous atmosphere, its flowing and frozen liquids, its trembling plants, its creeping, crawling, climbing creatures, the croaking things with wings that hang on rocks and soar through fog, the furry grass, the scaly seas."
—AMERICAN WRITER EDWARD ABBEY

THE SECRET WORLD OF NATURE

There's much in nature that you know about and can see with your own eyes every day—a tree, a plant, the sea, a bee, the mountains, a desert. There's also much in nature that you can learn about and see either through travel or books and films.

Yet there's much about nature that you may never understand and never see for yourself. Without such things, though, the world as you know it wouldn't exist—wouldn't support your existence or the existence of so many other living things.

For instance, at this moment your body is being inundated with uncountable waves, forces, sounds, and particles. The earth's magnetic field, gravitational forces, X rays from naturally occurring radon, gamma rays and X rays from supernovas, and neutrinos from the sun are just some of the natural forces that bombard you as you read this book. The dog napping at your feet may be able to hear some sounds that are well beyond your range of hearing or pick up a scent that's totally undetectable to you; too, your cat may be able to pick up the ultrasound being emitted by a mouse in your house. If you turn the page of this book, you'll be moving a mountain of atomic matter that has settled on the page while you were reading.

Your senses are attuned to just the merest fraction of natural activity that surrounds you; your senses only allow you faint glimmers into the world of nature's strange and wonderful secrets.

I am in awe of this wide world of wonders.

"One vivid memory remains of passing through the city. A small boy, five or six at most, had picked up a dead monarch butterfly from a pile of litter beside the street. He was standing entranced, bending forward, oblivious to all around him. It seemed as though I were looking at myself when young. A door was opening for him, a door beyond which lay all the beauty and mystery of nature."

—AMERICAN NATURE WRITER EDWIN WAY TEALE

NATURAL HARMONY

You may take for granted the harmony of your world until it's disrupted; so, too, may you take for granted the harmony of the natural world until you see that it, too, can be disrupted.

Take, for example, an event that took place in the coastal town of Pacific Grove, California. Long known for its monarch butterflies, people would come to the town specifically to witness the return of the brilliant orange insects. The butterflies were elevated to the status of town symbol; their image was emblazoned on street signs, maps, and promotional materials.

But in the early 1990s, there was a dramatic decrease in the butterflies because increased development destroyed the shrubs and flowers that were their natural habitat. The houses, lawns, and pavements that were created for an expanding human population had, at the same time, evicted at least one species of natural creatures from their own homes. And because one precious living thing had been lost in that community, not only was the harmonious existence of the monarch butterfly disrupted, but also the harmony of Pacific Grove.

It's up to you to protect the harmony of your world. Today, pay attention to the development, landscaping, harvesting, and other actions that disrupt the natural and human harmony in your community.

I actively promote natural harmony in my habitat.

> *"As my eyes*
> *search*
> *the prairie*
> *I feel the summer*
> *in the spring."*

—CHIPPEWA SONG

LOOKING FORWARD TO THE SUMMER

Even though spring is just around the corner and summer is still a season away, you can already feel the summer in the spring. So now is a good time to think about the type of summer you'd like to have. Think about what you'd like to do around the house. While you may already have a lengthy list of household projects to accomplish, you might want to include something that connects you with the natural world around your home. Maybe you can think of a good place to place a birdhouse or hang a bird feeder, plot a small vegetable garden, start a few cooking herbs from seeds to later transplant to a window box, provide badly needed pruning for a backyard tree, or seed and maintain a chemical-free lawn.

Now is also the time to think about your summer vacation. While tentative plans may include visiting relatives or taking the kids to a theme park, you might also like to do something that connects you with nature. Maybe you can plan a few day hikes in the mountains or a weekend camping or canoe trip, a longer trip to one of the national parks, or sign up for a guided trip sponsored by an expedition group or nature organization such as the Appalachian Mountain Club.

This coming summer can be a time to accomplish much, catch up with friends and relatives, enjoy man-made thrills, and still have a naturally good time.

I plan a summer vacation that connects me with nature.

"All humans are frightened of their own solitude. Yet only in solitude can we learn to know ourselves, learn to handle our own eternity of aloneness."
—UNKNOWN

ENJOYING YOUR SOLITUDE

Loneliness can attack you like a disease. Physically, it can drain you like a potent strain of a flu, wearing you down to the point of exhaustion. And, like a long bout with the flu, it can also drain you emotionally and spiritually, eating away at your ability to think positively and to trust that you're okay during the times when you're alone.

You may think that the best antidote to loneliness is to be more social, make more plans with friends, or walk around a crowded shopping mall. But often what's best is to go somewhere where you can be alone, with yourself and your thoughts, where you can revel in the glory of your aloneness and delight in what that experience reveals of your spirit.

Diarist Anne Frank once wrote, "The best remedy for those who are afraid, lonely, or unhappy is to go outside, somewhere where they can be quite alone with the heavens, nature, and God. Because only then does one feel that all is as it should be and that God wishes to see people happy, amidst the simple beauty of nature. As long as this exists, and it certainly always will, I know that then there will always be comfort for every sorrow, whatever the circumstances may be."

Today, find time to be alone with yourself and nature. Let this time of solitude strengthen you and help you to believe in yourself, your value, and your worthiness.

I revel in myself in my moments of solitude.

"The rains bring us trees and flowers; the droughts bring gaping cracks in the world. The lakes and rivers sustain us; they flow through the veins of the earth and into our own. But we must take care to let them flow back out as pure as they came, not poison and waste them without thought for the future."

—AMERICAN POLITICIAN AL GORE

PRESERVING THE ENVIRONMENT

The world's current ecological problems—pollution, acid rain, destruction of the rain forests, and the depletion of the ozone layer, to name a few—remind you that you're part of a complex web of life. Major catastrophes such as oil spills or the release of harmful chemicals into the atmosphere can affect everyone and everything, from the bottom of the chain of life to the top. Whether you experience this impact indirectly by paying more at the store for your vegetables, or whether you experience it firsthand by seeing your crops whither and die, the balance of nature is so delicate that any harm done today may be felt for a long time. Some of nature's balance can be readily restored; a soaking rain may save your crops. But it can take years to restore purity where there was poison, to replenish growth from stripped soil, to reestablish a nearly extinct species.

Yet you may question the impact that you, as one person, can have on healing the damages wrought by centuries of civilization. While you may never be able to recreate the ideal environment or even see it recreated in your lifetime, you can take positive action every day. What can you do? Plant a tree. Set up a recyling area in your home or health-care facility. Join an organization dedicated to the preservation of sand dunes, conservation land, or natural habitats. Make a lasting contribution!

I preserve the environment for now and the future.

"I am going to venture that the man who sat on the ground in his tipi meditating on life and its meaning, accepting the kinship of all creatures, and acknowledging unity with the universe of things was infusing into his being the true essence of civilization."

—OGLALA SIOUX CHIEF LUTHER STANDING BEAR

STILLING YOUR MIND

Meditation is the process of emptying your mind of stressful thoughts so you can experience physical relaxation and inner peace. It's a way to open yourself up to "communicate" not only with your "inner self," but also with a spiritual "guide" such as a Higher Power. In making this contact, you gain knowledge, inspiration, and guidance about the people, places, and things in your life so you can handle them more calmly, effectively, and objectively. As well, you gain a connection with the natural world and, in so doing, come in touch with the easy, flowing pace of a more natural way of living.

How do you meditate? There are no hard-and-fast rules. Some people sit in a quiet, candlelit room, their eyes closed, breathing slowly and deeply; some listen to soothing music or a guided meditation tape; some chant one word or focus on a single object such as the flame of a candle; some use running or walking as a soother; and some go outdoors to let the sounds of nature and the beautiful surroundings calm them.

To still your mind, think of the surface of a tiny pond on a sunny, windless, warm spring day. There's nothing to disturb the surface of the water; there's nothing, too, to disturb the depths. In such a still surface, the things in your life are mirrored undistorted so you can perceive your world with clarity and vision.

I still my mind to restore peace of mind.

"What a pity flowers can utter no sound!—A singing rose, a whispering violet, a murmuring honeysuckle,—oh, what a rare and exquisite miracle would these be!"

—AMERICAN CLERGYMAN HENRY WARD BEECHER

A NATURAL CHORUS

On one of his writing assignments, naturalist Edwin Way Teale was sent to a chicken farm on the edge of a small New Jersey village. One of the men who fed the poultry was rumored to have the oddest collection of musical instruments on earth.

The old chicken feeder told Teale that he had had visions, and in one vision he had watched 126 angels, each playing a different musical instrument. He took this as a sign that, during his time on earth, he was to reproduce all the instruments he had seen. Teale examined fiddles with three necks instead of one, a harp so huge it could be played from a second-story window, violins with crook necks, and odd combinations of harps and violins. The man told Teale that one of his smaller violins had sold for five hundred dollars because of the sweetness of its tone.

When Teale asked the man what special wood he had used to make such a sweet tone, the man told him that he got his wood from a lumberyard, but that he had been guided to certain boards, ones "that rang like a bell when he thumped them." The man told Teale that "all the resonance and beauty of tone in the finished product was inherent in the fibers of the wood"—not in the carving or finishing of the wood or even in the skill of the musician.

Today, when you listen to the spring sounds, think about what it would be like if all of nature could sing. Imagine sounds that would be just as sweet, melodious, and soothing—if only the flowers and trees could sing, too!

I imagine the song that could be created by an enormous natural choir!

"In the spring I have counted one hundred and thirty-six different kinds of weather inside of twenty-four hours."

—AMERICAN HUMORIST AND WRITER MARK TWAIN

APRIL'S WAYS

April can be one of the most fickle months of the year. She deludes all living things into thinking that spring has arrived—she encourages you to take down storm windows, rouses bulbs from their long winter slumber, urges trees to get their juices flowing, then gleefully wallops humanity and nature with snow or freezing rain. She teases you outdoors on a bright, sunny day, then torments you with showers for the rest of the week. She convinces you that a light jacket is all you need, then sucks in a deep breath and blows out a great gust of chilling wind. She takes the frozen ground, defrosts it into mush, then refreezes it, leaving ugly clumps and clods.

And yet the unpredictable month of April is often revered. "At its best," writes John Burroughs, "April is the tenderest of tender salads made crisp by ice or snow water." Henry David Thoreau pens, "The first sparrow of spring! The year beginning with younger hope than ever! The faint, silvery warblings heard over the partially bare and moist fields from the blue-bird, the song-sparrow, and the red-wing, as if the last flakes of winter tinkled as they fell!"

American humorist Dorothy Parker, however, expertly bridges the gap between the sentiments of those who find spring's unpredictability bothersome and those who find it glorious. "Every year," she writes, "back Spring comes, with the nasty little birds yapping their fool heads off, and the ground all mucked up with arbutus. Year after year after year."

Today I laugh at April's unpredictability and glory in her beauties.

"It's only when we truly know and understand that we have a limited time on earth—and that we have no way of knowing when our time is up—that we will begin to live each day to the fullest, as if it was the only one we had."
—SWISS-BORN U.S. PSYCHIATRIST, THANATOLOGIST, AND WRITER
ELISABETH KÜBLER-ROSS

LIVING EACH DAY TO THE FULLEST

You know that you have only a limited amount of time on earth. You may have less time than others; you may have more time. But you know that you're not immortal. At some point you'll no longer see the beauty of a sunrise or a sunset, speak with and touch a loved one, hear the sounds of nature or your favorite music, laugh at the antics of a child or grandchild, enjoy a run on a winding forest path, drive your car, swim in a lake, attain a business success, eat a delicious meal, find a cracked-open robin's egg on the grass, feel the wind on your face, cry, sing, dance, and make love.

Knowing this gives you an advantage over nature. Without a concept of time other than indications given by daylight and darkness, temperature fluctuations, and seasonal variations, the natural world doesn't know about its mortality. So the natural world can't plan ahead. The natural world can't appreciate its limited time on earth. The natural world can't put off something today in order to enjoy a once-in-a-lifetime experience.

Time is precious; every minute of this day is significant. So savor each moment you have before you. Let nothing escape your notice. And make time to work, to play, to laugh, to love, to give, and to live as fully and completely as you can.

I resolve to live well today.

"In walking, just walk. In sitting, just sit. Above all, don't wobble."
—ZEN SPIRITUALIST YUN-MEN

DOING THE IMPOSSIBLE

How many times have you been discouraged at the immensity of a project or goal that faced you? Maybe it was the desire to lose several pounds or to quit smoking. Perhaps it was doing something that stretched your capabilities. Maybe it was taking a risk that tapped into one of your biggest fears. Or perhaps it was doing something you've dreamed of doing, but always put off.

It's easy to say something's impossible, to refuse to take a risk, to bow to what your fears want you to do, and to resume old, familiar habits. But nothing in nature thinks in this way. Nature doesn't understand the term "impossible," and so every living thing believes anything is possible. Trees sprout from the steep sides of cliffs and reach towering heights. Ants lift amazing amounts of weight. Scrawny males challenge much larger males to mating battles, and win. Surefooted mountain creatures pick their way along pencil-thin paths, oblivious to the dizzying height and the certain death that greets them with one slip of a hoof.

Doubting yourself is the best way to undermine any success. Thinking too much about what lies ahead or what may possibly happen if something goes wrong talks you out of taking a chance. Feeling that your achievements would be so small that they would be insignificant belittles your capabilities and prevents you from developing your strengths.

Today, decide what you want to do, then set a course that leads you toward your goal. Hold steady to your course with faith, persistence, and a refusal to use the word *impossible*.

Today, I make the impossible possible.

"Do right always. It will give you satisfaction in life."
—PAIUTE PROPHET WOVOKA

BELIEVING THE RIGHT STORY

One of the most famed western artists, Frederic Remington, began his career picturing American Indians as savage opponents to hearty Anglo-Saxon adventurers. What appealed to him most were not the centuries of smoke, dust, sweat, blood, and toil that had been expended in the settling of the West, but the nostalgic, romanticized, and often fictionalized view of rugged cowboys, masculine military figures, and bloodthirsty Indians. In 1899, his portrait *Missing* depicts a white man who had been captured by the Indians, walking on foot through a scorching-hot desert with a noose around his neck, being led by arrogant-looking Indians on horseback.

But at the beginning of the next century, Remington adopted the figure of the Indian as a sympathetic symbol of the twilight of "old America." *The Luckless Hunter,* a 1904 painting, shows an Indian hunched on the back of his horse, wrapped in a blanket in twilight, empty-handed, alone. Remington had made a complete turnabout in his interpretation of his subject matter.

When Remington realized that the savage Indian from his early works had come to be perceived as an accurate representation of the era of western expansion, he felt that it was more important to be true to the Indian culture and what it stood for—freedom, strength, and existing in natural harmony. He ceased portraying misperceptions of the Indian and instead called attention to their plight as vanishing Americans, forcibly removed from their ways and from the land as a direct result of cold-blooded American expansion.

I crave an accurate picture of American history.

"People from a planet without flowers would think we must be mad with joy the whole time to have the things about us."

—ENGLISH NOVELIST AND PHILOSOPHER IRIS MURDOCH

FLOWERY DELIGHTS

Imagine what your life would be like without flowers. There would be no bulbs bursting from the ground every spring, no flower gardens, no wildflowers growing by the sides of the road or springing up in fields and marshy areas, no dogwoods or fruit trees offering up fragrant blossoms, no vegetables with flowers to herald the arrival of a cherry tomato or squash, no buttercups to hold under your chin, no petals to pick off one at a time to determine another's love for you, no corsages for the long-awaited prom, no Valentine's Day gift, no table centerpiece, no color and aroma to offset funereal somberness, nothing to climb up a trellis, nothing to press between the pages of a book.

Too, there would be no butterflies, no bees, no hummingbirds. No lily-pad chaise longues for sunning frogs. Nothing for insects to munch upon. No need for ladybugs or caterpillars. No need, too, for spiders or for birds.

Imagine living on this planet without flowers. What could ever replace a daffodil or a daisy? A rose or a rhododendron? A lily or a lilac? Loosestrife growing wild; orchids thriving in cultivation.

Throw out your vases. Forget about telling your housepainter that you want your house painted the color of a morning glory. Don't step carefully in the woods; there are no lady slippers you can harm.

Having to live on this planet without flowers would be like watching a black-and-white television. You could do it—but would you want to?

I go out of my way to see and smell flowers today.

"*Men argue, nature acts.*"
—FRENCH PHILOSPHER AND AUTHOR VOLTAIRE

RESOLVING CONFLICTS

Never in the history of the world has there been a war between two different species. While many animals fight over mates, food, and territory; while some sea creatures maintain a predator-prey relationship; while insects brawl with one another from time to time; and while living, growing things constantly compete for water, light, and space, nature doesn't go to war over such things. Nature takes action and, in so doing, avoids lengthy confrontations, arsenal manufacture and stockpiling, strategic planning sessions, senseless slaughter and the eventual monument tributes and honor rolls, environmental destruction, and tedious peace negotiations.

Not only does humanity argue far too much—from country versus country to race versus race to religion versus religion to gender versus gender—but argues in order to achieve dominance, annihilation, victory. Humanity grows angry and then responds to this anger vocally, vehemently, and violently; in the end, little is resolved while much is lost. It has taken nearly half a century for relations between Japan and the United States to improve, and yet there are many today who still see the Japanese as the enemy—a country and a people to be feared and hated.

If humanity could behave more like nature and learn how to act rather than react, then resolution would not be years in coming—and millions of dollars and lives later—but would be immediate and long-lasting.

I seek to release anger by resolving all conflicts promptly.

"It is a beautiful and a blessed world we live in, and while life lasts, to lose the enjoyment of it is a sin."

—AMERICAN CLERGYMAN TALBOT WILSON CHAMBERS

ENJOYING YOUR BLESSINGS

A story told by Dr. Bernie Siegel, author of *Love, Medicine and Miracles,* gives good advice about enjoying your blessings and appreciating more the circumstances of your life, no matter what they are:

A farmer who depends on his horse to plow is working his field one day when the horse drops dead. The people of the town say, "That's very unfortunate," but the farmer says, "We'll see." A few days later, somebody feels sorry for the man and gives him a horse as a gift. The people of the town say, "How fortunate," but the farmer says, "We'll see." A couple of days later, the horse runs away. "How unfortunate," say the townspeople, but the farmer says, "We'll see." A few days later, the horse returns with a second horse. "How fortunate," say the townspeople, but the farmer says, "We'll see." One day, while out riding with his son, the boy falls and breaks his leg. "How unfortunate," say the townspeople, but the man says, "We'll see." A few days later, the army comes to the man's farm to draft young men for war, but they can't take the boy because he has a broken leg.

The story can go on and on; the point is, the farmer refused to let the circumstances of his life color his attitude toward life. He enjoyed all those things he had been given for the time in which he could enjoy them, and he trusted that those things that he didn't enjoy so much wouldn't last forever. So rather than see the events in your life as either fortunate or unfortunate, you need to appreciate the blessings they bestow upon you at the moment.

I appreciate all of the blessings in my life.

*"The four largest national parks in the Rockies—Yellowstone, Waterton/
Glacier, Banff, and Jasper—are currently of no real or lasting importance
to the region's biological health. They are like the large, showy muscles of
a bodybuilder who has ceased to work out. They're not going to last; the
cardiovascular system's been ignored. The wild, fresh blood can't get from
one big muscle to the next."*

—NATURALIST AND WRITER RICK BASS

WORKING FOR THE ROCKY MOUNTAINS

Whenever Rick Bass gives talks on the critical situation that
exists in the Rockies—how the big trees that grew in the
Yaak Valley, creating the only rain forest in the United States,
have been clear-cut by corporations; how grizzlies, who so desperately need space, are down to less than two percent of their
former range; how the big animals in the region, the animals
so necessary to saving broad, intact ecosystems, now struggle
to exist at single- or, at most, double-digit populations; and
how important it is to contact senators and state representatives
about these things—his audience "shifts, squirms, yawns, rolls
eyes, checks watches. No shit, Sherlock, who's up next? We
all know the Rockies are being lost, they're thinking. But what
I'm thinking is, if we all know it, then why is it happening?"

What are you doing right now about the loss of treasured
lands to corporations, about the shrinking populations of valuable animals whose only predator is man, about the short
amount of time that's left for this once-vital, once-valuable region of America?

Connecting with nature means taking responsibility for
nature. Nature doesn't exist just for your vacation, for your
exciting "back to the wilderness" treks, or for your camera. "I
see too much play in the Rockies these days," concludes Bass,
"and not enough work."

I become actively involved in ways to save the Rockies.

"All birds, even those of the same species, are not alike, and it is the same with animals and with human beings. The reason Wakantanka does not make two birds, or animals, or human beings exactly alike is because each is placed here by Wakantanka to be an independent individuality and to rely upon itself."

—TETON SIOUX SHOOTER

DEVELOPING INDIVIDUALITY

Nature teaches an important lesson in individuality through the nesting habits of birds. Long ago, it was believed that all birds nested in the same way, laying their eggs in depressions on the ground or in natural cavities such as holes in trees. But, over time, bird nests became as varied and individualized as their occupants. Some birds, such as nighthawks, sandpipers, short-eared owls, and grouse, continue to lay their eggs in simple depressions on the ground. But trumpeter swans form nest mounds on ponds; female mallards nest at the edge of ponds, lining the nest with their own down feathers.

Other species prefer to nest in holes; woodpeckers chisel nest cavities in rotting trees, while kingfishers and bank swallows dig burrows in river and stream banks. Red-tailed hawks and goshawks opt for high-rise living, along with osprey and bald eagles, although the ospreys favor man-made structures such as power poles, and eagles like to build nests in trees using very large sticks. Female hummingbirds make tiny nest cups of seed down, mosses, or lichen, using cobwebs to bind their nests together. Robins plaster cup nests with mud and line them with soft grasses. Orioles hang pouchlike nests from branches.

To be an individual, you need to go through life constructing your own "nest," singing your own song, and flying on your own path.

I strive to distinguish myself as an individual.

"Many of us aspire to walk softly with respect and patience for all life on this planet. However, when the need for pest management arises, this goal is too often forgotten."

—PEST-MANAGEMENT SERVICE PERSON TRISHA ROSA

HOLISTIC PEST MANAGEMENT

The first thing you probably do when you see ants march into your home, attempt to work outdoors in the midst of mayflies, watch your pet scratch at fleabites, prepare for mosquito season, or seek to eliminate slugs, grubs, beetles, and other scavengers and ravaging insects and rodents from your garden is to purchase armloads of chemical sprays, powders, lotions, and "bombs" or enlist the help of an exterminator or lawn-and-garden-treatment service. But while such things may provide temporary relief or yield a luxurious lawn and pest-free garden, they can sometimes have devastating, adverse, and irreversible physical and environmental impacts.

Many holistic alternatives are widely available and, when used properly, can be long-lasting and very effective. The first rule of holistic pest management is based on the premise that any pest needs a habitat in which to survive, one that provides water, air, food, warmth, access to a nest, and protection from the elements. So eliminating the conditions that create an ideal environment for the pest "uninvites" them from your home, garden, lawn, pet, and self.

Too, many herbal remedies have scents that repel certain pests. Bathing a dog in eucalyptus soap or rubbing pennyroyal into your cat's coat as well as soaking collars in such things or making scented satchels for their bedding can deter fleas. Planting sage, garlic, peppermint, and lavendar can deter mosquitoes, which are not fond of these scents, from your backyard.

Before I use chemicals on pests, I seek to eliminate them holistically.

"Look. This is your world! You can't not look. There is no other world. This is your world; it is your feast. You inherited this; you inherited these eyeballs; you inherited this world of color. Look at the greatness of the whole thing. Look! Don't hesitate—look! Open your eyes. Don't blink, and look, look—look further."

—ZEN SPIRITUALIST CHÖGYAM TRUNGPA

HARMONY WITH YOUR HERITAGE

When you go outdoors—hiking, boating, camping, white-water rafting, mountain climbing, canoeing, and many other ways—you do so because you want to. You go out for the fun of it, the pleasure of it, the challenge of it, the stress-relieving elements of it, and the shared companionship of it. As well, you go out to learn more about the natural world and its living things.

But do you know that you go out also because you *have to*—because you feel the pull of nature's heritage deep with you? You have to look at the world, marvel at it, feel your connection to it, wonder at it, be inspired by it. "There are circuits and juices in every person," explains writer Douglas H. Chadwick, "that are the heritage of millions of years of evolution and survival. . . . They need exercising. Add a twinge of fear and wonder, and they can bring the world into focus with astonishing clarity. In such a setting, far from the clutter and clang of modern life, you find your senses opening wide, flowing easily, like the river, touching everything. . . ."

Today, let nature show you that you have a place in the living heritage of life. Every time you go outdoors, look around you at the passion, the challenges, the grandeur, the beauty, the discipline, and the opportunities represented by all of nature's wonders.

I know that each and every natural wonder is a part of me.

"*The sky is round, and I have heard that the earth is round like a ball, and so are all the stars. The wind, in its greatest power, whirls. Birds make their nests in circles, for theirs is the same religion as ours. . . . Ev'n the seasons form a great circle in their changing, and always come back again to where they were.*"

—LAKOTA SIOUX HOLY MAN BLACK ELK

WELCOMING NATURAL CYCLES

Growth in your life, as in nature, comes from the natural process of cycling through the seasons of your life. Each day, you're in a constant state of growth—from the personal changes you undergo, the risks you take, the challenges you face, the decisions you make, the people you meet, the gains you realize, the setbacks you suffer, the illnesses and injuries you heal and grow stronger from, the new experiences you have. Each day, too, you're in a constant state of decline from the effects of aging on your mind and body, from losses and failures you may experience, from periods of low energy, and from times of adjustment, reassessment, and realignment. Yet each day you're in a constant state of renewal, channeling your energy and strength into new endeavors and different paths, and spreading your enthusiasm to others.

Yet you've gone through such cycles many times before; you'll be going through them again in the future. Today's subtle greening of the leaves upon the trees has taken place many times before; nothing can reverse the natural progression of growth, decline, rebirth just as nothing can reverse the natural progression of your life. Welcome such "recycling" as evidence of everlasting life and growth. Live by the words of the Cherokee, who used to say, "It is coming quickly," when nature was about to change.

I am about to change; I welcome the change.

"So then the year is repeating its old story again. We are come once more, thank God! to its most charming chapter. The violets and the May flowers are as its inscriptions or vignettes. It always makes a pleasant impression on us, when we open again at these pages of the book of life."
—GERMAN POET JOHANN WOLFGANG VON GOETHE

SPRING CLEANING

For you, this spring season may signal a time for household as well as personal renewal—a time for cleaning out your closets, basement, and garage; a time for going over your whole home or apartment, from steam cleaning your carpets to polishing your windows; a time for beginning a diet or exercise program.

Yet this can also be a time when you pursue an action to improve the natural life around you. If you live in the city, you can join a garden club or city-park cleanup crew, organize a neighborhood recycling drive, or "adopt" the care of a zoo or aquarium reptile or animal. If you live in the suburbs, you can work with others in your community to beautify a common area, collect signatures to prevent further development, and voluntarily maintain parks and trails. If you live in the country, you can protect the water sources, wildlife, and wildflowers that are indigenous to your area or even introduce new living things as well as work hard to ensure that the natural peace and harmony are not disrupted, disturbed, or destroyed by humans.

Let the pleasant and inspiring impression that spring makes upon you motivate you to do good things not only for your own environment, but also for the larger, natural environment in which you live. The actions you take will benefit nature and, as well, may encourage others to join in enthusiastically, thereby increasing the good that can be done this season.

I spring into caring for my natural environment.

"I can remember once as a child—I was about six, and I'd walked out in the springtime in Virginia—and down the road from where we lived was a field of flowers. It was something about the way the sun hit the flowers and the butterfly on my arm, I was just totally, totally happy for about ten seconds. Totally perfectly happy."

—ACTRESS, AUTHOR, AND SPIRITUALIST SHIRLEY MACLAINE

TOTAL, PERFECT HAPPINESS

When was the last time you experienced a moment of such profound happiness—a time in which you felt such a great connection with your life, your world, and your planet and such an intense stirring from deep within your soul—that if, at that particular moment, you could have effectively captured the essence of the feeling and bottled it, there would have been no other name for it but *happiness*?

Too often what makes you happy is your salary, the location of your home, your profession, your possessions, your appearance, your achievements. Too often your happiness comes from being with a particular person, visiting or vacationing in a particular place, or participating in a particular pastime. Why can't you experience happiness from nothing in particular or from a combination of little things that can't be purchased or possessed—the sun on the flowers, for example, or a butterfly on your arm?

Today, let this morning make you happy—totally, perfectly happy. As English novelist and playwright Edward Bulwer-Lytton once observed, "I was always an early riser. Happy the man who is! Every morning day comes to him with a virgin's love, full of bloom and freshness. The youth of nature is contagious, like the gladness of a happy child."

This morning, I feel happiness.

"Land is also time. The greening of time is a clock whose hands are blades of grass moving vertically, up through the fringe of numbers, spreading across the middle of the face, sinking again as the sun moves from one horizon to the other."

—AMERICAN WRITER GRETEL EHRLICH

MAKING THE MOST OF THE LAND

On a clear spring day in 1952, Gertrude Lepine looked out of the window of her one-room Stowe Hollow, Vermont, schoolhouse and had an illuminating thought: if she stopped teaching, she could return to the farm where she grew up. That night, she called the school superintendent and quit. Then she returned to the 670-acre farm her father had purchased in Mud City, Vermont, during the Depression.

Since 1952, Gertrude and two other sisters who later joined her have run the family's rambling dairy farm, tending to the farmhouse, sturdy barn, uneven fields, and their herd of Jerseys. Their day begins at 3:30 A.M., feeding and milking the herd. After the first milking, the sisters eat breakfast together—a hearty meal of eggs, cereal, milk, and thick slices of homemade bread slathered with butter and jam. A variety of chores keeps them busy until the second milking, in the late afternoon or early evening.

The sisters, who are all in their late sixties, are realistic about being able to run their farm for much longer; last year, the farm lost several thousand dollars, and they've had no takers on the option of renting the barn and continuing farming. Soon the cows will be sold at auction. But the sisters have kept their roots and lived the length of their lives on the land. And they've sold the farm's development rights to the state, preserving their land as farmland so their heritage as farmers will live on for future generations.

I carry on traditions of land that's important to me.

"I stopped to hike a trail into a blackwater swamp of tupelo and bald cypress. . . . I had this powerful sense of life going about the business of getting on with itself. . . . Things were growing so fast I could almost feel the heat from their generation: the slow friction of leaf against bud case, petal against petal. For some time I stood among the high mysteries of being as they consumed the decay of old life."
—AMERICAN WRITER WILLIAM LEAST HEAT MOON

FROM WINTER INTO SPRING

A prime example of nature's continual growth is provided by the leaves trees shed by the thousands in autumn near woodland streams. Each leaf that cascades to the ground is critical to the continued life in the stream in the spring. When the leaves drop into the water or are blown in by the chill autumn winds, they become soaked. After immersion, they provide an abundance of organic carbon—a substance found in once-living things—for aquatic insects and crustaceans known as "shredders." The shredders literally shred the leaves and other dead plant life, further breaking down the rich source of carbon that's fed into the water; as well, the nourished shredders themselves become a prime food source for trout and other fish in the stream, which then provide you with nutritious food that you cook in your frying pan.

Spring couldn't happen without the support of the other seasons of the year. The clear streams that now rush to fill ponds and lakes are a result of last winter's snowfall; the snow and ice melt high in the mountains and then filter down to the lower elevations. One such stream begins on Mt. Washington in New Hampshire, cascades into the majestic Glen Ellis Falls, which feeds the Saco River, which then spills out into the Atlantic Ocean, providing clean, fresh water for a new beginning all over the planet.

I learn the sources of this spring's growth.

"The field has eyes, the wood has ears; I will look, be silent, and listen."
—DUTCH PAINTER HIERONYMUS BOSCH

SPIRITUAL INVISIBILITY

Can you see the wind? Can you hear how the tree changes from bare limbs and brown leaves to lush green? Can you see the fragrance of flowers floating on the breezes? Can you hear the joy and celebration of the earth as it loosens and softens in the warm spring sun and rain?

While you can't actually see or hear such invisible things, you can witness the evidence of them—the wind turning the leaves on the trees, for example—as well as imagine that the buds might actually make sounds as they stretch open, just as you do when you awaken in the morning and prepare to get out of bed. Because of this, you know such things exist.

So, too, is it in the human world. There are many things you can't see or hear but that you know exist. You can't see or hear love, for example. You can't see or hear forgiveness. You can't see or hear serenity. And yet you know such things exist because you feel them. Too, you probably have never seen God or heard a Great Holy Spirit's voice, but you see the evidence of a Higher Power's creation and heed the messages that the Creator sends to you. Because of this, you trust in the existence of an all-powerful Being—a Being who may be silent and invisible, but is vital to your spiritual development and daily existence.

Allow yourself to see nature without always needing a true image. Let nature speak to you today in its silent ways. Learn to live by the words of Salish logger, actor, and poet Chief Dan George, who once remarked, "The faintness of the stars, the freshness of the morning, the dewdrop on the flower, speaks to me."

I see the invisible; I hear the inaudible—nature communes with me.

"For lo, the winter is past, the rain is over and gone;
The flowers appear on the earth, and the voice of the turtle is heard in
* our land. . . ."*

—THE SONG OF SOLOMON 2:10–14

NATURE'S INTERDEPENDENCY

There's a story about a king who suddenly awakens in the middle of the night and summons the kingdom's wisest seer into his bedchambers. "O Great Seer," the king moans, "my sleep is troubled, for I do not know the answer to this question: What is holding up the earth?"

"Your Majesty," replies the seer, "the earth rests on the back of a giant elephant."

The king sighs in relief, and then goes back to sleep. But it isn't long before he awakens in a cold sweat and once again summons the seer to his bedchambers. "Tell me, Great Seer," the king says, "what is holding up the elephant?"

The seer replies, "The elephant stands on the back of a giant turtle."

The king reaches for his bed candle to blow out the flame, then stops. "But—"

The seer holds up his hand. "You can stop right there, Your Majesty," he says. "It's turtles all the way down."

Nature supports all living things; no one thing could ever live successfully on its own. Every living thing, for example, needs the earth, water, and air. In this supportive network of living things, all of creation can be seen to be interdependent. What this means is that you may often find yourself in the position to be assisted or to offer assistance to someone or something else. When this happens, willingly lend a hand or grab onto the one that's being offered to you.

I offer support to others; I take the support that's offered to me.

"Each of us needs to withdraw from the cares which will not withdraw from us. We need hours of aimless wandering or spates of time sitting on park benches, observing the mysterious world of ants and the canopy of treetops."

—AMERICAN POET AND ENTERTAINER MAYA ANGELOU

FINDING YOUR NEST OF PEACE

A bird builds its nest by first searching for the perfect twigs, pieces of string, weeds, scraps of paper, and other natural and man-made materials. Then it patiently interweaves these materials until its nest achieves the right shape, size, depth, and warmth. No two birds' nests are alike, even within the same species; each has its own unique blending of materials that makes it distinguishable from other nests.

So, too, do you need to have your own special "nest" for yourself. Because you may devote a lot of time to the care of a spouse, child, or aging family member or because you may have troubles, illness, worries, or decisions that need your time and attention, it's important to find or create a "nesting" space in which you can be with your own thoughts and feelings. This "nest" can be a favorite room in your home, in your garden, a particular spot on a seawall or stone wall, or a bench in the park that's shaded by a centuries-old tree.

But your nest doesn't always have to be a place. Sometimes your nest can be derived from intangible things that bring you peace—a picture of a loved one, a soothing cup of tea, a discarded blue-jay feather—or from living things that comfort you—the sound of your cat's gentle purr, the feel of your dog's warm tongue on your face, the serenade of the morning songbirds.

Today, find your nest of peace so you can spend time away from others in order to savor precious moments and take time just for yourself.

I seek my nest of peace today.

"Lord make us mindful of the little things that grow and blossom in these days to make the world beautiful for us."

—AMERICAN WRITER AND EDUCATOR W.E.B. DU BOIS

PERCEPTIONS OF PERFECTION

Everyone and everything in the world has imperfections. Just as there's no such thing as a perfect person, neither is there a perfect living thing. There are certainly very attractive people, there are certainly highly creative people, and there are certainly quite charismatic people, but there are no perfect people. Too, in nature there are wonderfully fragrant roses, there are roses with soft, velvety petals, and there are symmetrically shaped roses, but there are no perfect roses.

Life teaches you that every living thing is valuable and has its vital contribution to make, even when it's not perfect. As Ralph Waldo Emerson once commented, "What is a weed? A plant whose virtues have not yet been discovered." Every living thing has its own expression, its own capabilities, its own skills, its own way of being.

Nothing you can do, say, think, or imagine ought to convince you that you—above every other living thing—can be perfect, even when you've spent years aiming for such perfection. Being able to attain perfection is as impossible as being able to find the pot of gold at the end of the rainbow.

Why waste time trying to be perfect or attempting to do everything "right"? Nothing in nature struggles after such a goal; the rose is simply the rose. The point of life is to do your best and enjoy yourself while doing so. Let go of unrealistic perfectionistic expectations and you'll find that your best effort—not your perfect effort—is what really matters.

I accept my life on its own imperfect terms.

"Only in America. Where else would someone have the—is the word audacity?—to dream up a concept like this? First, acquire a 350-acre parkland in suburban New Jersey. Then, breed a herd of wild animals— zebras, lions, baboons, Bengal tigers, kangaroos and giraffes. Let them roam, charge $60 for a family of four to drive around and gawk at them, and call it a 'safari' at 'an exotic wildlife preserve.'"

—BOSTON GLOBE STAFF WRITER LINDA MATCHAN

HUMANE CAPTIVITY

Visitors to Six Flags Wild Safari Animal Park in Jackson, New Jersey, are greeted by ticket takers dressed in ersatz camouflage outfits and hats, allowed access by car into a drive-through gift shop operated by a man in a little thatch hut, and charged nearly two dollars for a soda. A drive through the park during ostrich-breeding season means the birds may rush at certain cars, staking claim to what they have come to associate with food. The area set aside for baboons has a "monkey bypass road" for those who want to drive through quickly, as the baboons have a tendency to hop on top of the cars as well as damage them. And the sign posted at the entry gate, calling the park "the world's largest safari," often prompts protest, such as the one of a ten-year-old boy, "Like, what happened to Africa?"

And yet Six Flags—with its 4.5-mile drive, themed sections, and free-range design that keeps the humans in the "cages" of their vehicles—provides exciting and unique opportunities to witness animal activity as well as to be greeted up close by a variety of animals that are familiar, such as elephants and buffalo, as well as unfamiliar animals such as ostrich, wallabies, and dromedaries.

Today, plan a trip to a top-rated zoo or wildlife preserve in order to see wildlife that's being kept in humane conditions.

I research the quality of a zoo or wildlife preserve before a visit.

"The sea is feline. It licks your feet—its huge flanks purr very pleasant for you; but it will crack your bones and eat you, for all that, and wipe the crimsoned foam from its jaws as if nothing had happened."

—AMERICAN PHYSICIAN AND WRITER
OLIVER WENDELL HOLMES, SR.

PROTECTING THE COASTLINE

As powerful as the ocean is—as mighty as its range, as profound as its depths, as destructive as its force—it is at your mercy. Everything you do on land ends up at the sea. Agricultural pesticides and toxins used in manufacturing are flushed into coastal waters. Gasoline from cars gets washed into the ocean. Overfishing threatens marine life. Trash chokes and kills.

The American Oceans Campaign is an organization whose mission is "to protect and preserve the vitality of coastal waters, estuaries, bays, wetlands, and deep oceans." Here are some things you can do to show your commitment to that mission and save a coastline near you.

- Properly dispose of beach trash and recyclables. Even if it's not your trash, pick it up. What you carry in, be sure you carry out.
- When planning a picnic on the beach, leave packaging at home. Pack what you plan to eat in reusable containers.
- Dispose of toxic products such as household paints and pesticides at facilities provided by your city or county, or work with local officials to establish such facilities. Do not dump such products into a sewer system.
- Organize or participate in a beach cleanup day.
- Establish an Adopt-a-Shore program where participants volunteer to maintain the cleanliness and safety of a particular section of the shoreline.
- Petition deep-sea fishing expeditions to limit catches.

I leave only my footprints on the beach.

"A dream may let us deeper into the secret of nature than a hundred concerted experiments."

—AMERICAN PHILOSPHER, POET, AND ESSAYIST
RALPH WALDO EMERSON

A VISION IN THE CRAZY MOUNTAINS

Plenty Coups was tribal chief of the Mountain Crow people who was honored with the name Aleekchea'ahoosh, translated as "Many Achievements," or "Plenty Coups." In the tradition of the Plains Indians, as a young man he went alone into the wilderness—the Crazy Mountains—in quest of a vision, or medicine dream. The dream, it was believed, would give him a personal guardian and reveal the sacred objects, or medicine, that would be a source of power to him throughout his life.

The dream that Plenty Coups had was considered a great vision by the Crows, for it foretold of the ultimate destruction of the buffalo and the need for the Crow people to remain friendly with the white man in order to remain safely in their homeland. Plenty Coups worked all his life for harmony between the whites and his people and, as a legacy, left forty acres that are now a state park, "to be used in perpetuity for the Crow people and used as a public park by them and others irrespective of race and color."

The personal guardian for Plenty Coups was the chickadee. During his vision quest, Plenty Coups said that a voice told him that the chickadee "is least in strength but strongest of mind among his kind. He is willing to work for wisdom. . . . Develop your body, but do not neglect your mind, Plenty Coups. It is the mind that leads a man to power, not strength of body."

Reflect on the meaning of a past dream or a "vision" you may have had. What can you learn today from this?

I use my dreams to guide me and offer me wisdom.

"I once had a sparrow alight upon my shoulder for a moment while I was hoeing in a village garden, and I felt that I was more distinguished by that circumstance than I should have been by any epaulet I could have worn."
—AMERICAN WRITER AND NATURALIST HENRY DAVID THOREAU

TRUSTING IN POSSIBILITIES

There's a story about a poor peasant farmer who was sentenced to death but miraculously obtained a reprieve by assuring the king that he would teach His Majesty's horse to fly within the year. Even though the king's advisers protested against his decision, exclaiming that the ruler was being duped by a mere peasant, he stuck by it.

"And just how do you think you'll ever live up to your promise?" a fellow prisoner asked the farmer.

"Within the year," the farmer explained, "the king may die. Or the horse may die. After all, in a year, who knows what will happen? Maybe the horse *will* learn to fly!"

If, at times, you feel your life or a particular circumstance in your life is hopeless, you need only look to nature to see that changes happen every day. So, too, do miraculous events. Baby robins plunge several feet out of a tree, frantically flap minuscule wings, perhaps catch an air current or a gentle breeze, and fly to a safe landing. A mother bat flies into a cave littered with thousands of bats and locates her own pup, distinguishing its cries from those of hundreds of other pups. A calf rejected by its mother and left to starve is willingly adopted by another and nursed to health. A dog that loses a leg to cancer resumes play as if it had lost nothing.

Today, remember that nature continually shows you that anything is possible.

I trust that the circumstances of my life can change for the better.

"And bending across the path as if saying prayers to welcome the dawn, were long grasses which were completely overpowered by the thick dew."

—KENYAN WRITER GRACE OGOT

A PRAYER FOR LOSS

You may find it hard to face a new day when you've experienced a loss in your life. Try as you might to "put on a happy face," to accept that what has happened "is for the best," or to trust that "nothing happens without a reason," sometimes all you can focus on is the loss of a true companion—a life partner, a trusted confidant, a loving parent, a furry friend.

One way to ease your pain and sadness is to start the day with a comforting prayer. The following prayer, of anonymous origin, emphasizes that loss is never permanent when you trust in the natural eternity of life:

> *Do not stand at my grave and weep.*
> *I am not there. I do not sleep.*
> *I am a thousand winds that blow.*
> *I am the diamond glint on snow.*
> *I am the sunlight on ripened grain.*
> *I am the gentle autumn rain.*
> *When you wake in the morning hush,*
> *I am the swift, uplifting rush*
> *   of quiet birds in circling flight.*
> *I am the soft starlight at night.*
> *Do not stand at my grave and weep.*
> *I am not there. I do not sleep.*

I pray for comfort as well as strength to help me through my loss.

"No one can write knowingly of weather who walks bent over on wet days."

—AMERICAN ESSAYIST E. B. WHITE

WEATHERING THE WEATHER

When was the last time you willingly went outdoors for a walk in the park, in your neighborhood, or in the woods on a rainy day? More often than not you stayed indoors, drove to a nearby mall or store, went to the movies, or, if you had to go outdoors, hid under the canopy of an umbrella as you raced from one shelter to another.

But there's so much that you missed! Go for a walk on a rainy day, and you'll know how brooks, creeks, and rivers are formed. The tiny rivulets you see at your feet run quickly by to a newly formed stream; it takes hundreds of them to make a brook, hundreds more to create a creek, hundreds times hundreds more to flow as a river. Even the tiniest of drops of rain have the power to stream down city streets, rapidly fill depressions on a road or sidewalk, surge into storm drains, urge leaves, sticks, and other debris along with them—all on a merry romp.

A day doesn't have to be "picture-perfect" in order for you to enjoy it. Some of the most exciting and rewarding experiences result from times of driving rains, swirling winds, thunderous sounds, and brilliant flashes in the sky. As writer Hugh Prather once opined, "What would I discover about the cottonwoods if when I walked to the mailbox I listened to them instead of looked at them? What would I find out about the rain if I didn't run inside?"

Today, look up at the rain falling down from the sky instead of down at the ground. Rush outdoors to get into the rain instead of running indoors to get out of it.

I appreciate all the different weather in my life.

"We behold the face of nature bright with gladness, we often see superabundance of food; we do not see or we forget, that the birds which are idly singing around us mostly live on insects or seeds . . . we do not always bear in mind, that, though food may not be superabundant, it is not so at all seasons of each recurring year."

—ENGLISH NATURALIST AND WRITER CHARLES DARWIN

THE VALUE OF FEEDING THE BIRDS

Think about where you shop for food. Now imagine this store closes. Where do you then shop for food? Now imagine that this store, too, closes. Where do you then food shop? Continue with this process of finding a new food source, losing that source, and then finding another. And another. And another. At first you'll frequent other stores in your neighborhood. Then in the nearest city. Then in the next nearest city. Eventually you may need to shop out of state, then out of that state, then out of another state. Remember, too, that as you're going through this process, so are others. Fewer stores mean more competition for food as well as limited supply and selection. What happens when there is only one store left, and this store must supply food for every person in every state in the United States?

One single action, which may impact on only one single species, can actually affect the future of the planet's entire ecosystem. Deforestation in Central America, for example, does more than just destroy trees and strip away valuable topsoil. The North American summer insects that winter in those forests are also destroyed, and without the insects, the population of North American songbirds, which need insects in their diet, declines. Your local birds may need your help supplementing their diet; provide them with ample seeds and plant flowers that attract insects they like.

I am a dependable food supplier for birds in my area.

> "If we go on using the Earth uncaringly and without replenishing it, then we are just greedy consumers. We should take from the Earth only what are our absolute and basic necessities: things without which we cannot survive. The Earth has an abundance of everything, but our share in it is only what we really need."

—MAGAZINE EDITOR, DIRECTOR OF SCHUMACHER COLLEGE IN
ENGLAND, AND FORMER JAIN MONK SATISH KUMAR

A VALUABLE RESOURCE

Imagine you must live the rest of your life on this planet with the assistance of only five things. Think about what things you would choose. How many of the five are possessions, such as a car? How many are necessities, such as food? How many are so essential to your life that you could not live without them, such as water?

If you're like most people, water wasn't even a consideration. You take for granted that there will always be enough water to drink and bathe in. Yet this attitude causes you—and millions of others in the world—to waste and to pollute this valuable resource.

Years ago, when Mahatma Gandhi visited Indian Prime Minister Nehru, he asked for a morning jug of water to wash his face and hands. Nehru poured the water as the two men talked about the problems of India. Gandhi forgot to wash, but the jug was empty. Nehru said he would fetch another jug, but Gandhi began to cry. Nehru reminded him that the city had three great rivers—the Ganges, the Jumnar, and the Saraswait—and that he didn't need to worry about water.

But Gandhi shook his head. "Nehru, you are right. You have three great rivers in your town, but my share in those rivers is only one jug of water a morning and no more."

I treasure water as a valuable resource and use only what I need.

"Old age, to the unlearned, is winter; to the learned, it is harvest time."
—YIDDISH PROVERB

LIVING WITH THE SEASONS

Seasons teach you about transitions. Just as winter slides into spring, spring into summer, summer into fall, and fall into winter, so, too, does infancy ease into childhood, childhood into adolescence, adolescence into youth, youth into midlife, midlife into maturity. The natural seasons that occur outside you as well as the seasons of change that occur with you provide you with a valuable life lesson: they let you know that just as all things must pass, so, too, must all things return. So while every new beginning brings you closer to an end, every ending has within it the hope of a future celebration.

Seasons, then, are valuable teachers that can convey to you the subtle lessons of how to live better. Respect the seasons, and you'll be more ready to accept the give-and-take that's a natural part of seasonal constancy and flux. The love that seems eternal now may soon be a memory; an illness that seems unbeatable now may soon give way to health; a pain or sadness that seems all-consuming now may open the doors to happiness. Perhaps this is why writer Pico Iyer observes that the seasons "teach us that suffering is inevitable, and in that inevitability is a constancy that helps take the edge off suffering. We cherish flowers more than evergreens, precisely because they do not last."

As well, the seasons teach that there are no hard-and-fast divisions. Just when you think winter is over, an unseasonable blizzard reminds you that there are, as well, overlaps in life. Thus, the winter of your life can, as well, be thought of as the spring—a time of hope, renewal, and growth.

I embrace the seasons of my life.

"The subtlety of nature is greater many times over than the subtlety of the sense and understanding; so that all those specious meditations, speculations, and glosses in which men indulge are quite from the purpose, only there is no one by to observe it."

—ENGLISH ESSAYIST AND PHILOSOPHER FRANCIS BACON

SOWING THE SEEDS

Have you ever thought about the many varieties of flowering plants in the world—some 250,000 species that provide a wealth of flowers, fruits, and vegetables—and how they continue to exist and flourish without human assistance?

Many of the flowering plants have evolved in ways that enable the transfer of seeds from one plant to another or one location to another. The catkins, or flowers, of an oak or hazel tree dangle on a delicate stem in order to be blown about by the wind; the shaking releases the pollen, which is then transported to other flowers. Sycamore and maple trees have their seeds wrapped in a propellerlike fruit that "helicopters" away from the tree in the wind. Daisies have light seeds attached to a "parachute" of hairs, which enable travel over great distances. Besides the wind, birds are great gardening assistants; Charles Darwin once reported he was able to grow eighty-two plants from the seeds taken from the feathers of a single bird.

Too, the aroma emitted by flowering plants has evolved in ways that attract their own particular pollinator-of-choice. Since birds are attracted to color and not odor, the red and orange flowers they're drawn to usually have no scent. However, bees love sweet-smelling scents such as those emitted by the clovers, and fly-pollinated flowers such as birthwort and the calico flower entice their pollinators by emitting an odor that smells like rotting meat.

Today I sow the seeds for future flowering plants.

"This is what I had come for, just this, and nothing more. A fling of leafy motion on the cliffs, the assault of real things, living and still, with shapes and powers under the sky—this is my city, my culture, and all the world I need."

—AMERICAN WRITER ANNIE DILLARD

CAREFUL COEXISTENCE WITH NATURE

After a year of rigorous training; weeks of struggle against cold, wind, ice, snow, acute mountain sickness, and oxygen starvation; fifty-seven hours without sleep; injury; and overwhelming tiredness and weakness, *Outside* magazine writer and technical climber Jon Krakauer reached the summit of Mt. Everest on May 10, 1996. But rather than feel the exuberant release of emotion he had expected, as he straddled the famous Tibet–Nepal peak he "just couldn't summon the energy to care . . . twenty-nine thousand twenty-eight feet up in the troposphere, there was so little oxygen reaching my brain that my mental capacity was that of a slow child. Under the circumstances, I was incapable of feeling much of anything except cold and tired."

Going out into nature should never be so grueling, so debilitating, so filled with hardship—Krakauer left the summit and returned to camp in time to beat the sudden, furious blizzard that claimed the lives of inexperienced climbers, some of whom had paid as much as $65,000 to place their feet on top of the world, as well as their seasoned guides who tried to save their lives—and so competitive that you're deprived of the time and the energy you need to enjoy what you've set out to see.

Strive to keep your experiences in nature simple, realistic, and safe. Whether you go out on a river, hike a mountain, journey underground or under water, or soar in the sky, do whatever you do in moderation. Take no chances, be physically and mentally prepared, and conserve your energy.

I respect nature as well as myself so we can coexist safely.

"The shell must be cracked apart if what is in it is to come out, for if you want the kernel you must break the shell."

—GERMAN PHILOSOPHER AND MYSTIC
JOHANNES "MEISTER" ECKHART

BECOMING MORE OPEN

Not letting others know who you really are—your thoughts, your feelings, your dreams, your goals, your background, and your wants and needs—is like being a seed that, when planted, refuses to sprout and ends up rotting in the ground. Rather than push its way to the life-sustaining surface of the ground so it can reveal its blossoming growth, it remains hidden, seemingly protected, and yet more at risk by not rising to the surface.

Opening up to others can be a life-enhancing, rewarding experience. While risking full openness with others—even a close friend or a life partner—isn't always easy, the discomfort and vulnerability you feel or anticipate you'll feel can be offset by sharing little bits of yourself at a time—gradually breaking through the surface of the ground—and may eventually diminish over time as you feel the support, caring, concern, nurturing, and love from others who respect you more when you're being honest and open with them than when you're guarding your feelings and not letting them get to know you.

While you don't have to open up to everyone in your life, it's important to at least open up to someone. Today, know that you have choices. You can choose to keep yourself in your protective shell or you can crack the shell and expose some of what lies within. Do so, and you allow others—as well as yourself—a chance to see not only who you are, but also who you can be.

I risk openness and, in so doing, am rewarded by greater intimacy.

> "The chess board is the world, the pieces are the phenomena of the universe, the rules of the game are what we call the laws of Nature. The player on the other side is hidden from us. We know that his play is always fair, just, and patient. But also we know, to our cost, that he never overlooks a mistake, or makes the smallest allowance for ignorance."
>
> —ENGLISH BIOLOGIST THOMAS HENRY HUXLEY

PLAYING A FAIR GAME

So many things in nature present you with opposing points of view—good and bad, benefits and detriments, gains and losses. A spring rain provides valuable water for new crops, yet too much rain can drown the young plants. Sunshine provides the body with vitamin D, and yet too much sun can burn and lead to skin cancer. A coat made from an animal's fur can keep you warm, and yet contribute to the extinction of a species.

For every move you make that affects the universe, the universe counters this move with one of its own. Make a move out of greed, exploitation, vanity, or ignorance, and you will suffer the effects not once, but repeatedly, until you make a move out of genuine concern, a desire for equality, and a reliance on intelligence.

According to Greek myth, when Prometheus stole fire from the gods and gave it to humans, he was punished by Zeus by being chained to a rock and, every day, an eagle tore out his liver, an organ that restored itself during the night. If the moves you make on earth today desire to destroy, then you, too, will be destroyed. But if the moves you make aspire to create, then you will be treated fairly, justly, and patiently.

I play the game of life with sportsmanship, always showing my fellow player courtesy and respect.

"I sat there and forgot and forgot, until what remained was the river that went by and I who watched. On the river the heat mirages danced with each other and then they danced through each other and then they joined hands and danced around each other. Eventually the watcher joined the river, and there was only one of us. I believe it was the river."

—AMERICAN WRITER NORMAN MACLEAN

ADDING ENJOYMENT TO YOUR DAY

Are there things in your life that you love to do? Albert Schweitzer loved to work in his clinic in Lambarene, Africa. John James Audubon loved to paint American birds and wild animals. Eleanora "Billie" Holiday loved to sing. John Greenleaf Whittier loved to write. Amelia Earhart and Charles Lindbergh loved to fly. Henry David Thoreau loved spending time at Walden Pond. And Rachel Carson so loved the ocean and being a marine biologist that she has been credited with helping to bring an ecological awareness to contemporary America through her powerful writing.

When you love what you do, you can be creative and passionate. You can be energetic and enthusiastic. You can be joyful and positive. You can feel strong and confident. You can make a difference in your life and in the lives of others. And you can be so focused on what you love to do that external "rewards"—money, recognition, respect—pale beside the physical, emotional, and spiritual rewards you get simply from being able to do what you want to do.

What is it that you enjoy doing? Working with children? Being creative? Camping? Fishing? Hiking? Canoeing? Singing or dancing? Volunteering? If you haven't been able to include this love in your life lately or on a regular basis, today make a definite plan to spend some time with it.

I devote time to doing something I love.

"Some divers talk so much about sharks that you would think they were the only fish in the sea. It is as if the beautiful great land forests are described only in terms of poisonous snakes and panthers. Can you imagine going into the woods aware only of those animals, so that you miss the calmness and the thousands of other animals, the beautiful and the shy?"

—AMERICAN WRITER MARY LEE SETTLE

THE TRUE STORY ABOUT WILDLIFE

Equating wildlife with ferocity is one of the many misconceptions that have been disseminated by those who would like nothing more than to be able to hunt, trap, and poach indiscriminately and, in so doing, gain some sort of self-worth and power from conquering creatures who are, in many ways, both harmless and defenseless. Much-maligned creatures such as coyotes, wolves, sharks, rattlesnakes, lions, alligators, and bears are portrayed as evil killers who have insatiable, bloodthirsty appetites and will, if allowed to proliferate, ravage the planet, invade cities, and kill innocent pets, children, and farm animals.

In reality, however, fleas, ticks, and mosquitoes are far more annoying and menacing in terms of the diseases they spread than any species of wildlife. And while it's true that bears have attacked joggers and campers, coyotes have killed sheep and chickens, alligators and sharks have mauled swimmers, and rattlesnakes have inflicted painful and dangerous bites, more often than not such actions were out of retaliation, territorial defense, fear, or hunger in a shrinking living space.

The next time you read or hear about a sensational act committed by a particular species of wildlife, provide a voice of reason. Respond by telling the true story about such wild creatures—their shyness, their beauty, and their importance to the planet.

I provide an accurate view that defends wildlife.

"To be overcome by the fragrance of flowers is a delectable form of defeat."
—AMERICAN WRITER BEVERLEY NICHOLS

APPRECIATING MORTALITY

Once there was a king who ruled over a spacious and magnificent kingdom. The king so loved his land that he would often ride his horse across it, especially in the springtime, to marvel at the natural beauty and bounty of the land and the fields of breathtakingly brilliant and fragrant wildflowers.

One day, as he was out surveying his domain with his nobles, he stopped at a scenic spot and cried out, "To think that one day I must die and leave this behind! Wouldn't it be wonderful if we could live forever? Then we'd always be able to enjoy what we have for an eternity. We'd never have to give it up—none of it!"

All the nobles except one nodded in agreement. "Not me, sire," the one noble replied. "I wouldn't want life to be everlasting. And neither would you!"

The nobles gasped at the audacity of such a direct contradiction to the king's expressed wish. The king turned to the dissenting noble and said in an icy tone, "Do tell, noble, why you know this would be so."

"Well, sire," the noble began, "if life were everlasting, then the first king would still be among us—the one who so hated the natural beauty of these fields that he ordered them continually plowed so nothing would grow on them. I would still be a farmer, and you, sire, would still be a clerk."

The king thought for a moment about the noble's words. Then he smiled. "I'm foolish to even think about living forever," he said. "You have shown me, wise noble, that to truly appreciate what I have while I'm alive, I need to be able to let it go."

I appreciate the grandeur of life while I'm alive.

"Except for our higher order of minds we are like the little moles under the earth carrying out blindly the work of digging, thinking our own dark passageways constitute all there is to the world."

—WRITER BESS STREETER ALDRICH

A VISION OF HARMONY

John Donne wrote years ago that no man was an island, that each human being was "a piece of the continent, a part of the main." This means that every person, place, and thing is a part of humanity—a part of a larger pattern of harmony that intrinsically links each together in a dynamic web of life.

To understand this principle of oneness, think about a loved one you may have lost. Do you remember what your first holiday gathering after this loss was like? You may have felt a definite void, a sense that a vital piece of you and your family was missing, a feeling that the gathering was in some way imbalanced or "out of synch." Later on, there may have been a time when you had good news to share and, in your excitement, reached automatically for the phone to dial the once-familiar number before you stopped short with the recollection that the special person was no longer there. Once again, you may have felt your world disrupted, a pattern to which you had grown accustomed taken away from you, leaving you with the feeling of being disconnected from the world around you.

Whenever you feel as if you've lost your vision of oneness in some way and begin to see yourself as an island, you lose your ability to live in harmony with the world around you. That's when you need to reach out to others so you can open your eyes and see the integral part you play in the much larger pattern. You may be only one link in the great chain that connects you to and with all of life, but you're a very vital link.

I restore my vision of oneness with the world.

"Statistically, the probability of any one of us being here is so small that you'd think the mere fact of existing would keep us all in a contented dazzlement of surprise."

—AMERICAN BIOLOGIST AND WRITER LEWIS THOMAS

MEANINGFUL RELATIONSHIPS

Jutting majestically out from the granite sides of a 2,500-foot canyon in the Kofa Mountains of Arizona are the only native palm trees in the entire state. How do the tropical plants live year after year in the dark, almost perpendicular sides of the narrow gorge? How can they flourish when the sun reaches them only two hours in a day? Botanists who have studied this incredible phenomenon have concluded that the stone walls of the canyon reflect enough light and store enough warmth throughout the day to enable the trees to survive in the seemingly uninhabitable environment. Thus, it isn't an oddity of nature or mere coincidence that the trees happen to grow out of those particular canyon walls; rather, there's a supportive relationship that has been created between the environment of the canyon walls and the needs of the palm trees that allows the trees to grow.

What may sometimes seem to be mere coincidences in your life can prove to be meaningfully related. Think of how you met your life partner, what made you decide to attend the college you did, how you found your current job, why you're living where you are right now. Were such things "blind luck" or examples of synchronicity?

If you believe in synchronicity rather than luck and happenstance, then you'll also believe in the words of writer Anne Morrow Lindbergh: "Each cycle of the tide is valid; each cycle of the wave is valid; each cycle of a relationship is valid." In day-to-day living, everything is meaningful.

I trust that there is meaning to many occurrences in my life.

"A good marriage is that in which each appoints the other guardian of his solitude. Once the realization is accepted that even between the closest human beings infinite distances continue to exist, a wonderful living side by side can grow up, if they succeed in loving the distance between them which makes it possible for each to see the other whole and against a wide sky.

—GERMAN POET RAINER MARIA RILKE

GROWING SEPARATELY, GROWING TOGETHER

Sunrise and sunset together represent the measure of a day. When the sun rises, the moon sets; when the moon rises, the sun sets. Without such a relationship between the sun and the moon, a day would have no beginning as well as no end.

You and your partner together compose a relationship, but the success of your relationship depends upon whether there are times when you can be as separate as the sun and the moon. Although you may share much in common, can you both think, act, and feel as two individuals?

Too often when you've been in a close friendship or intimate relationship for a long time, establishing and maintaining a sense of individuality can be threatening. You may feel that taking separate paths from one another, even for short periods of time, will force you apart or in some way damage the peaceful resonance you've formed in your relationship.

Yet time spent apart, with others or by yourself, is not only essential to both people in any relationship, but also strengthening for the relationship. Healthy relationships—that is, the best relationships—are made of two individuals, not one, who can both seek out and enjoy a variety of friendships and outside interests. Separation from one another is necessary to help you to connect with one another.

I encourage and support separateness in my relationships.

"The rocks are where they are—this is their will. The rivers flow—this is their will. The birds fly—this is their will. Human beings talk—this is their will. The seasons change, heaven sends down rain or snow, the earth occasionally shakes, the waves roll, the stars shine—each of them follows its own will. To be is to will and so is to become."

—ZEN SPIRITUALIST D. T. SUZUKI

DOING YOUR WILL

Knowing who you are and what you want from your life isn't always easy. You may look around at others and think, "I wish I was as happy in my career as she is," "I'd like to have as nice a home as he has," or "I wish I had interesting hobbies like she does." But while comparing and contrasting yourself to others is often human nature, it's not part of nature. No living thing looks outside its species or even within its own species to consider how it "measures up" to the habits, interests, standards, or behaviors established by others. While a creature might adopt or mimic what another creature does—a way of hunting food or a method of fashioning a dry, safe shelter—no creature conforms its way of life to the way another creature lives. It remains true to its own will.

Because you live in a society that approves of individuality only to the extent that such a desire for singularity falls within the boundaries of conformity, it can be hard to be true to your will. You grow up bowing to peer pressure and struggle to "fit in." You obey your parents' wishes and follow your teachers' guidelines. You work in a way dictated by your boss or company. You meet the needs of your partner.

Today, begin your day by doing something that's truly your will. Break out of a pattern, wear a different style of clothing, follow a dream. Be who you really are rather than who others think you are or would like you to be.

Today I do my will and, in so doing, become more myself.

"O, great blue sky; see my roaming here. I trust in you, protect me!"
—PAWNEE SAYING

A DOOR TO A GREATER LIFE

Nearly two hundred years ago, President Thomas Jefferson asked soldier, plantation owner, and his personal secretary Meriwether Lewis to cross the Mississippi River to see if there was an all-river route to the Pacific Ocean. At that time, Jefferson's request was quite bold, for no one knew how far the continent stretched or what kind of terrain or terrors existed in the wilderness. Some doubted the president's selection of Lewis to head up the expedition because of the man's lack of exploration skills. But Jefferson had faith in Lewis's leadership skills and knew that Lewis would master the other skills he needed. In fact, Lewis spent two years before the expedition focusing on key areas of study to make the report for his mission as complete as possible—botany, zoology, ornithology, astronomy, and cartography. In the end, the three-year trek involved incredible physical and emotional distress—it took months to move upstream against the current of the Mississippi; it took even longer to cross the Rockies on foot and horseback. But Lewis was instrumental in the expansion of the United States, first in the newly acquired Louisiana Territory and then in the eventual surge to the west.

There will always come a time in life when you have to make a significant change, follow a new guideline, take a different path, or do something new. The outcome will not always be certain. But if you can be courageous, approach each new trial with optimism, be enthusiastic, and trust that your every step is being guided by a spiritual resource that can give you unending strength, then you can believe that life is an exciting adventure of discovery.

I alter my vision of life by opening a new door in my life.

"The soul would have no rainbow had the eyes no tears."

—MINQUASS PROVERB

SURVIVING THE STORMS OF LIFE

You know that all wounds need time to heal, whether the wounds be physical, emotional, or spiritual. But when you've been wounded—by an illness or injury, by the loss of a relationship or loved one, or by a sense of hopelessness and despair—you may believe that you'll never be able to heal. You may feel that from this moment on, you'll always be in pain or you'll always feel sad, empty, hopeless, depressed, lost, and lonely. Suffering will become your permanent state of living; your suffering will have no end.

Yet no present hour ever endures; nothing in the universe stands still. Torrents of rain yield glorious sunshine and magnificent rainbows. The saying "And this, too, shall pass away" provides an apt reminder that the world's a scene of perpetual change, constant in its inconstancy, fluctuating from sorrow to joy.

Rather than sit around and bemoan your suffering, use this difficult time to work with the natural cycles of change—the passings and comings of life. First accept that, eventually, this moment of struggle will pass. Then, rather than focus on the agonizingly slow passage of each minute, strive to see the opportunity that can come out of your crisis—look for the rainbow after the storm. Greek playwright Aeschylus once said, "By suffering comes wisdom." So think about what you can learn from your experience. Then be willing to look beyond your dilemma to what lies beyond the horizon. Look outside yourself—to the sunshine, the lush greenery, and the sights, sounds, and smells of forthcoming summer life—and what's inside will soon be healed.

I let my tears cleanse my soul.

> *"The cult of wilderness is not a luxury; it is a necessity for the protection of humanized nature and for the preservation of mental health."*
> —FRENCH MICROBIOLOGIST AND ENVIRONMENTALIST
> RENÉ DUBOS

THE SERENITY OF THE WILDERNESS

Where do you go when you need peace of mind—a time and space in which you can soothe the intense stress and stimulation that bombard you so often in a day? Where do you go to escape from the invasive sounds of jackhammers as well as the pervasive shouts of your own children?

The call of the wilderness urges you to climb up mountains, paddle down streams, traipse through the briars and brambles, pitch a tent in forests, and roam sandy shorelines. The call of the wilderness offers you a safe haven—a place in which to escape, to get away from it all. The call of the wilderness asks you to hitch your soul to the marvelous silences of brilliant sunrises and breathtaking sunsets, to the big mountains that heave themselves up toward the heavens, to the fashionable hues and tints with which the sky adorns itself, to the stark contrasts presented by rugged mesas and gently rolling hills. The call of the wilderness is an invitation to a marvelous museum that's chock-full of specimens that represent centuries of fascinating, challenging study.

Peace of mind comes from the time you spend in contemplation of all the glories that large industries, cinematic special effects, cable networks, and technological wizardries can never capture. These glories must be discovered. For, as writer Wallace Stegner says, "We simply need that wild country available to us, even if we never do more than drive to its edge and look in. For it can be a means of reassuring ourselves of our sanity as creatures, a part of the geography of hope."

I discover peace of mind in the wilderness.

"Suddenly, as a ship leaves an estuary, we came out on to the steppe: a dazzling open sea of green. I never saw that colour before. In other greens, of emerald, jade, or malachite, the harsh deep green of the Bengal jungle, and the sad cool green of Ireland, the salad green of Mediterranean vineyards, the heavy full-blown green of English summer beeches, some element of blue or yellow predominates over the others. This was the pure essence of green, indissoluble, the colour of life itself."

—ENGLISH ARCHITECTURE AND ART CRITIC ROBERT BYRON

COLOR YOUR WORLD

Scientific research has proven that color can play a significant role in influencing your mood. Think about how you feel when you see a brilliant red cardinal or a bright yellow finch, a red rose-drenched sunrise, the surprisingly beautiful violet-blue shade of a just-opened morning glory, the blue-green expanse of the sea. Then think about how you feel after three or four days of gray, overcast skies. The bright and vibrant colors evoke a positive stimulus to your senses, while the gray, dark colors depress your senses, making you feel lethargic and blue.

Similarly, the colors you wear and the tints with which you decorate your living space can reflect the positive or negative feelings you have about yourself and your life. Sometimes dressing in a more brilliant or soft color can subtly change your mood from sadness to happiness. Sometimes imagining that you're surrounded by a healing color—a healthy pink, for instance—or a brilliant white light can help lift your spirits.

Today, imagine you have a palette of beautiful colors with which to "paint" yourself and your world. Close your eyes and visualize colors that glow within and around you, creating a powerful and positive energy. Take these colors with you throughout the day so you can be a joyous, walking rainbow.

I "paint" myself with vibrant colors.

"What lies behind us and what lies before us are small matters compared to what lies within us."

—AMERICAN ESSAYIST, POET, PHILOSOPHER
RALPH WALDO EMERSON

CREATIVE RISK-TAKING

All growth in life springs from the tension between limits and desires. You can believe that you can't do anything about a limitation and simply give up, or you can believe that there's got to be another way around the limitation—and then strive to find it.

In a parable related by creativity consultant Roger Von Oech, two frogs fall into a bucket of cream. The first frog, after frantically thrashing about for several seconds trying to seek footing, concludes there's no way out of the bucket, accepts its fate, and drowns. But the second frog does whatever it can to stay afloat, thrashing about minute after agonizing minute until all his churning gradually turns the cream into butter. Though exhausted by his efforts, the frog then finds his footing and hops out of the bucket.

You may believe that there's no way around any of your life-limiting circumstances. Yet as Rollo May writes in his book *The Courage to Create,* "The creative act arises out of the struggle of human beings with and against that which limits them." You can be like the frog that believes it can't do anything about its situation and gives up, or you can be like the frog that refuses to accept defeat.

Dig deep within yourself to find the determination to struggle against your limitations. Be creative. Invent new ways of doing things. Change old attitudes. Revise former behaviors. Try out new paths. In short, don't be afraid to try to make some things in your life "butter"!

I create ways to move beyond my limitations.

"I began to have an idea of my life, not as the slow shaping of achievement to fit my preconceived purposes, but as the gradual discovery and growth of a purpose which I did not know."

—ENGLISH PSYCHOLOGIST AND DIARIST JOANNA FIELD

ENJOYING A DIFFERENT PACE

"My concept of time has changed," begins a journal entry written by a woman who just turned forty. "And, because of this, my concept of myself has changed, too. For years I've always lived life at a grand pace. I've been at the top of my class since high school, became a scholarship athlete in tennis who later turned semipro, and then, with a partner, started a tennis school for promising young athletes. When my friends would tell me about a book they had read, a movie they had seen, or a vacation they had taken, I would wonder how they ever found the time. Because for me it was always, 'Go, go, go.' I thought that slowing down was bad, that once I slowed down, it meant I wouldn't be a success.

"Then my partner got married and left the business to me. I couldn't run it alone, and I couldn't find someone else to take her place. I put in longer and longer hours and started feeling tired all the time. After a routine checkup, my doctor told me that I had to find a healthy outlet for my stress.

"So I signed up for a weeklong camping and hiking trip with the Appalachian Mountain Club. I didn't think I could keep up with everyone because I was so tired and burned out, but I did. I had a pack on my back and fashioned a strong stick for support, and I found myself going up modest elevations and enjoying myself thoroughly at the group's reasonable pace. It was then that I realized I didn't have to run through my life anymore. I could walk. I could take my time. In going slower, I've become more aware of who I am."

I take my time to get to know myself.

"I learned many English words . . . could recite some of the Ten Commandments . . . I knew how to sleep in a bed, pray to Jesus, comb my hair, use a toilet . . . I learned that a person thinks with his head instead of his heart."

—SUN CHIEF

LOYALTY TO YOUR OWN BELIEFS

In 1871, as part of President Grant's "peace policy" to keep Indians on reservations and "transform them" into whites, church groups were encouraged to appoint reservation agents throughout the west. The agents brought assistants to the reservations who built churches and supplied the Indians with Bibles, started schools that taught the Indians the white man's history, opened trading posts where money was exchanged rather than goods, and laid out farms instead of allowing Indians to hunt, plant, and live in their own ways. By forcing them down the "right path," or the white man's way, the Indians were forced to suppress what was in their hearts and souls.

So, too, it is with you when you're forced to believe in something you don't feel in your heart. The Fox Indians tell this story about such coercions: "Once there was an Indian who became a Christian. He became a very good Christian; he went to church, and he didn't smoke or drink, and he was good to everyone. He was a very good man. Then he died. First he went to the Indian hereafter, but they wouldn't take him because he was a Christian. Then he went to heaven, but they wouldn't let him in—because he was an Indian. Then he went to hell, but they wouldn't admit him there either, because he was so good. So he came alive again, and he went to the Buffalo Dance and the other dances and taught his children to do the same thing."

I remain true to what I believe in my heart and soul.

"I dread success. To have succeeded is to have finished one's business on earth, like the male spider, who is killed by the female the moment he has succeeded in his courtship. I like a state of continual becoming, with a goal in front and not behind."

—IRISH-BORN ENGLISH DRAMATIST AND CRITIC
GEORGE BERNARD SHAW

PRACTICING NONRESISTANCE

Life is a flow of energy. Yet too often people seek to stop that flow when they've achieved a sought-after goal or realized a lifelong dream. After the thrill of their accomplishment has worn off—the marathon has been run, the mountain has been climbed, the work project has been completed, the house has been purchased, the degree has been earned, and the new clothing size has been attained—unless there are new goals to accomplish, the hard-earned "victory" rest may gradually turn into lethargy and, in some cases, resistance to setting a new goal or dreaming a new dream.

Yet to resist is to impede life's natural flow of energy—a flow that encourages you to move, to make progress, to evolve, to grow, to change. Nonresistance in nature is epitomized by a mighty river. Its constant goal is to flow wherever it finds openings—over cliffs, between boulders, across any and all obstacles. Even if the river is dammed, the cliff removed, or the boulders shifted, the river will continue to flow by simply changing its course. The direction may be affected, but the river's flow will not.

Nonresistance keeps the rivers flowing, your heart beating, the tides going in and out, the clouds floating high in the sky. Today, set your sights on a new goal. You can make it one that is easy to achieve or harder to attain, but it's imperative to make another so you can continue ever onward.

I set a new goal so I continue to make progress in my life.

"Maybe it's best to treat happiness like a deer in the forest. Sometimes it will emerge from the woods and pay you a visit. But it dislikes undue attention. And if you chase it, it will run away."

—WRITER PHYLLIS THEROUX

LOVING CONNECTIONS

One day a member of a tribe living in a remote area in central Brazil left his village and journeyed to São Paulo. After spending a few years experiencing the bustling modern city of millions of people, he went back to his small village of three hundred. When he got home, he told the members of the tribe why he had returned. "Here," he said, "we know each other and are with each other." He explained that even though he had looked for happiness in the city, he hadn't found it; rather, the close personal and social connections typical of his way of life in the tribe were what was lacking in the city and what truly made him happy.

Tribal societies treat all of their members equally—both young and old, married or unmarried, learned and ignorant, brave and shy. In tribes, younger family members, as well as everyone in the village, share in all responsibilities, triumphs, and tragedies, and it's this ongoing connection that brings great happiness to all members, for it bonds them together in harmonious, nurturing, and loving ways, like a variety of plants that all root in the same garden.

Writer Terry Berger once wrote, "The garden is a metaphor for life itself. Although not all of us are gardeners, we all plant the seeds of family and friendship. And yes, we must carefully tend them to make them grow." No matter where you live—in the city or the country, alone or with others, far away from family members or close by—remember to tend your "garden" every day. Give time, attention, and love to those in your "tribe," and you'll be happily rewarded.

I find my happiness in my "garden" of friends and family.

"All right, I know the ecologically correct line: 'They won't bother you if you don't bother them.' But who knows what bothers a bear? Take that fellow who was innocently jogging in Grand Teton National Park in August 1994 and ended up contributing an entire muscle group, the sartorius, to some grizzly's brunch. . . . Not to mention any number of sleeping campers whose sleeping bags were somehow mistaken for hot-dog rolls."
—WRITER BARBARA EHRENREICH

KEEPING THE WILD THINGS WILD

The bear is rapidly becoming one of "nature's outcasts"—a living thing that has become objectionable to man and is viewed as so evil and dangerous that it must be eradicated by poisons, by guns, by relocation.

And yet it is humanity that has made this creature into an outcast. A bear's preferred foods are beechnuts, acorns, apples, blueberries, and raspberries. But vanishing territory and the availability of trash has created a generation of bears that have been subjected to humanity and know no fear. In fact, a new breed of bear—the "Dumpster" bear—has been created. Bears as young as three and four years old have been observed eating out of trash bins and have even wandered into people's homes in search of food. According to Carroll County (New Hampshire) Fish and Game Commissioner Richard Patch, such Dumpster diving is being passed down from bears to the next generation. "If you're a bear," Patch comments, "would you rummage around in the woods working for a meal, or just go to a Dumpster and eat all you want and know there will be more there tomorrow?"

Be mindful of the wild creatures that live near you and whether they have become dependent upon humanity for survival. Ensure that all wild creatures have enough space and preferred foods in the wild to survive.

I protect the territory needed by wild animals.

"Life and love are life and love, a bunch of violets is a bunch of violets, and to drag in the idea of a point is to ruin everything. Live and let live, love and let love, flower and fade, and follow the natural curve, which flows on, pointless."

—ENGLISH AUTHOR D. H. LAWRENCE

THE MEANING OF LIFE

What is the meaning of life? Ask the violet that sprouts on your lawn, and if it could answer it might say, "This." Ask a honeybee as it forages for food, and it might say, "This." Ask the salmon that swims upstream during spawning season, and it might say, "This." Ask a morning songbird, and it might say, "This."

To all of nature's living things, "This" as a meaning of life needs no further translation. And yet to human beings, the translation is sought after, demanded, required, analyzed. Human beings need to know their purpose, while the rest of nature views itself *as* the purpose.

Humanity wonders, *Is the meaning of life to love?* Nature loves. Humanity wonders, *Is the meaning of life to be happy?* Nature exudes happiness. Humanity wonders, *Is the meaning of life to aspire to greatness?* Nature is the epitome of grandeur. Humanity wonders, *Is the meaning of life to leave behind some form of a legacy?* Nature "fills the air and earth with a prodigality of seeds, that, if thousands perish," observes Ralph Waldo Emerson, "thousands may plant themselves; that hundreds may come up, that tens may live to maturity; that at least one may replace the planet." Humanity wonders, *Is the meaning of life to protect the planet?* Nature is the planet.

Today, realize that the point to life is that there is no point. All you must do is simply live, love, and love the fact that you live.

My life has meaning simply because I'm alive.

"Nature is always hinting at us. It hints over and over again. And suddenly we take the hint."

—AMERICAN POET ROBERT FROST

CLEANING UP THE PLANET

Ralph Steadman, a British artist, cartoonist, and writer, once described this scenario. "If each of us was given a suitcase, a personal compartment to fill with ten items we could choose to take with us over the border into the new, clean millennium, who would choose an oil slick or nuclear waste? Who would choose the blackened stumps of a burnt-out rainforest? Who would choose a dying river or a dead whale?"

Over the years vested interests in fossil fuels and finite resources, immediate and oftentimes hasty solutions to pest and varmint control, and the need to meet the ever-increasing demands of a soaring world population have slowly devastated the planet's natural life, from a common flea to precious wetlands to the very air you breathe. The fallout from such ravages has been gradual and barely noticeable until fairly recently, when it was discovered that the remaining number of particular species could be counted on one hand, that dry winds easily blew away topsoil exposed from clear-cutting, that beaches had to be closed, and that fish and shellfish no longer were sold in fish markets and restaurants because of red tide or mercury contamination.

Now it's time to take nature's hint: the planet is in trouble, and your help is sorely needed. Today you need to remember that the Earth is not just your home, to be kept clean and properly maintained, but also a sacred, living planet. You need to roll up your sleeves and pick up after yourself and the other inhabitants.

Today I take an action that helps to save the planet.

"I had always pictured jungle as suffocating spaghetti tangles . . . a wicked salad that stank in your face and flung its stalks around you.

This was like a church, with pillars and fans. . . . There was nothing smothering about it, and although it was noisy with birds, it was motionless—no wind, not even a breeze in the moisture and green shadows and blue-brown trunks. And no tangles—only a forest of verticals, hugely patient and protective."

—AMERICAN WRITER PAUL THEROUX

CONQUERING YOUR FEARS

An old story once told by spiritualist Chuang-tzu describes a man who was so afraid of his own shadow and the sound of his footsteps that he ran away from them. But the more he ran, the louder the footsteps sounded and the more swiftly his shadow raced after him. The man's fears soon grew into panic, and he ran faster and faster until he finally died of exhaustion. What the man didn't realize is that if he had only stopped running and rested under the shade of a tree, the shadow would have disappeared and the footsteps would have ceased.

Sometimes a city park, a quiet suburban street, or an isolated trail through the woods may be filled with shadows and footsteps. So where can you feel safe and secure in order to spend a few moments of peace, quiet, and serenity in meditative communing with nature?

It has been said that the opposite of fear is faith. One torments you; the other comforts you. One imprisons you; the other liberates you. One paralyzes you; the other empowers you. Rather than run away from the outdoors, develop faith-filled alternatives to your fears. Stroll through a city park with a group of friends; skirt the unlit areas. Walk with your dog on suburban streets, through familiar neighborhoods. And hike through the woods on frequented trails with a friend.

I conquer my fears in safe and effective ways.

"It was when I began to find out the ways of wasps with other insects on which they nourish their young that my pleasure in them became mixed with pain. . . . Thus the old vexed question—How to reconcile these facts with the idea of a beneficent Being who designed it all—did not come to me from reading, nor from teachers, since I had none, but was thrust upon me by nature itself."

—ARGENTINE-BORN ENGLISH NATURALIST AND WRITER
W. H. HUDSON

SEEING THE POSITIVE IN THE NEGATIVE

There are thousands of species of parasitic wasps that lay their eggs on or in the body of a "host" insect—a gypsy moth, caterpillar, aphid, or beetle, or any one of the various leaf rollers. Other species, like the solitary potter and digger wasps, lay their eggs in individual cells constructed from mud; the mother wasp then provides her unborn offspring with the dead or paralyzed body of an insect or even a small invertebrate by "sealing" it into the cell with the egg so the larva can feed on the insect between hatching and pupation. In some species, the wasp is so skilled at using her stinger to deliver the paralyzing fluid into the host that she penetrates the main nerve ganglion so the host remains alive but immobilized as "fresh food."

As gruesome as this behavior may sound, the hosts upon which wasp young feed include some of humankind's worst pests, thereby regulating their numbers. And each wasp colony—which is founded, built, flourishes, and then collapses within a single growing season—has evolved into a highly socialized "society" that enables the colony to survive a multitude of disasters.

In your life you probably know those who "feed" off others—they take rather than give, use rather than help, lie rather than tell the truth. Yet there are good qualities about such people that need to be recognized; no one person, like no singular living thing, is all bad.

I recognize one good thing in every person I meet.

"The cottages have no dishwasher or microwave ovens, no televisions or telephones. ('People tell me they want air conditioning,' says Days, 'I tell them, 'Open the window.') Their layouts are all the same: galley-size kitchen, phone booth of a bathroom, two shoebox bedrooms, and a living room that holds a couple of rocking chairs, a couch, fireplaces that no longer work, and front windows that look out onto the beach."

—WRITER AND JOURNALISM TEACHER B. J. ROCHE

SUMMERTIME DREAMS

During the Depression, many people thought Joe Days was nuts to do what he did. Rather than lay off his construction crew, he kept his men busy building small cottages in North Truro on an isolated section of beach outside of Provincetown. For two years, Days and his crew kept building the cottages, which now number twenty-three. His wife named each after a different flower—from arbutus to zinnia.

Sixty-five years after the final nail was driven into Days's "cottage industry," Beach Point is no longer an isolated scrap of beach. A Holiday Inn and a Sheraton are just down the road. But while such plusher digs have vacancies throughout the summer season, Days's cottages are booked a year in advance for the following season. Many of the three-hundred-plus family renters regularly stay in the cottages and have done so for decades—same week, every year; older family members hand down their cottage time to younger family members. A hundred-name waiting list patiently pines for the possibility of a cancellation.

Do you have a summer routine you look forward to or special summer vacation plans you've made this year? Whether you're going on your annual trip to visit family members or trying out a new fishing spot in the mountains, know that it won't be long before you'll be enjoying this time away.

I look forward with anticipation to summertime plans.

"These days, even Thoreau's hut in the woods can sound pretty appealing. No phone, no fax, no beeper. No business dinners, business trips, or obligatory rounds of golf. No mix-and-match separates, programmable entertainment centers, state-of-the-art kitchen gadgets. Forget the commutes and car pools, the parking headaches. In fact, forget the car!"

—WRITER LAURA PAPPANO

IN SEARCH OF SIMPLICITY

How do you define simplicity? Perhaps it means having more time in which to do those things you want to do rather than cram all those things you have to do into every available minute. Maybe it means having less stuff to take care of—a job, a house, a boat, a vacation home—and fewer rarely used possessions that are piled high in closets or stored in attics, basements, and garages. Or perhaps simplicity is less about what you have and more about how you live—about maintaining the obligations and owning the possessions, but following a philosophy of living that makes your time on earth meaningful and valuable.

No matter what your definition of simplicity, its essence lies in getting rid of excesses. You can pursue your love of cooking without subscribing to several cooking magazines, accumulating stacks of cookbooks, and filling drawers with recipes. You can pursue the latest fashions without needing to buy every color of the same shoe or handfuls of ties. You can purchase a vacation home without furnishing it in the same way as your year-round home. You can encourage your children to be socially active without having to teach them how to use a Rolodex.

Begin to live more simply today by ignoring the initial stress you might feel from a "free" evening and by paring down your possessions to what you need rather than what you want.

Beginning today, I choose to live on a need level rather than a want level.

"Whenever the pressure of our complex city life thins my blood and be-numbs my brain, I seek relief in the trail; and when I hear the coyote wailing to the yellow dawn, my cares fall from me—I am happy."

—AMERICAN NOVELIST HAMLIN GARLAND

NATURAL RELIEF IN THE CITY

When was the last time you experienced a refreshing change of scenery? Oftentimes you don't have to go far from where you live or work in order to take a periodic "time-out" to collect your thoughts, resolve a problem, get in touch with your true feelings, calm your anxiety, and ease your stress.

Museums, botanical gardens, parks, historic trails, centuries-old cemeteries, docks and piers, and libraries provide quiet, mentally rejuvenating places for you to visit when you want to take a break from office politics and pressures, the stale smells of subways and parking garages, and conflicts with partners and children. Getting outdoors or experiencing some of what "city nature" has to offer you near a window overlooking a garden, under a stand of trees where chirping birds frolic, near a fountain or tiny basin of water, or standing on the edge of a dock watching the ships sail in and out of a busy harbor can provide you with a pleasant escape and a relief from the chaos and confusion of the city.

Sometimes when hiking a mountain trail or canoeing on a river through the wilderness is completely out of the question, "getting away from it all" is as easy as stepping outside onto your balcony and tending to your box garden. The natural experience surrounds you whether you're in the city or the country; it's just a question of seeking it out and then making good use of it before the pressures of day-to-day life get the better of you.

I seek nearby, stress-relieving natural relief.

"Sometimes it seemed to him that his life was delicate as a dandelion. One little puff from any direction, and it was blown to bits."

—WRITER KATHERINE PATERSON

SOARING IN STRENGTH

When a bird hops around on the ground, it becomes vulnerable and weak; at such a time, it would be easy for a cat to quickly snatch the bird in its mouth. Yet when the bird is in flight, it becomes powerful and strong.

You, too, can be like that bird—weak and vulnerable as well as powerful and strong. Yet too often you may be more conscious of your weaknesses and vulnerabilities and let them dictate how you feel about yourself. One of the greatest mistakes any human being can make is to spend too much time and effort trying to correct or deal with one or more weaknesses rather than to focus on developing one or more of their strengths.

Don't worry if you're not as fleet of foot as others. Don't belittle yourself if you rent an apartment because you can't yet afford your own home. It's okay if you still can't make up your mind what you want to be when you grow up or if you can't seem to resolve issues with your parents or your life partner. It's human to struggle to achieve a goal.

A proverb of unknown origin states, "Even when a bird is walking, we sense that it has wings." Today, you can soar with your strengths in mind, or you can let your weaknesses ground you. Focus on what you do right rather than what you do wrong, focus on what you can do rather than what you can't, and focus on moments of success rather than times of failure.

I let my strengths make me strong.

"The search is what anyone would undertake if he were not sunk in the everydayness of his own life. To become aware of the possibility of the search is to be onto something. Not to be onto something is to be in despair."
—WRITER WALKER PERCY

ADDING ZEST TO YOUR LIFE

A story has been told about Zen spiritualist Chuang-tzu, who was walking with a friend one day along a riverbank.

"How delightfully the fishes are enjoying themselves in the water!" Chuang-tzu exclaimed as he peered down into the water.

"You are not a fish," his friend said. "How do you know whether or not the fishes are enjoying themselves?"

"You are not me," Chuang-tzu responded. "How do you know that I do not know that the fishes are enjoying themselves?"

When you believe that nothing will change or ever get better in your life, chances are pretty good that nothing will change or get better. If you do little to facilitate change, you'll have little change. So if you're stuck in a rut or plagued by the same problems, you need to recognize that much of it is your own doing—and, as well, much of it can be your own "undoing," simply when you start to search for possibilities.

Writer Robertson Davies recommends that the best way to add some spice to your life is to become interested in life in general. "Curiosity," he writes, "is the great preservative and the supreme emollient. Not, of course, curiosity about theater or history alone or at all, but curiosity about *something*. Enthusiasm. Zest. That is what makes life a delight."

I delight in searching for something new in my life.

"To live fully, outwardly and inwardly, not to ignore external reality for the sake of the inner life, or the reverse—that's quite a task."
—GERMAN-JEWISH MYSTIC AND WRITER ETTY HILLESUM

SEEING ALL OF LIFE

The ultimate boundary to human life is death. What your life is like depends on how you live within that boundary—on how well you live in the world within yourself as well as within the confines dictated by death's limitations. If your world contains sickness, aging, and death, then these become inevitable parts of the "scenery" of your world. If, on the other hand, you see health, wisdom, love, pleasure, serenity, and other similarly positive elements, then these become scenic vistas in your world that you're able to experience and enjoy.

Ancient sages believed that the existence of a timeless reality is possible—a world in which there's an eternal awareness of life, an existence that either can't or won't see boundaries. Renowned physicist Albert Einstein espoused such liberation from boundaries when he said, "At such moments one imagines that one stands on some spot of a small planet gazing in amazement at the cold and yet profoundly moving beauty of the eternal, the unfathomable. Life and death flow into one, and there is neither evolution nor eternity, only Being."

If you can view death not as a boundary or a restricting force in your life but just another transformation in life, death no longer represents an end point, an extinction, a limiting factor in how you live your life today. To live fully today, you must be true to life. Value the moment, act on it, live in it. See yourself as timeless, your life as limitless, and your being as immortal. Then you'll realize that the whole of life lies in the verb *seeing*.

I see all of life as immortal.

"We are like butterflies who flutter for a day and think it is forever."
—AMERICAN WRITER AND SCIENTIST CARL SAGAN

ABOUT THE SIERRA CLUB

Return to your childhood hometown, and you'll probably discover the impact that development and growth has had upon some of the natural locales you once used to frequent. Gone is the pond in the woods where you used to skate in the winter and swim in the summer; gone, too, are the woods that once surrounded the pond. Gone is the giant oak tree that functioned as your front-yard lookout tower; gone, too, are the great oaks that lined your street. Gone is the pasture where horses used to graze; gone are the horses and the nearby farms.

When John Muir founded the Sierra Club in 1892, the 182 members immediately started protecting America's forests and wild lands. For more than a century, the Sierra Club has played a key role in safeguarding more than 132 acres in America's national-park and wilderness systems. Were it not for the continuous hard work of the Sierra Club—today with over 500,000 members in every congressional district and an added expansion into other areas of environmental protection issues—no one knows how many wild and scenic places around the country might have been destroyed.

You can stop development that sacrifices valuable land resources and take action on major concerns that threaten the integrity of natural areas and wildlife—acid rain, global warming, and the protection of rain forests. Join the Sierra Club or another influential grassroots conservation organization. Remember that in protecting your universe, you're protecting your destiny.

I participate in conservation goals to protect my universe for many lifetimes.

"Sure, there may be life on other planets—if you call that life. But humans are still the only intelligent life—right? The wagons will circle to defend this last bastion of human conceit."

—NATHAN MYRHVOLD, GROUP VICE-PRESIDENT AND CHIEF
STRATEGIC DAYDREAMER AT MICROSOFT

THE CENTER OF THE UNIVERSE

In the second century, Ptolemy postulated that the whole universe rotated around the Earth, and for years humans proudly believed that they were the center of the universe. But in the 1400s, Copernicus theorized that the Earth revolved around the sun; Galileo provided proof with his telescope. The authorities at the time were livid—how dare anyone challenge the supremacy of the planet! To do so was a threat to man's supremacy, for if the planet man lived on was not the center of the universe, then perhaps man wasn't the most intelligent and superior being in the universe. Authorities threatened to burn Galileo alive, so the scientist recanted.

In the centuries since, human beings have proven to themselves time and time again that both Earth and man are superior. Earth sends rockets and astronauts into space; earthlings can land on the moon as well as nonchalantly bullet through space and then return to safety without a splashdown. Man can uproot massive trees, keep ferocious animals in cages, and tame beasts several times his size. Man can nearly eradicate a species and then miraculously bring it back.

But in 1996, man and Earth received a challenge to their superiority—evidence of life on Mars. Perhaps Earth is not the only planet that sustains life; perhaps other intelligent—or even more intelligent—life-forms exist. Rather than view Earth or man as special, you need to view all of life itself—in any of its forms and wherever it is discovered—as special.

I accept that I am part of a very special, life-giving universe.

"I can tell my children that the way to get honor is to go to work and be good men and women."

—CHEROKEE CHIEF RUNNING BIRD

A COOPERATIVE SPIRIT

In business, the best leader is often the one who can motivate others to achieve a common goal so that all the members of the group believe, once the aim is accomplished, that they've done the work together. Because of this, the best leader knows when to act, when to be passive, when others are receptive, and when others won't listen. The best leader, therefore, is the one who presents himself or herself as an equal to others— neither oppressively leading nor passively following, capable of rolling up sleeves and digging in to do whatever work needs to be done—despite established "roles" or job titles—always ready to give praise and reluctant to criticize or judge, and skilled at building cooperation by exhibiting cooperation.

In nature, there's a good amount of cooperative spirit that's exhibited. Geese that fly in formation, for example, follow their "flight leader" until the leader drops back from the point of the V, at which time another goose will automatically take its place without causing the group to fall apart. Natural cooperation happens in other ways: a gentle summer rain provides water for green living things; a receding tide exposes food for gulls; dead leaves drop around a tree, slowly decay, and provide the tree with a rich source of nourishment. What you learn from such natural cooperation can be applied to fostering a cooperative spirit where you work. Everything you do can become an integral part of the overall organization; everything you do influences coworkers and helps to shape them in positive ways.

I am a worker who cooperates with others and helps them to succeed so everyone succeeds.

"We call it seventh-generational thinking. Seven generations ago, our ancestors loved us so much that we are still here as a people. We have to create a world not only for today, but for seven generations to come. The young people from this camp are going to be messengers for the future."
— CHAIRMAN OF THE CHEYENNE RIVER SIOUX TRIBE
GREGG BOURLAND

INDIAN SUMMER

Twenty-year-old Alana Marshall prays every morning to lose her anger. By the time she was eighteen, she had had three children; her brother, a gang member, was killed in an arson fire. Given a choice between entering an alcoholism-treatment center or spending the summer at Camp Wolakota Yukini, she opted for the camp. With her adopted horse Coda, she is learning the traditions of her Indian heritage with other troubled Indian youth as she seeks out a better future for herself at the "spiritual boot camp" on the Cheyenne Indian Reservation.

Each of the campers at Wolakota Yukini come from troubled Indian reservations. Each is trying to break the grim cycle of alcoholism and despair by living as their ancestors did—in teepees, by traveling on horseback, by learning their Indian language, and by participating in ceremonies led by tribal elders. Camp life is rigorous, structured, and strict. Campers rise at dawn to pray. Teepees are packed and moved every week. Campers must tend to the horse that has been assigned to them for the summer. Fighting and swearing are forbidden; those who break rules must do push-ups or pull extra guard duty. Prairie survival is stressed, along with respect for the earth and an understanding of the connectedness of all living things.

This summer, explore the youth programs that are available to troubled youth as well as city-bound youngsters. Volunteer time to a program or sponsor a child so he or she can experience, for a short time, a different way of life.

I support summer youth programs that instill good values.

"There is a secret world beneath the thousands of miles of power lines that crosshatch New England, covering hundreds and thousands of acres. It is also a forbidding world, with its stark, skeletal towers—one where medical studies say humans should not live. Yet naturalists say the grasslands, shrubs and meadows of the power lines play a vital role in supporting New England wildlife."

—WRITER ROYAL FORD

HIDDEN ASSETS

Sometimes industry and the environment can strike up a mutually beneficial relationship that helps nature to flourish without affecting consumer demands and lifestyle. Beneath the Hydro-Quebec power lines in New Hampshire, for instance, the Massachusetts-to-Canada electrical source has provided a valuable habitat for a variety of wildlife. The power company continually fights the growth of large trees beneath the lines, leaving low-growth shrubs and bushes that support a variety of wildlife. Blueberries, blackberries, elderberries, strawberries, checker berries, black cherries, and wild pasture roses feed bees, butterflies, birds, black bears, deer, fox, coyote, and moose. Honeysuckle, dogwood, hazelnut, and sumac bushes provide shelter for mice, shrews, rabbits, and other small animals, which supplement the fox and coyote diets as well as provide perfect hunting grounds for red-tailed, red-shouldered, and broad-winged hawks. Such a habitat could easily be destroyed, however, if the power company used powerful pesticides to keep the trees at bay.

You can take an active role in encouraging your local power company to use mechanical methods, such as periodic large-growth cutbacks or the application of safe herbicides, to protect a power source as well as the hidden assets it provides.

I support industry that protects the environment.

"When one has been long at sea, the smell of land reaches far out to greet one. And the same is true when one has been long inland. I believe I smelled the sea rocks and the kelp and the excitement of churning sea water, the sharpness of iodine and the under odor of washed and ground calcarous shells. Such a far-off and remembered odor comes subtly so that one does not consciously smell it, but rather an electric excitement is released—a kind of boisterous joy."

—AMERICAN WRITER JOHN STEINBECK

NATURAL SMELLS

Because you have a sense of smell, there's much that you can detect. You know, for instance, even with your eyes closed, if your partner or child is hugging you. You know, from a mere whiff, the brand of your perfume, deodorant, or shampoo. You know whether gas is leaking in your house or something is burning on the stove. You know when the pie or cookies are almost ready to take out of the oven. You know, within seconds of stepping outside, that a neighbor is cooking dinner on a grill. You know when the pizza has arrived. You know when a magazine is promoting a new perfume. You know when the trash needs to be taken outside. You know when milk is bad.

But does your sense of smell also let you know when you're nearing the ocean or driving past a dairy farm? When a thunderstorm is about to start? When you're near a lilac bush? When a water source is a stone's throw away? Do you know what dirt smells like? A rock? A leaf? A berry? A buttercup?

Nature has smells that reach out to you, touch you, alert you, entice you, repel you, scare you, soothe you. Open your sense of smell to nature's aromas, and you may discover odors that can touch your heart, fill you with anticipation, and trigger a memory of a beloved person or special time and place in your life.

I breathe in the beautiful smells of nature.

"I knew that living in the wilderness would offer challenges, and I wasn't sure I was up to them. . . . I thought I couldn't do without my morning cup of coffee. . . . I didn't think that I could be wet without being miserable. . . . I was afraid that I couldn't sleep on a thin rubber mat. . . . I thought I'd hate being dirty. . . . I doubted I could survive without my usual distractions. . . . I worried I'd feel ill at ease in a wild place. . . ."

—BOSTON GLOBE COLUMNIST LINDA WELTNER

SELF-DISCOVERY IN THE WILD

What do you think you might discover about yourself if you had to live in the wilderness for a short time? When columnist Linda Weltner set off for southeast Alaska on a kayak trip with her husband and a Zen Buddhist trip leader, she had misgivings about being able to reconcile her "citified" self with an uncivilized environment. But what she discovered was that a morning cup of hot tea was as satisfying as her usual cup of coffee, with great gear she could stay warm and dry on the coldest and wettest days, physical exhaustion allowed her to fall blissfully asleep on any surface, icy salt water provided as cleansing a body wash as a shower, there was joy in doing one thing at a time rather than four things at one time, and a wilderness locale could be made as cozy as home.

Sometimes the self you thought you knew and with which you've felt comfortable for decades can be challenged through a similar "shake-up"—a journey into the wilderness, adding a morning walk or run to your daily routine, choosing to pack a lunch filled with homemade or homegrown goodies instead of eating out, making a backyard garden or planting some herbs in a window box, or planning a weekend away from home. Sometimes a change of scenery or a break in a pattern or routine can give you the opportunity to see who you are in a whole new light.

I challenge myself and, in so doing, liberate myself.

"The wildwood birds . . . sang in concert, without pride, without envy, without jealousy. . . ."

—CHEROKEE INDIAN POKAGON

CONQUERING JEALOUSY

When you experience jealousy, you become a participant in a strange kind of competition. Your goal is to defeat an "opponent," yet oftentimes you don't know who or what your opponent is. Is it your partner, or the amount of time your partner spends at the office? Is it your friend's new outfit, the way your friend looks in the new outfit, or your friend? Is it your next-door neighbor, or the fact that your next-door neighbor maintains a beautiful backyard garden?

You may think you're jealous of a person but then find, upon closer examination, that it's not the person, what he or she is doing, or what he or she possesses that's making you feel jealous. Rather, jealousy stems from self-interest and self-destruction; you're jealous because you compare yourself with others, seeing how you measure up, and decide that others are better, have more, are more attractive, and so on. You engage in a one-sided battle in which your adversary is, in reality, yourself.

Yet none of nature's living things feels jealousy. Ralph Waldo Emerson once observed that "These roses under my window make no reference to former roses or to better ones; they are for what they are; they exist with God to-day. There is no time to them. There is simply the rose; it is perfect in every moment of its existence." So, too, are you perfect in each moment of your existence. Today, build upon this inner security by developing a more accurate perception of who you are in relation to yourself, not to others.

Today I focus on three qualities that make me happy with who I am.

"Quick as a breath, quiet as a whisper, the doe glides off into the forest. Sometimes when I see a deer this way I know it is real at the moment, but afterward it seems like a dream."

—AMERICAN ANTHROPOLOGIST RICHARD K. NELSON

KNOWING WHAT'S REAL

Have you ever gone through a difficult or trying experience and thought at the time, "I can't believe this is happening?" Everything seems to take on an aura of unreality; you can't grasp that your loved one is really gone, that you really passed the bar exam, that you really survived a car accident without a scratch, or that you really saw a deer disappear into the forest.

There's a Zen parable about a man who is walking across a field one day and encounters a tiger. Frightened of the beast, the man flees. The tiger chases after him. Suddenly the path ends and the man stops just before he would have fallen over the edge of a steep cliff. Frantically looking around him, he sees a wild vine. He grasps it and swings himself over the edge of the cliff. The tiger sniffs at him from above and begins pawing at the vine. The man looks down to where, far below, another tiger has come, waiting to eat him. As beads of perspiration drip down the man's face, two mice—one white and one black—begin to gnaw away at the vine. Little by little, the fibers of the vine part. The man looks around him, and then sees a luscious strawberry nearby. Grasping the vine with one hand, he reaches out and plucks the strawberry with the other. He begins to eat it. How sweet it tastes to him!

Living fully and completely in each moment gives you the opportunity to experience all that life has to offer—the heart-breaking as well as the breathtaking—so you can know what's really real.

I pay attention to each moment of each day.

"Life is always walking up to us and saying, 'Come on in, the living's fine,' and what do we do? Back off and take its picture."

—WRITER RUSSELL BAKER

FINDING YOUR ALIVENESS

Imagine that you have the opportunity to take a coast-to-coast trip across the United States. You can stop wherever you'd like, spend however long you want at any location, and have no set timetable. Are you going to focus solely on reaching your destination and simply drive there as quickly as you can? Or are you going to release the need to arrive at a specific time and simply enjoy the scenery, the people you meet along the way, and the interesting places you happen upon?

Every day you have the opportunity to go on a "cross-country trip"—a once-in-a-lifetime adventure. How do you wish to spend your time? If you focus on getting from one place to the next—from breakfast to lunch to dinner or from the morning newspaper to the afternoon mail delivery to the network news—then you'll certainly reach your appointed destination. But what if you allow yourself to get sidetracked from time to time—you water your plants and then eat breakfast or weed the garden and have a snack as you read the morning paper or take a walk and then eat a late lunch and maybe rent a movie for the evening? Wouldn't the lack of a set schedule help you to enjoy every minute and sometimes stop to savor a unique opportunity?

"Aliveness," says writer Richard Moss, "is not necessarily about feeling better, curing ills or solving problems; it is about feeling more, being in touch with a larger dimension of awareness." Today, see what happens when you get in touch with that larger dimension.

I open up to a larger dimension of awareness.

July 2

"In the four months since we came here the nights have warmed, the sea has grown softer, the green, still wintry water of March has turned . . . to blue. . . . There is a hatching of butterflies, and on the mountain there are many sweet things for the bees; in the gardens, after a rainfall, you can faintly, yes, hear the breaking of blooms. And we are waking earlier, a sign of summer, and stay lingering out late in the evening, which is a sign, too."

—AMERICAN WRITER TRUMAN CAPOTE

BEGINNING A MEANINGFUL JOURNAL

Reading the above few sentences written by Truman Capote about a time and place in his life and how such things affected him can make you feel as if you were right there with him. His words describe the sensual impact that the world outside made upon him and, without being given the details of how his day-to-day life unfolded, you get a pretty good idea of how he spent his days and nights.

If you have kept a diary or journal and now reread some of your entries, what you may realize is that you've created an itinerary or logbook of your life rather than an experiential interaction with the world around you. This may be evidenced by your constant rehashing of unresolved problems or conflicts, a self-absorbed focus, or endless venting of anger, frustration, and confusion.

Today, you can start a diary or journal that can function as a record of your connectedness to all living things, of the development of a highly sensual relationship with the natural world around you, and of the meaningfulness of the little things. Use your diary or journal to take a refreshing and positive look at life, to praise your achievements, and to focus on the good in life. Entrust your diary or journal with your special secrets, longed-for dreams, and heartfelt desires.

I begin a diary or journal that will be a pleasure to reread years from now.

"One thing I'd like to know most of all: when those ants have made the Hill, and are all there, touching and exchanging, and the whole mass begins to behave like a single huge creature, and thinks, what on earth is that thought? And while you're at it, I'd like to know a second thing: when it happens, does any single ant know about it? Does his hair stand on end?"
—AMERICAN BIOLOGIST AND WRITER LEWIS THOMAS

NATURE'S ACCOMPLISHMENTS

Do you think that human beings are the only living things that experience a sense of pride and accomplishment from their achievements? Do you think that human beings are the only living things capable of feeling and showing emotions? Do you think that human beings are the only living things that dance for joy, shout with happiness, or murmur with contentment? Do you think that human beings are the only creatures capable of stepping back from an achievement and thinking, "Look at what I've done? Isn't that amazing?"

While the answers to such questions will probably always be based on opinion, intuition, and theory rather than actual proof, what is most important is how you respond to the creations of nature's living things. You can marvel at the bird's nest that's interwoven with strands of grass and your dog's shed hair, the massive wasps' nest that hangs suspended from a tree branch, the activity that bustles around an anthill. In *The Life of the Spider,* French entomologist J. Henri Fabré tells how a large spider in his house provided entertainment for his whole family: "Big and little we stood amazed at her wealth of belly and her exuberant somersaults in the maze of quivering ropes; we admire the faultless geometry of the net as it gradually takes shape . . . the work becomes a fairy orb, which seems woven of moonbeams."

I admire the work of nature's creatures.

"But for the last two days it has been the great wild bee, the humblebee, or 'bumble,' as the children call him. . . . As I wend slowly along, I am often accompanied by a cloud of them. They play a leading part in my morning, mid-day, or sunset rambles, and often dominate the landscape in a way I never before thought of—fill the long lane, not by scores or hundreds only, but by thousands. Large and vivacious and swift."

—AMERICAN POET WALT WHITMAN

THE SOURCE OF HONEY

Open a jar of honey this morning to spread on your toast or sweeten your cup of tea, and you're tasting the fruit of the labors of thousands of bees—up to twenty thousand in a particular hive—who travel hundreds of miles to gather the nectar needed to make the honey. This honey is extracted from millions of combs and is actually created within the forager bees, after the nectar travels through each bee's esophagus into the honey sac, where it is then converted by enzymes the bee secretes into a mixture of glucose and fructose. Other bees in the hive—the house bees—then begin their specialized task of "pumping" water out of the nectar by fanning their wings, assisting the chemical process that results in honey. Then, the hive works together to fan the moisture out of the honey in order to reduce it to its finished state. All this, so you can enjoy your morning teaspoon of honey!

It's vital to learn where the things that you use in your daily life come from as well as how the source may have been treated. Bee harvesters know that in order for a hive to be productive, the unity of the hive needs to be maintained, and the hive itself should never be disrupted. Have the manufacturers of the products you use, eat, or wear been as conscientious in taking from their source?

I ensure that no natural life has been disrupted or harmed to create any of the products I use.

"It were happy if we studied nature more in natural things, and acted according to nature, whose rules are few, plain, and most reasonable."
—ENGLISH QUAKER LEADER WILLIAM PENN

ABIDING BY NATURE'S LAWS

American theologian Tryon Edwards once remarked, "The leaves in autumn do not change color from the blighting of frost, but from the process of natural decay.—They fall when the fruit is ripened, and their work is done.—And their splendid coloring is but their graceful and beautiful surrender to life when they have finished their summer offering of service to God and man." So, too, it is with your life; for anything worthwhile to be accomplished, you need to act in accordance with the natural processes of life.

There's the story of a man who, for years, had owned a peach orchard. One year he harvested a crop of much smaller peaches than usual. He apologized to all of his customers, explaining that his orchards needed constant attention. He said that it took him an entire day just to prune one tree properly, and with over five hundred trees to tend, he couldn't keep up.

"This makes me very upset," he confided to one of his regular customers. "I can't prune all of my trees myself, and I can't afford to hire extra help. I tried rushing the job, but ended up severely damaging some of the trees in my haste. So I decided to let the trees grow as they wanted to. And this is what happened." He sighed as he indicated the smaller peaches with a wave of his hand.

The customer took a bite of a smaller peach. "This is the most delicious peach I've ever tasted," she said. "Even though the peaches are smaller, they're even more tasty. Maybe you used good judgment in letting the trees grow as they wanted to."

Today, abide by the words of German philosopher Immanuel Kant: "Everything in nature acts in conformity with law." Live by nature's simple, basic rules.

I respect natural law rather than strive for outcomes I desire.

"There's a certain odor wafting through the night air in some neighbor-hoods. . . . It's gotten so bad that it seems that you can't take out the trash or get a tool out of the garage without practically tripping over a skunk or inhaling a lungful of foul air. . . . William Maloney said that two skunks have taken up residence in his garage—along with the family's two pet rabbits. 'The skunks walk around like they own everything,' he said."

—NEWSPAPER REPORTER GLORIA NEGRI

TRUE OWNERSHIP

When one of nature's "wild things" enters human terri-tory—whether that wild thing be a coyote in a farmer's chicken coop, crabgrass on a manicured suburban lawn, or rats in a city alleyway—often the first reaction is not to eradicate the intruder immediately but to express miffed astonishment at such encroachment.

Yet while you may view your "territory" as that space de-termined and protected by a legal document such as a lease or mortgage, your personal living space, or what lies within the boundaries of a stockade or barbed-wire fence, wildlife neither comprehends such ownership nor abides by it. For nature "owns" everything, and because of this, all wild things are the true owners of your property. The coyote that raids a chicken coop believes the chickens are on her territory; the crabgrass that invades the lawn believes the grass is on its territory; the rat that roams the city alleyways views such spaces as its terri-tories. So there's nothing unusual about a skunk that would consider Mr. Maloney's garage its shelter and Mr. Maloney's property its territory. The skunk walks around like he owns everything because he does. To all things natural, the world has no property lines. To all things natural, the world—and all things in it—is its territory.

I respect the right of all living things to reside on my property.

"On the seventh day of the seventh month pick seven ounces of lotus flowers; on the eighth day of the eighth month gather eight ounces of lotus root; on the ninth day of the ninth month collect nine ounces of lotus seeds. Dry in the shade and eat the mixture and you will never grow old."

—YIN SHAN CHENG YAO

ACCEPTING YOUR AGE

Not a day goes by when you don't hear of a new "weapon" in the eternal battle against aging. Sometimes a product or procedure is marketed specifically to the older market, claiming to keep skin looking young, for example. Other times a product is rumored to have age-reversing effects, and like wildfire, the rumor spreads.

Yet how important is your age? Is it your age that determines what you can or cannot do? Is it your age that determines how you should act, how you should dress, how you should feel? Western civilization isn't always kind and respectful of its elder citizens. American society teaches its children to look at an older person and say, "I hope I'm never like you," rather than "I want to be just like you." Yet traditional cultures often hold their elders in high regard, seeing them as storehouses of wisdom to be transmitted to the next generation. The Pueblo Indians, in fact, believed that their elders' rituals helped the sun to rise each morning.

Today, rather than be tempted to try a new "recipe" for looking or feeling young or younger, respect the place in life that you fill because of your age. Forests are filled with young saplings as well as towering trees that have lived for centuries, and each benefits the other.

Which is more important—how young I look or how young I feel?

"We never saw ourselves as 'environmentalists.' We were simply hard-working, good citizens trying to raise our kids and provide a safe, healthy life for our families. Our fight was for our own survival. We came to understand that since it is our community, and our lives, we have the right and the responsibility to actively participate in decisions affecting us."

—PENNY NEWMAN, DIRECTOR OF THE CENTER FOR
COMMUNITY ACTION AND ENVIRONMENTAL JUSTICE

DEFENDING YOUR COMMUNITY

In 1965, when Penny Newman and her husband set out to find the "perfect" place to start a family, they settled upon the community of Glen Avon in Southern California. They bought a home, raised two children, and had a wonderful life until 1978, when heavy winter rains resulted in acrid-smelling rainwater and a gray frothy foam on puddles. Then "frightening things began to happen. Tennis shoes and jeans began to fall apart; bloody noses were commonplace. Like other children in the community, my boys had red, sore, irritated skin. Shawn developed double vision and severe headaches." What Newman later discovered were the Stringfellow Acid Pits, a hazardous-waste dump used in Glen Avon since 1955. Open pits on a seventeen-acre site held over 34 million gallons of chemicals such as solvents, pesticides, and acids. The winter rains had caused the ponds that housed the liquids to overflow, and when the dam threatened to burst, officials released a million gallons directly into Glen Avon.

Newman helped form Concerned Neighbors in Action. After seventeen years, the community settled with the polluters for $114 million. While the money won't replace friends lost to cancer or children's surgeries and transplants, "it does provide some vindication for the suffering we as a community went through and allows us to rebuild our lives. And it acts as a deterrent."

I become a concerned neighbor so I can defend my community.

"The best place to find God is in a garden. You can dig for him there."
—BRITISH PLAYWRIGHT GEORGE BERNARD SHAW

YOUR SPIRITUAL GREEN THUMB

You're being reborn every minute of the day; every cell in your body is constantly changing. In fact, you're not even the same person you were just a few short minutes ago. This means that if you want, you can shift your attention from a focus you may have in your life—your career, your finances, your relationship, your hobbies—onto other interests and desires from time to time in order to keep your energy level high and your interest level at a peak. Then you can feel more hopeful, full of zest, carefree, free-spirited, in love with life, and become more closely attuned to nature and to a spiritual presence that can assist you in feeling more meaningfully connected to life.

Remember that you get what you cultivate in your life. Think of yourself and your life as a garden, and then keep in mind what would happen if you didn't plant new seeds each year, tend to them, and cultivate their growth. Think, too, what would happen if you planted only one vegetable or one flower and not a variety of seeds. You'll either have a garden so choked with weeds that nothing will reach fruition or a garden that will yield just one crop.

But if, from this moment on, you begin to focus on tending your garden wholeheartedly and with the desire to encourage all growth, you can give birth to a garden that's filled with soft, green shoots of exciting new growth—a garden that truly touches your heart and soul and connects you with the true Giver of Life. As Walt Whitman once declared, "A morning-glory at my window satisfies me more than the metaphysics of books."

I cultivate the garden of my existence.

"The sky struck me wordless. At the head of the valley was a perfect rainbow—seven layers of light arching between two mountain peaks that had gone silver. The rainbow was so bright the spires of the spruce trees below seemed lit like candles. If light could make sounds, we would have heard a symphony."

—WRITER JEFF RENNICKE

BEING TOUCHED BY NATURE

Have you ever witnessed something in nature that touched you in a profound way? Perhaps you came upon a herd of deer standing on the top of a hill at sunrise that made you catch your breath. Maybe a brilliant flash of lightning caused you to gasp. Perhaps the rare sighting of an American bald eagle filled you with hope. Maybe a newborn calf tottering on weak legs made you smile.

While a scientist could provide you with explanations as to why you came across the deer in that area, what caused the lightning's brilliant flash, the number of American bald eagles now in existence, or the reason for a calf's weak legs, the scientist couldn't tell you why such things touched you the way they did. What's important is that such things touched you in ways that eluded words.

The fact that a rainbow is created by the refraction of light through rain droplets doesn't make the rainbow any less brilliant or breathtaking when you see it, nor can it take away the sense of joy you may feel at its brief appearance at the end of a rainstorm. To early Christians and Jews, a rainbow was a ray of heavenly light radiating from above. To Africans, the birds on Noah's Ark were so overjoyed to see a bow of light in the clouds after forty days and forty nights of rain that they flew through it, leaving behind their brilliant colors.

I care less for explanations about nature; I care more for my emotional reaction to nature.

"You cannot stay on the summit forever; you have to come down again. So why bother in the first place? Just this: what is above knows what is below, but what is below does not know what is above. One climbs, one sees. One descends, one sees no longer, but one has seen. There is an art of conducting oneself in the lower regions when one can no longer see, one can at least still know."

—NATURALIST AND WRITER RENÉ DUMAL

SAVING THE PLANET

Here are ways to pass off the responsibility of saving the planet to others:

- Refuse to talk about environmental issues.
- Ignore warnings of potential long-term dangers; they are scare tactics by those who wish to stop progress.
- Take no risks—climb no mountains, ford no streams, take no new paths through the woods.
- Buy products tested on animals; purchase fashion accessories made from animal parts; clothe yourself in animal skins.
- Kill anything that bothers you.
- Go outside as little as possible.
- Believe that what little you could do would never help the planet.

Here are ways you can help to save the planet now and for future generations:

- Avoid unnecessary waste; recognize that resources are finite.
- Rediscover nonmaterial values that protect the environment.
- Do things that bring you joy and fulfillment.
- Take a risk—climb a mountain simply because it's there.
- Remember that you have only this one planet to inhabit.
- Respect life; love yourself and all living things.

I take responsibility for this planet.

> "The morning dawns with an unwonted crimson; the flowers more odorous seem; the garden birds sing louder, and the sun ascends the gaudy earth with unusual brightness; all nature smiles, and the whole world is pleased."
>
> —AMERICAN THEOLOGIAN DAY KELLOGG LEE

MAKING YOUR MORNINGS DIFFERENT

When you start your day, is your mood often positive and full of energy? Or do you find yourself beginning the majority of your days tired, grumpy, and unable to feel interested in the day that lies ahead?

Too often, operating on little sleep, dealing day after day with work and family pressures, and striving to handle the "normal" stresses of everyday living can make morning the time you dread most. Sometimes it may be all you can do to resist hitting the "snooze control" on your alarm clock yet another time, quickly shower and then throw together a reasonably presentable outfit, and stay alert for the morning commute.

Yet how might your morning be different if instead of focusing on time, on deadlines, on obligations, and on responsibilities, you focused on what's outside your home or apartment—the natural world that's slowly coming to life? Perhaps if you started today to notice the color of the morning sky, the new growth in your garden or window box, the particular songs of this morning's birds, and the brightness of the sun, you'd be less focused on how much you dread the day to come. Perhaps, too, you could notice the same things on each successive morning so you could compare and contrast the mornings; then you might realize each day dawns a bit differently. Each day wears a different outfit and begs you to notice it.

I observe this morning through new eyes; I start today as a new person who has a new, positive outlook on this day.

> *"A perfect summer day is when the sun is shining, the breeze is blowing, the birds are singing, and the lawn mower is broken."*
>
> —JAMES DENT, IN *CHARLESTON* (WEST VIRGINIA) *GAZETTE*

CELEBRATING THE JOY OF LIFE

What makes a day truly joyful to you—a day that, for whatever the reason, feels as if it should be celebrated? Maybe the day is a special occasion, such as your birthday or anniversary. Perhaps the day is the first of your vacation. Or maybe the day is one in which a planned activity, such as mowing the lawn, must be postponed, leaving you with time in which you can be spontaneous.

Joy is most often a wonderful surprise—totally unexpected, and yet never undesired. You may spend most of your life struggling to achieve some level of happiness and think, when you're happy, that you're also joyful, but happiness and joyfulness are two different emotions. Happiness is an outcome, a by-product, that springs from things—a promotion, a raise, a goal that's achieved—rather than coming from the heart, where joy resides.

Joy is a gift that's given to you even when it's not your birthday, a holiday, or an anniversary. Joy happens simply because joy *is*. Joy is spontaneous. Joy is playful. Joy is lighthearted. Joy is lively. Joy is one with the moment, one with life. Joy is the true soul of happiness.

Life teaches you to welcome joy when joy comes to you, but not to desire joy as a goal or as an expected outcome for things that are sought after, worked hard for, or struggled over. You can't just say, "Today I'll be more joyful," and expect that joy will suddenly appear. But what you can do from now on is to celebrate and embrace the good in life as much as you can, in the hopes of discovering the joy of life.

Joy of life comes from enjoying my life.

> *"[When] you walk along a country road and notice a little tuft of grass . . . the next time you pass that way you [must] stop to see how it is getting along and how much it has grown."*
>
> —AMERICAN PAINTER GEORGIA O'KEEFFE

CONTINUAL GROWTH

When you were growing up, your parents might have made you stand with your back against a doorjamb so they could measure how much you had grown since the time of your last measurement. After being carefully marked with the day's date in pencil, the doorjamb—which would remain unpainted for decades and retain the marks that not only measured your upward progress but also that of your brothers and sisters—served as a reminder that you were continually growing.

Nature, too, is continually growing. Even though a woods, a field, or even your lawn may seem to look the same from one day to the next at this time of year—lush with shades of green and rich with full growth—if you took time to truly notice a particular dead branch in the woods, a certain large rock in a stone wall that borders the field, or a tuft of grass in the corner of your yard, you would see a difference in such things every day. Look now and perhaps you'll see that the branch has been moved by a nocturnal, insect-foraging creature. Maybe the rock displays a different gray hue at this time of the morning. Or perhaps the grass in that corner sparkles as the sunlight reflects off its thin layer of morning dew.

You, too, are ever-changing. Even though it has been years since the last mark was made on the doorjamb, you're still growing in a multitude of other ways—physically, emotionally, intellectually, and spiritually. Each day encourages a new mood, a different philosophy, a shift in attitude, the assimilation of a new bit of knowledge. Each day encourages growth.

I grow in subtle, yet profound ways every day.

"The power that makes the grass grow, fruit ripen, and guides the bird in flight is in us all."

—RUSSIAN-BORN AMERICAN NOVELIST ANZIA YEZIERSKA

THE POWER WITHIN

Author, publisher, and metaphysical lecturer and teacher Louise Hay recommends that you imagine that your thoughts are like drops of water. As you repeat thoughts over and over to yourself on a daily basis, you may first notice a small stain on the carpet on which you're standing. Later on, you may notice a much larger stain. A short time later, you may find you're in the middle of a small puddle, then a pond, and—as your "thought-drops" continue—you're in a lake and then in an ocean. The question she then asks you to consider is: "What kind of ocean are you creating with your thoughts? Is it one that is polluted and toxic, or one that invites you to enjoy its refreshing waters?"

"Unpure" thoughts are those that gradually corrode your insides with their constant negativity. "Unpure" thoughts are those that divert fresh thoughts from feeding the stream of your mind, creating instead stagnant pools of nothingness. "Unpure" thoughts are those that slowly gnaw at your roots, gradually cutting off nourishment and depleting your strength. "Unpure" thoughts are those that blow you over with great gusts, preventing you from standing on your own two feet.

"Pure" thoughts, however, are those that give you confidence, strengthen your mind and spirit, affirm your worth, point you in the right direction, help you to reach out for support, encourage you to trust your own judgment, show you that you have value, enable you to recognize your good qualities, and make you take risks. Today, listen to just the pure thoughts and you'll realize that the power that lies within you is vital and self-affirming.

I think in ways that enable me to respond positively to myself.

"I go about looking at horses and cattle. They eat grass, make love, work when they have to, bear their young. I am sick with envy of them."
—AMERICAN WRITER SHERWOOD ANDERSON

ADULT PLAY

Do you ever feel an urge that entices you to be free of responsibilities, to forget about making ends meet, to take a break from the drudgery of work? When you feel such an urge, you may think that you need a vacation or a weekend away from home. But maybe what you really need is to play—to run, to jump, to climb, to belly flop, to skip, to hop, to tumble, to roll. Maybe what you really need to do—for just a short time—is to be a child.

When you're a child, all you may want to do is to be an adult; when you're an adult, you may long for the childhood days of feeling free and carefree. Even though, as an adult, you're free to make your own decisions and to do all those things you could only dream of doing as a child, you're never free to return to a long-ago time or to live in childlike ways—dependent, nurtured, protected, provided for. "How free had I really become?" wondered writer Michael Welzenbach one summer night as he stared with envy at the swings in the playground across from his apartment building. *"What on earth are you thinking?. . . . A grown man down there on the swings? What would everyone think? . . . [W]asn't freedom the self-confidence to stop on impulse and do a somersault on the lawn? To make a snow angel and not be concerned what anyone might think?"*

So what if you have bills to pay today or a job to go to? Take some time to be a child and simply play—laugh, romp, and enjoy an activity from a distant summer day.

I make time for "recess" in my activities today.

"But ask now the beasts, and they shall teach thee; and the fowls of the air, and they shall tell thee: Or speak to the earth, and it shall teach thee: And the fishes of the sea shall declare unto thee."

—JOB 12:7–8

NATURE'S CLASSROOM

Diane Dreher, author of *The Tao of Inner Peace,* tells the story of a midwestern farm boy who was the only one in his family to go to college. He felt privileged to be accepted to a state university. After years of hard work, he earned a graduate fellowship, this time to a fancy eastern school. There, he often felt embarrassed when his classmates asked if he had read this or that learned book; he often felt way out of his league going to school in a big city and trying to converse with classmates who sounded so intellectual and knowledgeable. So he would remain quiet as his classmates discussed theories and authors he didn't know. But then, one day, he decided to tell the truth. "No, I haven't read that book," he responded when asked. "Could you tell me more about it?"

Just as you can expand your knowledge by taking a course, reading a book, or learning from others, so, too, can you expand your knowledge by taking an interest in nature. Nature is like a magnificent university filled with brilliant teachers; it offers locations around the world, with countless classrooms that specialize in thousands of subjects. "Consult Nature in everything and write it all down," urged Italian artist and engineer Leonardo da Vinci. "Live in the fields, and God will give you lectures on natural philosophy every day," proclaimed American poet and essayist Ralph Waldo Emerson. And German theologian Meister Eckhart once opined, "If I spent enough time with the tiniest creature—even a caterpillar—I would never have to prepare a sermon."

I learn a great deal from attending nature's classroom.

"Live Like You'll Die Tomorrow. Farm Like You'll Live Forever."
—BUMPER STICKER ON THE TRUCK OF ORGANIC COTTON
GROWERS RODGER AND SANDY SANDERS

ORGANIC AWARENESS

When you munch on an ear of corn, a carrot, a peach, or a handful of grapes, are you eating more than just the vegetable or fruit? When you pull on a T-shirt and a pair of shorts, are you wearing more than just cotton or a cotton blend? Just as packaged foods come with labels that list ingredients, so, too, should fruits, vegetables, meats—and even the clothes you wear—come with a listing of any and all sprays, pesticides, preservatives, and waxes used in the process of producing the sweetest corn, the crispiest carrot, the juiciest peach, the tastiest grapes, the softest fabric.

Products that are grown on farms that are not organic are often doused with chemical fertilizers and sprays during their growth in order to repel insects that would damage the crops. But such chemicals also poison the earth and necessitate that you carefully wash anything edible prior to eating it. Organic farming, on the other hand, uses crop rotation and diversity, insectaries, fish fertilizers, and rich compost in order to produce a tasty but oftentimes not-as-enticing-looking fruit or vegetable. Too, nonorganic cotton growers generously saturate their cotton plants to repel bugs while organic cotton growers allow the fluffy white cotton plants with their delicate pink-and-white flowers to teem with insects. And yet the fabric that's produced from the organic cotton—and then used, undyed and untreated, in clothing, undergarments, socks, bed linens, and other items—is just as soft, breathable, and easy to care for as the items made from sprayed cotton.

I pay attention to whether the products I eat or wear are organic.

"It was a morning in early summer. A silver haze shimmered and trembled over the lime trees. The air was laden with their fragrance. The temperature was like a caress. I remember—I need not recall—that I climbed up a tree stump and felt suddenly immersed in Itness. I did not call it by that name. I had no need for words. It and I were one."

—LITHUANIAN-BORN AMERICAN ART HISTORIAN, CRITIC, AND
COLLECTOR BERNARD BERENSON

SEEKING ONENESS

Being "one" with the moment—feeling so connected with a particular time and space that you are conscious only of that instant—rarely happens in the hustle and bustle of everyday life. Rare is the person who feels "at one" with his or her job, with the crowd that waits for the next available subway car, with the carpool route or the screaming children in the van, with the long lines that wait to be admitted to a show. Oftentimes you can feel this "oneness" during a morning workout—sometimes indoors, in a gym—but usually when you're outdoors, on your run, during a lively tennis match, or out on the golf course on a warm, sunny day.

Writer Anne Morrow Lindbergh once described a time when she experienced this sense of oneness. "Yesterday," she wrote, "I sat in a field of violets for a long time perfectly still, until I really sank into it—into the rhythm of the place, I mean—then when I got up to go home I couldn't walk quickly or evenly because I was still in time with the field."

To truly experience oneness, you need to suspend any sense of time and its natural progression so you can be in the moment. You need to focus your mind on where you are rather than be physically in one space and mentally in another. You need to lose your control so you can let the time and place control you.

I follow the gentle rhythm of a place outside of me so I can be one with it.

"Nature gives to every time and season some beauties of its own; and from morning to night, as from the cradle to the grave, is but a succession of changes so gentle and easy that we can scarcely mark their progress."
—ENGLISH NOVELIST CHARLES DICKENS

THE SEASONAL PASSAGE OF TIME

Nature is always able to transform itself; it does so by constantly renewing itself with vigor and fresh life in ways that seem both obvious and dramatic. In the spring the robins return from their winter homes and noisily chirrup from sunup to sundown; ice melts on rivers with groans, pops, and moans; bulbs box their way out of the hard earth and slam their colors upward through the melting snow. Summer yields a steady and energetic growth; the air is alive with swarms of insects and thick with clouds of pollen; vegetables and fruits swell massively; greenery winds, twists, and tunnels everywhere. Autumn bursts forth with majestic colors and tosses its edibles to the ground in mad generosity to creatures in pursuit of the free bounty. Winter then blows into town with fury, releasing its anger at once again being excluded from all the fine-weather fun and frolicking.

Yet the seasonal cycles of nature are subtle; without a calendar distinction, it might be hard for you to determine when winter is over, when spring begins, when summer starts, and when autumn sets in. Yet to live as the Puri Indians once did, who had only one word for yesterday, today, and tomorrow and whose only way to express the distinction between the three was to point backward for yesterday, forward for tomorrow, and overhead for the passing day, is to be able to live within the seasonal passage of time. Does it matter if today is Monday or Sunday? Does it matter what date or time it is when you're reading this? Live in the moment, enjoy the progression of the seasons, and always point overhead.

I live in the moment offered by the season.

"In dwelling, live close to the ground.
In thinking, keep to the simple.
In conflict, be fair and generous.
In governing, don't try to control.
In work, do what you enjoy.
In family life, be completely present."

—*TAO TE CHING*

"RULES" FOR NATURAL LIVING

The Tao provides simple and basic "rules" for more rewarding day-to-day living; the following list recommends some simple and basic "rules" for more natural day-to-day living.

- Walk barefoot sometimes. Let your bare feet delight in touching the earth.
- Let the wind play with your hair; imagine the breeze to be the fingers of a passionate lover.
- Smell everything; if you can't recognize a smell, make up your own name for it.
- At work, drink from a coffee mug, not Styrofoam cups. Use one paper towel, not a few. Take notes on the backs of sheets of scrap paper.
- For friends and family members who seem to have everything, "adopt" a wolf, dolphin, or other creature for them as a holiday or birthday present.
- Ride your bike. Take a hike. Canoe. Carpool.
- Plant one tree each month.
- Build a birdhouse or bat house.
- Always carry out what you carry in.

I add to this list with other "natural rules" of my own.

"Lighning seems to have lost its menace. Compared to what is going on on earth today, heaven's firebrands are penny fireworks with wet fuses."
—AMERICAN ESSAYIST E. B. WHITE

NATURAL VERSUS MAN-MADE

When you were growing up, it might have been a big deal to be able to hold a lighted sparkler in your hand at night and pretend you were the keeper of heaven's stars. Nowadays a single sparkler no longer generates much interest with today's youth; rather, massive, cover-your-ears fireworks displays that cost thousands of dollars seem to be the norm. When you were growing up, a delightful summer evening's entertainment might have been to collect fireflies in an old mason jar. Nowadays the entertainment value of catching fireflies is ranked low; instead, catching the latest action-adventure-murder and mayhem-knock-'em-dead thriller is far more entertaining. When you were growing up, the hoot of an owl, the sounds of crickets, or the incessant throaty sounds of peepers may have lulled you to sleep. Nowadays, even if such sounds could be heard through a bedroom window late at night, they're often drowned out by the sounds of a blaring television or overpowered by headphones clamped tightly over ears.

When you witness such shifts in today's youth from the pursuit and enjoyment of simple or natural wonders to total immersion in man-made creations for their pleasure, it's up to you to provide a balance between the two. Because movies, fireworks displays, and the television play major roles in the lives of today's youth, they should not be denied. But today's youth should also not be deprived of the opportunity to play with a sparkler, catch a firefly, listen to the sounds of the evening, or sit by a window watching a lightning storm.

I show those younger than me entertaining and exciting natural wonders.

"When you ride in a boat and watch the shore, you might assume that the shore is moving. But when you keep your eyes closely on the boat, you can see that the boat moves. Similarly, if you examine many things with a confused mind, you might suppose that your mind and nature are permanent. But when you practice intimately and return to where you are, it will be clear that there is nothing that has unchanging self."

—ZEN SPIRITUALIST DOGEN

ADJUSTING TO LIFE'S EBBS AND FLOWS

Have you ever dug into an ant's nest? The first reaction of the little creatures to your intrusion is to do everything possible to save their lives, their nest, and its contents. So what the ants do is act immediately. They scurry around, moving the larvae into a safer underground chamber. Exposed contents of the nest are relocated to unseen passages. The hill of grains of dirt is gradually rebuilt. In a matter of minutes, the ants are again safely underground and ready to resume the normal flow of their daily routines.

How do you react when some catastrophe or unplanned event occurs? Do you want to crawl under a rock in order to escape having to deal with any change—all the while bemoaning the impermanence of life—or are you as resilient as the ants, ready to take positive action no matter what time of day or what you're doing at the time you need to shift your focus?

Today, remember that life is full of constant change and that each change needs a response from you. Even a rock experiences life in this way, constantly being acted upon by the elements, by earth's gravitational pull, by stresses and pressures placed upon it, even though its nature appears to be permanent. Every event in life is part of life's constant cycle of change. So, too, is your mind and nature part of this ever-changing impermanence.

As the events in life change, I change in response.

"Nature does nothing uselessly."

—GREEK PHILOSPHER ARISTOTLE

UNDERSTANDING THE "MASTER PLAN"

Do you ever wonder why some things in nature exist, why certain creatures behave as they do, or what purpose is fulfilled by a seemingly useless or pesky living thing?

Dutchman's pipe, one of California's most beautiful native vines, serves as a host to the pipevine swallowtail butterfly. In fact, this particular butterfly is so host-specific that it will only lay its eggs on the leaves of that vine, which later provide food for the larvae. Stinging nettles, which inflict fiery stings on human skin and, within minutes, result in little white blisters that itch terribly, feed dairy goats, attract the caterpillars of tortoiseshell and peacock butterflies, and help neighboring plants withstand lice, slugs, and snails during wet weather because of a high iron content. Pigeons, called by some "rats with wings," termed a public nuisance, and often synonymous with filth and poverty, are not only part of the human environment, but also have striking similarities to human beings. Their vision is far superior to humans, and even with a brain smaller than a fingertip, they can perform certain tasks beyond the capability of any computer. Too, pigeons not only commit new images to memory at lightning speed, but also organize images into logical categories as do humans when conceptualizing. Dandelions, the bane of every groundskeeper and lawn fanatic, have medicinally beneficial roots, assist in the ecology of ninety-three different species of insects, provide abundant nectar and pollen for bees, stimulate nearby fruits and flowers to ripen through the ethylene gas exuded at sunset, and produce latex, which, for years, has been used to produce rubber. These are just a few examples that prove that nothing in nature is useless.

The world in which I live never ceases to amaze me.

"Nature imitates herself. A grain thrown into good ground brings forth fruit: a principle thrown into a good mind brings forth fruit. Everything is created and conducted by the same Master,—the root, the branch, the fruit,—the principles, the consequence."
—FRENCH MATHEMATICIAN AND PHILOSOPHER BLAISE PASCAL

NATURALLY DIVINE GUIDANCE

Have you ever marveled at how fate has drawn you to different people, certain situations, or a new location? Maybe you met the person of your dreams by a chance encounter or an interesting turn of events. Perhaps you stopped at a store you've never been in before and discovered a childhood friend working there. Maybe you just happened to meet up with someone on a wilderness sojourn who had valuable information to share that you needed or had been looking for. Or perhaps a spontaneous hike through a field enabled you to add a sought-after bird to your list of sightings.

There's a lesson to be learned from each person you meet and each chance encounter you have. Your contact, however brief or long, happens for a reason. As spiritual writer Ruth P. Freedman has commented, "There is a divine plan of good at work in my life. I will let go and let it unfold." Although not all the lessons you'll learn will be easy or all the contacts you make feel wonderful—some people may treat you badly, and some enticing opportunities may not work out—all will have given you a valuable lesson.

Trust that your life is being guided not only by the decisions you make, but also from the input of a divine resource. Rather than marvel at chance meetings and amazing connections with nature and people, accept such things as fulfilling a useful purpose. Every lesson you learn is meaningful.

I trust that there's a divine, natural plan in my life.

"If you stand in a meadow, at the edge of a hillside, and look around carefully, almost everything you can catch sight of is in the process of dying, and most things will be dead long before you are. If it were not for the constant renewal and replacement going on before your eyes, the whole place would turn to stone and sand under your feet."

—AMERICAN PHYSICIAN AND WRITER LEWIS THOMAS

PROTECTING NATURE'S RENEWAL

At the end of Dostoyevsky's *The Brothers Karamozov*, a young man dies. After the funeral, his friend Alyosha reminds those who are gathered to mourn the loss through the custom of eating pancakes. The purpose is to mix the sweetness of life with the bitterness of death and to show the need for nurturing ongoing life.

In nature, death is a common occurrence. While some living things live longer than human beings, others come into existence for mere minutes. Because of the laws of predation, the young and the weak face a constant struggle with death. And because of the impact humanity makes upon nature, depletion, diversion, and decimation can prevent nature from continually renewing itself.

Just as nature leaves humanity alone to experience death, whether natural or man-made, such as through wars, so, too, should humanity leave nature alone to go about its cycles of decline and renewal, life and death. If nature must be affected, such as by development that places the continued survival of any living population in jeopardy, then this impact must be regulated. Nature has no way of communicating with humanity that something has become so dangerously depleted that the lives of an entire species may be in jeopardy. That's why it's up to you to set, promote, and defend environmental limits that protect and preserve nature before fatal and irreversible damage is done.

I let nature experience its natural deaths and constant renewals without my input.

"For proverbs are the pith, the proprieties, the proofs, the purities, the elegancies, as the commonest so the commendablest phrases of a language. To use them is a grace, to understand them a good."
—ENGLISH AUTHOR AND TRANSLATOR JOHN FLORIO

PROVERBS TO LIVE BY

Inspirational words can sometimes find their way into your life just at the moment you need them, providing you with the right focus to resolve a problem, the right words to ease your discomfort or pain, the right wisdom to make you think, or the right lightheartedness to make you smile.

Here are some proverbs that may have a place in your life today:

- With all things and in all things, we are relatives. (Sioux proverb)
- The rain falls on the just and the unjust. (Hopi proverb)
- Those who have one foot in the canoe and one foot in the boat are going to fall into the river. (Tuscarora proverb)
- The more you ask how far you have to go, the longer your journey seems. (Seneca proverb)
- You should water your children like you water a tree. (Hopi proverb)
- If you continually give, you will continually have. (Chinese proverb)
- Water which is too pure has no fish. (Zen proverb)
- Do not judge your neighbor until you walk two moons in his moccasins. (Northern Cheyenne proverb)
- There is no death, only a change of worlds. (Duwamish proverb)
- The words of God are not like the oak leaf, which dies and falls to the earth, but like the pine tree, which stays green forever. (Mohawk proverb)

I honor the proverbs of many generations and cultures.

"Nature is often hidden, sometimes overcome, seldom extinguished."
—ENGLISH ESSAYIST AND PHILOSOPHER FRANCIS BACON

ELIMINATING DECEPTION

Camouflage hunting clothes can be quite effective in hiding from the animal being hunted. Rather than look like a person, the outfit enables you to blend in with a pile of leaves, tree trunks, or the reeds by the edge of a lake. The appearance you create by using such clothing is illusory and false, and yet it appears to be real. Camouflage is used just as effectively by nature's living things. "Look at a tiger," encourages American poet Marianne Moore. "The light and dark of his stripes and the black edge encircling the white patch on his ear help him to look like the jungle with flecks of sun on it."

Being camouflaged while out in nature is cleverly deceptive, but being so camouflaged in the business world, with family members, or with an intimate partner or friends by "keeping up appearances" or playing a role they expect of you allows you to be deceptive in ways that create an effect that may not necessarily be true, allowing you to "hide" your true self, thoughts, and feelings from them.

Deception is one of nature's most misunderstood lessons. For nature doesn't use deception to lie, cheat, manipulate, avoid intimacy, or to be dishonest in any way. Rather, nature uses deception for survival. Why, then, would you want to deceive others through the appearances you create? Sometimes you may be too afraid to let others see the true you; sometimes you may not even know who the true you is.

It has been said that the truth will set you free. Today, rather than camouflage your ideals, who you are, and what you need, let someone else see you as you are.

I share my true self with another.

"This is the summer of Patrick's pumpkin plant, its vines creeping across the backyard, its roots burrowing deep into our fantasies of a slower, simpler life. That Patrick's pumpkins grew at all in the rocky, unprepared soil hard by our 70-year-old house is testament to a child's faith in nature."

—BOSTON GLOBE COLUMNIST EILEEN MCNAMARA

EXPERIMENTING WITH NATURE

When Eileen McNamara's son wanted to grow a pumpkin plant in their backyard, she told him how the plant needed well-drained loam and well-rotted manure. She gave him a lecture on the difficulties of gardening in their location and the amount of room a mature pumpkin plant would need. But Patrick's response was, "Mom, let's just plant it." It wasn't long before "Patrick's pumpkin plant busted out of the herb garden, catapulted across the lawn and climbed the hemlock hedge that separates our litter of bicycles and baseball bats from the immaculately tended greensward next door."

Patrick's pumpkin plant astounded the entire family. Everyone took turns with the watering can and in measuring the enormous yellow blossoms. The neighborhood became involved, too. One neighbor took it upon himself to fertilize the plant. Another slipped a board beneath the fruit to prevent rot. A third took time out during her dog walks to stop and inquire about the pumpkin's progress.

Then, describes McNamara, "Because we came outside to check the pumpkin plant, we saw the robin's nest [and] her babies: all needy beaks one day, all flown the next . . . we saw the wasps' nest [too]." As the plant continued to grow, the family spent time together turning each pumpkin to prevent flat sides and planning the artistry they'd use in making their own jack-o'-lanterns.

I encourage my family to share in a summer nature experiment.

"Travel by canoe is not a necessity, and will nevermore be the most efficient way to get from one region to another, or even from one lake to another—anywhere. A canoe trip has become simply a rite of oneness with certain terrain, a diversion off the field, an art performed not because it is a necessity but because there is value in the art itself."

—NATURALIST AND WRITER JOHN MCPHEE

THE VALUE OF NATURAL ARTS

Just because some things are no longer necessary to the way you live your life doesn't mean that such things can't be revisited, reused, reemployed, reexperienced. A fire in a fireplace can still provide warmth, keep a kettle of soup warm, and shine light upon a book. Vegetables grown in a home garden plot or balcony pot can still dress up this evening's salad or be blanched and canned to enjoy this winter. A personal letter can still be handwritten and posted to arrive at a friend's house. A musical instrument can still be whittled from a piece of wood. Pine needles can still be gathered to make a soft, forest bed. Animals can still be tracked through the woods by the prints, markings, and scat they leave behind. The wind can still forewarn of a storm. A canoe can still take you to a mid-lake island or distant shore.

Of course you always have the option to turn on a furnace or your stove or flick on the electricity, stop by a grocery store or farm stand to pick up fresh or canned vegetables, E-mail or fax to your friend, purchase a CD or a finely handcrafted musical instrument, pump air into a plastic-coated mattress or sleep indoors, visit animals in a zoo, turn on a weather radio, or steer your motorboat to the island or distant shore.

But what do you gain from always relying upon modern technology? What purpose does such efficiency serve?

I keep the past ways alive by valuing forgotten arts.

"We are all happier in many ways when we are old than when we were young. The young sow wild oats. The old grow sage."
—BRITISH STATESMAN SIR WINSTON CHURCHILL

HOLDING ON TO HAPPINESS

In 1987, journalist Nancy Mairs wrote an article about happiness, which she highlighted with a brief, but personally moving description of her midlife experiences. She wrote: "If anyone had told me then that by the time I was forty-three I would be crippled and George would have cancer and my beloved family would have begun to die, I would have cried out, 'Oh, no! I could never stand the pain!' But if anyone had told me that, in the presence of these realities, I would find myself, without warning, pierced by joy, I would have been stunned speechless, certain that my information was either perverse or outright mad."

Do you think that you can be happy, joyful, and confident no matter what life places in your path—the traumas as well as the triumphs? While there's much tragedy in life, when you're young such things appear to be quite unbearable. And yet when the same things occur in mature adulthood, you may realize that you not only know you can handle them, but can also handle them well.

Age as well as nature teaches a very valuable lesson over the years: the extent to which you can be content has little to do with what happens to you. Rather, happiness depends more upon your ability to find pleasure in life—in spite of what happens to you—and to hold on to that happiness. As American poet and essayist Ralph Waldo Emerson said, "Do what we can, summer will have its flies; if we walk in the woods we must feed mosquitos. . . ."

I adjust to life's circumstances in ways that contribute to my happiness.

"I no longer believe that there will be time, and time enough, for everything I want to do. That I can control many events. That my culture's standards of beauty and virtue are attainable or even desirable. . . . I've learned how to find beauty in places where I never would have searched for or found it before—in an edematous face, a lesioned and smelly body, a mind rubbed numb by pain. Pain. A burned-over district. Mortal lessons: the beauty of a ravished landscape."

—WRITER JAN GROVER

NATURAL REMISSION

In her observations of the Wisconsin Cutover, Minnesota writer Jan Grover likens the ravages of the cutover stand of Wisconsin timber to the devastation inflicted on the body of a friend by AIDS. Only under a protective coating, such as snow, she observes, do the million acres of land look beautiful. Once the snow melts, however, all the scars are evident—a topography of relentless and unfeeling use and abuse from being logged between 1860 and 1920, then sold by the railroad and timber companies to naive farmers who soon discovered that the thin soils severely shortened any potentially rewarding growing season. Human population in the area is scant; the ratio of bars to people, stumps to people, and unfinished homes and rusting trailers to people reveals humans are definitely in the minority.

Ravaging of any natural beauty, which is oftentimes done at a slow pace, can be irreversible. Like a cancer, it spreads from one vital location to the next. Yet while the difference between incurable diseases and destructive practices is that the cancers can be temporarily stopped while the destructive practices can be permanently ended, both cessations—whether temporary or permanent—ensure that life can go on, if only for a short while.

I prevent cancerous growth from spreading into the natural landscape.

"Mother Nature has let us flounder all night in the fog. We fight our way: she is telling us with her fog that life is not always a direct sighting; you don't always know where you are or where you are going; you can only keep fighting with a smile until it breaks and the new light is seen, then you are on your way again. It may be a new direction, but it is a life. Thanks for the fog."

—WRITER CHAPIN WRIGHT

TEMPORARY BLINDNESS

Once, long ago, a thick fog blanketed a seacoast village. Lost in the fog, a seabird that lived far away from the village on an ocean island uninhabited by man fluttered into the village and then landed, exhausted, on a dock. A fisherman who was mending his nets quickly tossed them over the seabird and ran to alert the others.

After the mayor of the village was informed of the unplanned visit by the rarely seen seabird, and knowing how the fog had made the villagers, who depended upon going out to sea every day, quite unhappy, he proclaimed the day to be one of celebration. A cage was fashioned to hold the bird. Pigs and lambs were slaughtered and placed on large spits. Musicians tuned their instruments. Children raced through the streets, shouting and playing raucously.

As everyone gathered in the village square, trumpets blared and a formal procession made its way through the crowd. The mayor delivered a lengthy speech about the good fortune the fog had brought the village, then removed the blanket from the bird's cage. The crowd gasped; the bird was dead. At that moment a respected elder of the village held up his hand. "Fear not, people. This is not the sign of a bad omen. Rather, it is a reminder to all that the bird that lost its way did so momentarily. It knew that as the fog lifted, its way would be clear. But the cage you placed it in was permanent. There was no way out."

I trust times of indecision and darkness to be temporary.

"In nature a repulsive caterpillar turns into a lovely butterfly. But with human beings it is the other way round: a lovely butterfly turns into a repulsive caterpillar."

—RUSSIAN AUTHOR ANTON CHEKHOV

DEFINING BEAUTY

To be able to grow more beautiful each day—both in appearance and in character—may be a goal you often find elusive. Daily stresses, pressures, conflicts, arguments, and fatigue can chip away at your ability to keep a smile on your face, a song in your heart, and kindness in your soul. The lack of time, energy, finances, and motivation can prevent you from achieving goals you know will help you to feel better about your appearance.

But what is beauty? In the human world, most people would equate beauty with a fashion model or movie star; few would remark that Mother Teresa was beautiful. In the natural world, most people would think of flowers as beautiful, or freshly fallen snow on pine trees, or a butterfly. Few would think of a caterpillar or even the lowly earthworm as beautiful.

Yet might beauty not be better defined by what someone or something does rather than how someone or something appears? English clergyman Gilbert White once remarked, "Earth-worms, though in appearance a small and despicable link in the chain of nature, yet, if lost, would make a lamentable chasm . . . the earth without worms would soon become cold, hard-bound, and void of fermentation; and consequently sterile. . . ."

Today, think of beauty as function rather than appearance. Look closely at a spindly tree struggling to survive in the park, for example, and you'll see the shade it provides and the home it makes for other creatures. You'll see that it's beautiful.

I see beauty in all living things.

"Sit in reverie, and watch the changing color of the waves that break upon the idle seashore of the mind."

—AMERICAN POET HENRY WADSWORTH LONGFELLOW

JOURNEY TOWARD SILENCE

Have you ever noticed how vitally important it is that everything and everybody be heard? People rarely keep silent in the company of others. Barking dogs are the suburban version of the town criers of the past. Shopping for food or riding in an elevator is invariably accompanied by a "pop-rock" tune. Turning on the radio is probably the first thing you do after you start the car. You wear headphones while you exercise. You shower in the morning to the traffic and weather report. You make love in front of the television.

Even in those brief moments of silence you may be able to snatch from time to time, you may find yourself mentally "conversing" with yourself by compiling lists of things to do, rehearsing a conversation you'd like to have, rehashing the dialogues of the day, or just incessantly chattering away to yourself, leapfrogging from one topic to the next.

Today, try to embark upon a different path—one that leads you into the silence of your soul. To do this, you need to cut off all outside auditory distractions as well as your inner voice. Start this journey toward silence for just a few minutes each day. After a week, gradually increase your time. The goal is to be able to stimulate other senses, such as sight, taste, touch, and smell, and, in so doing, be able to heighten your inner awareness in ways that enable you to think less in terms of what you need to do or what you have done and more in terms of who you are and who you are in relationship to the life that's around you.

I provide silent time for myself so I may know more about my world.

"Keep your hands open, and all the sands of the desert can pass through them. Close them, and all you can feel is a bit of grit."

—ZEN SPIRITUALIST TAISEN DESHIMARU

VARIABLE LIFE CYCLES

Decades ago, how life was supposed to be lived was structured and predictable. Because most people didn't expect to live longer than their fifties or sixties, it was essential that key personal and social tasks be accomplished by specific ages. That meant that schooling and job preparation, courtship and marriage, child rearing and home ownership, and retirement were assigned to particular periods of life and were supposed to occur only once in a lifetime. If you were a thirty-year-old unmarried woman, you were a spinster because your opportunity for parenthood had passed; if you were a twenty-year-old man who didn't know what he wanted to do for a living, you were a ne'er-do-well.

Yet today you can be a grandparent without even being a parent. You can date many people and marry more than once. You can be married and not have children; you can have children and not be married. You can be a freshman in college when your hair is gray; you can retire before your hair is gray. Whereas once the sands of time used to only flow downward through a narrow opening until all the sand ran out, today the sands of time are spread out over a wide beach—a beach that stretches around the planet. Today you're living a cyclical life plan rather than a linear one. Just as nature offers you midsummer as well as summer, your life experiences have no age restrictions; age no longer dictates periods of emotional, physical, or even fiscal growth. Education, work, parenthood, sex, recreation, and a variety of other life activities can blend into and influence one another at any age.

I enjoy the freedom of a cyclical life plan.

August 6

"Nothing is so tiresome as walking through some beautiful scene with a minute philosopher, a botanist, or a pebble-gatherer, who is eternally calling your attention from the grand features of the natural picture to look at grasses and chuckie-stanes."

—SCOTTISH POET AND NOVELIST SIR WALTER SCOTT

KNOWING NATURE SIMPLY

Have you ever climbed an *Alnus rubra*, covered your head and run away in fright from an *Eptsicus fuscus*, plucked a *Pulex irritans* from your dog's fur, found an *Ariolimax laevis* in your garden, used a powerful weed killer on *Taraxacum officinale*, swatted a *Musca domestica*, set out a trap for a *Mus musculus*, been besieged by *Sturnus vulgaris*, or stung by a *Vespula vulgaris*?

Sometimes learning that's based on memorization isn't as exciting as learning that's based on true experience; learning all the state capitals, for instance, isn't as stimulating as traveling to the states themselves. So it follows that knowing an official name of a natural living thing isn't always as vital as knowing what the name stands for—knowing that you've climbed a red alder tree, run from a big brown bat, nabbed your dog's flea, come across a light brown field slug, tried to get rid of a dandelion, chased a housefly, tried to trap a common house mouse, been inundated with common starlings, and been stung by a yellow jacket.

English writer D. H. Lawrence once wrote, "Where are the little yellow aconites of eight weeks ago? I neither know nor care. They were sunny and the sun shines, and sunniness means change, and petals passing and coming." Sometimes, quite simply, all you need to know about one of nature's living things is something as simple as its color.

I strive to keep what I learn about nature simple.

"There are many pleasures to be derived by drawing up to a comfortable rock or well-appointed stump and watching a stream go by. It is no coincidence that great cities consider fountains and pools among their most important assets. The soothing effects associated with water in any form take the sharp edges off the annoyances of daily life."

—WRITER NORMAN STRUNG

WATER'S FLOW

Of all the millions of adults who work each day to make a living on this planet, the proportion who must travel to work by boat or who are dependent upon water to provide them with their livelihood is quite small. Fishermen, farmers, cruise lines, and shipping companies are just a few of the professions that live off and from the water. But for the most part, you and your wide circle of friends and family are drawn to the water solely for recreational purposes.

Yet if you were told you could never swim or sail on the ocean again, never fish from a crystal lake, never wiggle your toes in a chilling mountain stream, never see a majestic waterfall, never toss crumbs to the ducks in a pond, never again hear waves crashing to shore, or shed tears as you're comforted by the soothing *there-there, shoosh-shoosh, there-there* of a babbling brook, you would probably be quite unhappy. Even the smallest of water sources would remind you of the greatest water source of all—the great expanse of salt water that cleanses the shores of all the continents, that's fed day and night by rivers and streams but is never filled, is never emptied, is never lowered even in the times of the worst droughts.

Water connects you to all that is living. Sit by the water today and listen to it; there's a great restfulness in the sounds, a patient murmuring, even though they are rushing as fast as they can to get ever closer to their source.

I experience the connection water makes to the life-sustaining waters of the ocean.

"Out there in the Milky Way and the world without end Amen, America was a tiny speck of a country, a nickel tossed into the Grand Canyon, and American culture the amount of the Pacific Ocean you bring home in your swimsuit."

—AMERICAN HUMORIST GARRISON KEILLOR

TWO RITUALS; TWO CULTURES

Picture in your mind two images. One is of the dealers on the New York Stock Exchange during an average business day, who stand shoulder to shoulder, frantically jostling one another as they wave their arms and raise their voices. Sweat pours down their faces and soaks their traditional garb of dark pants or skirt and light-colored shirt; their erratic gestures and movements go on for hours.

The second image is of Masai women, who stand shoulder to shoulder, frantically jostling one another as they wave their arms and raise their voices as they dance and sing. Sweat pours down their faces and soaks their traditional garb of brightly colored dresses and beaded headbands; their erratic gestures and movements go on for hours.

Although both rituals are similar and both are true to the culture in which the participants live, the Masai women's dance is just as important a feature of their society as the stock traders' "dance" is to their society. The Masai women, who are often regarded by Western cultures as strange or even primitive, use dance, song, and ritual to celebrate their sense of place and their role in the environment. The stock traders, on the other hand, use their ritualistic gestures and cries to celebrate the obsessive worship of money. While both cultures are vital, both need to learn from the other in order to celebrate the earth in lasting, meaningful ways.

I keep my culture's obsessions in perspective with the rest of the world's.

"Is there to be found on earth a fullness of joy, or is there no such thing? Is there some way to make life fully worth living, or is this impossible? If there is such a way, how do you go about finding it? What should you try to do? What should you seek to avoid? . . . What should you accept? What should you refuse to accept? What should you love? What should you hate?"

—TRAPPIST MONK AND AUTHOR THOMAS MERTON

THE JOY OF FISHES

One day renowned Taoist writer Chuang-tzu was crossing the Hao River with Hui-tzu. Chuang said, "See how free the fishes leap and dart. That is their happiness."

Hui replied, "Since you are not a fish, how do you know what makes fishes happy?"

Chuang answered, "Since you are not I, how can you possibly know that I do not know what makes fishes happy?"

Hui argued, "If I, not being you, cannot know what you know, it follows that you, not being a fish, cannot know what they know."

Chuang said, "What a minute! Let's get back to the original question, which was how did I know what makes the fishes happy. I know the joy of fishes in the river through my own joy, as I go walking along the same river."

Joy is something highly personal; joy varies from person to person. While you may feel joy when you spend a Saturday afternoon fishing on a river, someone else may feel revulsion, discomfort, and stress doing the same thing. So joy is something that you need to seek for yourself and to define as the feeling relates to what is in your heart, not in the heart of another. Avoid what you dislike, accept what is acceptable, and love what is most dear to you.

Today I define joy on my own terms.

"Summer is the time when one sheds one's tension with one's clothes, and the right kind of day is jeweled balm for the battered spirit. A few of those days and you can become drunk with the belief that all's right with the world."

—AMERICAN ARCHITECTURE CRITIC ADA LOUISE HUXTABLE

THE SERENITY OF SUMMER

Even though your life during the summer months may be quite hectic—long hours of daylight encourage you to be out every evening, weekends are filled with plans, houseguests come and go, and barbecues spark like wildfires throughout the neighborhood—you may find yourself more relaxed and content than during any other time during the year. You may find yourself rising in the morning to greet the bright new day rather than grumble at it. You may take better care of yourself by exercising more, eating greater amounts of fresh fruits and vegetables, and balancing work time more equitably with recreation and time spent with the family. And even though your life may be more hectic than at other times during the year, you may feel rested, energized, and invigorated.

Wouldn't it be great if you could store summer in jars, stack them in your kitchen cupboards, and then open them up at those times in the winter when you awaken on a dark, cold morning feeling as if you could hibernate for six weeks, when getting dressed to go out of your house is a project rather than a process, and when evenings and weekends are spent sitting in front of the television?

As relaxing as summer days and nights can be, growing dependent upon a season to help you relax prevents you from learning how to shed your tensions yourself. Today, enjoy the summer's tranquillity, but think of ways to cultivate your own sense of inner peace throughout the year.

I take lessons from the summer in how to relax.

"We have an unknown distance to run; an unknown river yet to explore. What falls there are, we know not; what rocks beset the channel, we know not; what walls rise over the river, we know not. Ah well! We may conjecture many things."

—NATURALIST AND EXPLORER JOHN WESLEY POWELL

RUNNING DOWN THE COLORADO RIVER

At the time he led an expedition of four small boats of ten men down into the Green and Colorado rivers on a thousand-mile journey into unknown canyon country, John Wesley Powell (1834–1902) was already a self-taught scientist, an innovative college teacher who led Illinois college students into the Rockies on the first student geological field trips, and a Civil War veteran who had lost his right arm at Shiloh. Even though Powell discovered the Escalante River and the Henry Mountains—the last unknown river and mountain range in the continental United States—as well as beautiful canyons during his famous river run, rather than view his trip as an adventure, he used it to provide practical government surveys and gather scientific information so Americans could understand the wilderness, adapt to its conditions, and use its resources sensibly. He wrote and published his *Exploration of the Colorado River* in the hope that it would gather support for further scientific exploration in the west, but the book's immediate effect was to make Powell a hero for introducing such magnificent canyon country to Americans. Since that time, many have made the pilgrimage to the Colorado River, yet no one has truly experienced the river the way Powell did as its first true explorer: "Ever before us has been an unknown danger, heavier than immediate peril. Every waking hour passed in the Grand Canyon has been one of toil."

I admire those who journey into an unknown to make it known to others.

"Hope and the future for me are not in lawns and cultivated fields, not in towns and cities, but in the impervious and quaking swamps."
—AMERICAN WRITER AND NATURALIST HENRY DAVID THOREAU

TRAVELING NEW ROADS

Think for a moment about a nearby city. Picture the many roads that lead to that city. One may be a winding country road. Another may be an efficient, eight-lane expressway. And still another may be rutted and filled with potholes.

No matter which road is taken, it leads to the same destination. But what will be different is the experience of the journey, depending on which road you take. One may result in a pleasant ride, filled with new sights, new sounds, new smells; the second in a monotonous, stop-and-go exercise in tedium; the third in frazzled nerves and a high level of frustration.

Now imagine that this city is your life. Every day you wake and need to choose a road that will take you into the city—into yourself. But which one will you choose? Even though the highway may seem to be the best, most direct choice, unexpected delays can make your journey on this seemingly simple route a nightmare. While the bumpy, pothole-ridden road may seem to be the least enjoyable road, it may end up providing you the greatest challenge and, ultimately, the greatest satisfaction. And the winding, tree-lined road may offer so many interesting diversions that you put off reaching your destination at a designated time so you can enjoy the journey more.

From one day to the next, you never know what you may discover about yourself or how you will discover it. There's always a new road to travel, if you're willing to try it out.

I travel on a new road of discovery each day.

"The American Indian is of the soil, whether it be the region of forests, plains, pueblos, or mesas. He fits into the landscape, for the hand that fashioned the continent also fashioned the man for his surroundings. He once grew as naturally as the wild sunflowers; he belongs just as the buffalo belonged. . . ."

—OGLALA SIOUX CHIEF LUTHER STANDING BEAR

LIVING WITHIN YOUR ENVIRONMENT

Can you imagine living in the desert without air-conditioning, in Alaska without cold-weather clothing, on an island without a motorboat, or in the plains without irrigation to keep your crops watered? Years ago, American Indians lived in all climates comfortably, staying both cool and warm, canoeing long distances on water, and with full bellies even in times of drought. Too, years ago, America's explorers set out on foot, horseback, or canoe on an adventure of discovery, carrying food and other provisions that often ran out long before the expedition came to an end, were lost or destroyed, or were used to barter for another sorely needed supply.

Today, "natives" who reside in a variety of climates believe they are adept at adapting to their environments, but their survival is rarely in jeopardy because of technology and the accessibility of all necessities. Today, "explorers" who set out to conquer wild rivers, teeming jungles, parched deserts, and majestic mountain peaks do so with such a large quantity of gear that locals are hired just to carry provisions; so, too, do locals have, as their job, to be the first to set out and "break trail" so others can merely follow in their footsteps.

Today, imagine you had to live without one of the "creature comforts" you've grown accustomed to; consider what today's lunch would be if it had to consist of what you harvest or trap. Could you be a true "native" or "explorer"?

I keep in mind how far I often am from being a true survivor on this planet.

"The people are afflicted with a eveil [sic], not much unlike, and almost as severe as, some of the plagues in Egypt. I mean the inconceivable swarms of muscatoes and sandflies which infest every place, and equally interrupt the tranquility of the night and the happiness of the day. Their attacks are intolerable upon man as well as beast. The poor cows and horses in order to escape from these tormentors stand whole days in ponds of water with only their heads exposed."

—AN UNKNOWN OBSERVER AT CAPE HENLOPEN, DELAWARE,
IN 1788

LEARNING TOLERANCE

In the 1930s, a man could make a dollar a day digging ditches for the Delaware Mosquito Control Commission, which, after some study, determined that the best way to get rid of some of the fifty-three species of mosquitoes was by disrupting the insects' life cycle by draining off the small, shallow ponds that served as breeding pools. Hand-dug ditches, up to twenty inches wide and twenty inches deep, one hundred and fifty feet apart, soon crisscrossed Delaware's marshes, which were then drained whether or not they were suitable breeding grounds for mosquitoes.

"Every time they dug one of those ditches," says naturalist writer Jennifer Ackerman, "it was like pulling the plug from a bathtub. The full effects are only now being uncovered. The rookeries of breeding waterfowl and other birds have shrunk or disappeared for want of pools in which to feed." Marsh grasses essential to the food chain were crowded out by tall reeds. Invertebrate populations were decimated. Some drainage ditches opened areas of marsh to more frequent flooding. And, ironically, "the small pools that formed behind the mounds of spoil created new breeding grounds for *A. sollicitans* "—the salt-marsh mosquito.

In some cases, leaving nature alone is the best way to deal with nature.

Today I accept mosquitoes as a natural part of summer.

"If one advances confidently in the direction of his dreams, and endeavors to live the life which he has imagined, he will meet with a success unexpected in common hours. . . . If you have built castles in the air, your work need not be lost; that is where they should be. Now put the foundation under them."

—NATURALIST AND WRITER HENRY DAVID THOREAU

THE POSSIBILITIES OF A DREAM

When ethnobotanist and award-winning nature writer Gary Nabhan attended the burial of his friend and mentor Howard Scott Gentry, he realized that the man who had been forty-nine years his senior had taught him a valuable lesson in pursuing a dream. Gentry's love had been the desert agave. In 1951 and 1952, he had planted dozens of seedlings, but it took nearly a quarter century for them to flower for the first time. To examine one specimen required several hours of cutting, skinning, sectioning, and then pickling. Hundreds of such specimens were detailed in Gentry's 670-page masterwork, *Agaves of Continental North America*, published in 1982, nearly fifty years after Gentry had begun his first agave collections.

Even after years of study and great achievement, Gentry realized that there was little he really did know about agaves. But his patience in waiting for the reward of a desert bloom showed him the joy of believing in his dream of learning everything about the plants. As American writer and naturalist Diane Ackerman has observed, "It is always like this for naturalists, and for poets—the long hours of travel and preparation, and then the longer hours of waiting. All for that one electric, pulse-revving vision when the universe suddenly declares itself."

When Gentry was too old to venture into the field with any frequency, Nabhan did so himself, taking the man's memory—and his dreams—with him.

I believe that dreams can come true.

"I would rather be ashes than dust! I would rather my sparks should burn out in a blaze than it should be stifled by dry-rot. I would rather be a superb meteor, every atom of me in magnificent glow, than asleep and permanent as a planet. The proper function of man is to live, not to exist. I shall not waste my days trying to prolong them. I shall use my time."

—WRITER JACK LONDON

MAKING EVERY ACT COUNT

What do you wish to be doing when it becomes too difficult for you to move around without the assistance of a cane, crutch, or wheelchair? What do you wish to be doing when you're told that an illness or disease is going to beat you down? What do you wish to be doing when death is breathing down your neck? If your answer is, "I want to be doing whatever I can, no matter how grand or how minor the action," then start today to ensure this will happen. Do everything—even the little things—as well as you can.

A story is told about an old man who was thin and frail, ravaged by an unmanageable disease. The doctor told those who had gathered around the man's bedside, "It's pretty hopeless. It doesn't look like he'll last through the night." So they left the man alone in order to prepare dinner, make telephone calls, and take a break before resuming their death vigil. But when they entered the room, they found the man sitting in his favorite chair next to his bed, which he had made so well there wasn't even a wrinkle on the bedspread. The man sat hunched over in the chair, his breathing labored and his weak arms and legs shaking. But then he coughed and raised his head to look at his astonished friends and family members.

"I wanted to leave this world feeling like I had accomplished something right up until the very end," the man gasped. "And I did. Now I can go."

Today, I put my heart and soul into even the smallest acts.

"Every moment Nature starts on the longest journey, and every moment she reaches her goal."

—GERMAN POET JOHANN WOLFGANG VON GOETHE

RISKING IT ALL

Imagine that you've been given the chance to return to any previous time in your life and change a decision you made at that time. The only drawback is this: You must lose everything that has happened to you since that time. In effect, what you're faced with is an opportunity to risk it all—to risk losing everything you've earned and all the people you've been blessed to know in the hopes that you'll end up in a much happier, more successful life for yourself.

What would you do? If you decide to return to a pivotal point in your life and explore the road you opted not to take, then you might think that you're an incredible risk-taker—someone who is unafraid to lose it all in the hopes of winning it all. But if you don't, does that make you any less of a risk-taker?

Taking risks is not always about loss, although often, when taking a risk, loss does occur; the crew of the *Challenger* and climbers who die during a climb confirm this. But the greatest risks are not those that have the greatest potential for loss; rather, sometimes the greatest risks are those in which you remain true to your beliefs and ideas, protect your security, trust in yourself and your capabilities, and live without regret over the past but hope for a better future.

Oftentimes the greatest risk is considering all the chances you could take and then having enough confidence in yourself to be able to decide whether something new and different is really what you want. The greatest risks are those that are made from freedom—freedom to choose, and then to live without regret over the choice that's made.

I am free to live my life in the way I choose for myself.

"In natural objects we feel ourselves, or think of ourselves, only by like-nesses; among men, too often by differences."
—ENGLISH POET SAMUEL TAYLOR COLERIDGE

A CELLULAR EXISTENCE

The most amazing thing about continual athletic conditioning—through daily workouts or training for speed or endurance—is that you can do this only because of the physical adaptations that take place at the cellular level. You gradually become stronger because your muscles become more enduring, your lungs more powerful, and your heart more capable of keeping up with the demands you place upon it. These things happen because of the mitochondria—the "energy factories" in the cells where nutrients are broken down and turned into raw power. With each breath you take in, whether that breath be one made as you run up a hill, as you prepare to execute a flip turn in a pool, as you negotiate white water in your kayak, or as you stretch and yawn upon rising in the morning of a shining new day, the mitochondria provide the oxidative energy you need. Without the mitochondria, you would die. In effect, you exist because of the mitochondria; you occupy a place in which thousands of these entities miraculously transform you every day into a single entity.

When medical essayist Lewis Thomas wrote his first book, *The Lives of a Cell,* he pointed out how arrogant it was for human beings to detach themselves from the natural world, for human beings share an existence with every other living thing because of the cellular nature of life. The cells "work in my interest, [with] each breath they draw for me," said Thomas, and concluded, "perhaps it is they who walk through the local park in the morning, sensing my senses, listening to my music, thinking my thoughts."

I take care of my cells, and they take care of me.

"Most of us have lost that sense of unity of biosphere and humanity which would bind and reassure us all with an affirmation of beauty. Most of us do not today believe that whatever ups and downs of detail within our limited experience, the larger whole is primarily beautiful."

—WRITER GREGORY BATESON

PRAISING THE EARTH

Rarely a day goes by without an article being published or a news report broadcast that focuses on the disappearing rain forests, global warming, air pollution and ozone depletion, declining biodiversity, failing fisheries, animal poaching and slaughter, poverty and famine due to overpopulation, and a multitude of other environmental problems. In the past, such things served as rallying cries that united people in efforts to right the wrong; today, such things serve to confirm what is already known—that the earth is a planet faced with enormous environmental problems.

Yet a great deal has been done in the past few decades to restore much of the planet's lost luster. Many dangerous pesticides have been banned, including DDT. New laws have resulted in noticeable and measurable improvements; the Clean Water Act, for example, has effectively shut off raw sewage that once flushed into bodies of water that are now stocked with fish, are swimmable, and, in some cases, even drinkable. Corporations have become more earth-conscious and are responsible for providing financial support for a wide variety of environmental causes. Many species have been pulled back from near extinction and reintroduced into their habitats. Today, take time to praise the earth—to see the beauty that has already been restored and the new growth that is springing back to life.

Today I focus on what's right with the planet.

"When hungry, eat your rice; when tired, close your eyes. Fools may laugh at me, but wise men will know what I mean."

—ZEN PHILOSOPHER LIN-CHI

CALLING A TIME-OUT

In the heat of an intense sports competition, one of the best strategies a coach can use is to call a time-out. When the players have a chance to step away from the action and take a breather, they're given the opportunity to replenish their depleted energy, review their strategy, and renew their efforts to win.

After the "heat" of time spent focusing solely on one facet of your life—your career, your family responsibilities, your relationship, your health, and so on—you may need to take a time-out. That doesn't mean that you have to stop what you're doing now forever. It just means that if you give yourself a chance to take a breather, you might be better able to assess how well you're balancing all the interests and activities in your life. Too, you'll have a chance to decide whether you need to readjust or redirect your energy so you won't discover—too late—that you can't do all those things you've always wanted to.

It has been said that the most successful people in life are those who have a three-dimensional outlook—a focus that's divided between work achievement, leisure-time pursuits, and the creation of a fulfilling personal life. Such people often demonstrate specific behaviors in maintaining this outlook. They have a strong sense of inner calm, which helps them to stay focused. They have clear goals and a sense of purpose, which guide their lives. And they have a sense of adventurousness, which gives them the courage to take risks and to think positively. Today, call a time-out. Take stock of your life. Think of how to achieve more balance so you can attain and maintain everything you want from life.

I strive to add more balance in my life.

"By late August, the leaves are dull, except here and there where the first fires of autumn color flash in the hills or along the highway. When I was your age, the fires were literal, and the sight of colored leaves always stirred the sense of smell, too, piles of leaves burning in front, it seemed, of every house, not just in my neighborhood but in America. I can conjure the physical sensation of that aroma now. . . ."

—AMERICAN NOVELIST JAMES CARROLL

AUTUMN'S APPROACH

In a poignant essay written for his child, writer James Carroll evokes the impact of seasonal changes as he thinks back on his own youth, when he would watch his father rake the fallen autumn leaves in their yard into a pile and then stand, leaning on his rake, watching the smoke drift up from the fire. Even though burning leaves today is illegal and his father is gone, Carroll remembers the end of summer as a time of sad family rituals—hammocks being folded away, unfinished Kool-Aid mix cartons shoved to the back of a shelf, a neighborhood deprived in the evening of the sounds of the Good Humor man, the end of after-supper games of hide-and-seek and capture-the-flag.

"The end of summer is to the year what sunset is to the day," writes Carroll. "An inch below the golden surface are feelings of loss. . . . The turning season reminds us that we live in time, on the Earth. . . ." The loss in autumn is of youth, of carefree joy, of vacations, of new friendships, of goals not quite achieved by summer's end, of more time spent outdoors, of greater activity.

But just as the chilly, late-August days and nights signal an end, so, too, can they imply a beginning. The lawn mower and lawn furniture now being packed away will be unpacked soon, the hammock rehung, pitchers of Kool-Aid mixed again. The summer, like every other season, will soon return.

I bid farewell to the summer and welcome autumn's return.

"Knowledge and timber shouldn't be much used till they are seasoned."
—JURIST OLIVER WENDELL HOLMES, JR.

DEVELOPING WISDOM

Here is one path to wisdom you can follow:

First, you believe everything that you're told, without being given any reasons, such as each animal that dies goes to heaven and becomes a star in the sky.

Next, you believe in most things, but express doubt about some things that you once accepted without question, such as your dog being a star in the sky, because a science teacher told you stars are billions of years old, and Max was only four.

Then you believe in nothing whatsoever. Was Max really a dog? Did he really die from being hit by a car, or was there a conspiracy? What about the grassy knoll he used to frequent?

After that you start to believe in most things, but express some doubt about a few other things. Max was great company. What about getting another dog?

Then you believe in everything again—except now you realize that you possess the reasons why you believe them. Max was a good dog, a good buddy. Therefore, Max is probably the most brilliant star in the sky.

Jazz musician Chick Corea offers this version of a similar path he followed to wisdom: "I searched through rebellion, drugs, diet, mysticism, religions, intellectualism, and much more, only to begin to find . . . that truth is basically simple—and feels good, clean, and right."

A tree that grows never questions its existence or the existence of all the trees around it; it simply grows and, in so doing, matures. So, too, should you. Recognize that knowledge isn't wisdom; wisdom is what you know and believe in.

I strive to become like seasoned wood.

"He is lucky who, in the full tide of life, has experienced a measure of the active environment that he most desires. In these days of upheaval and violent change, when the basic values of today are the vain and shattered dreams of tomorrow, there is much to be said for a philosophy which aims at living a full life while the opportunity offers."

—BRITISH MOUNTAINEER ERIC EARLE SHIPTON

GETTING IN MOTION

Life is meant to be lived in motion, for all living things are in motion. Deep below the ocean's surface, for example, aquatic plant life undulates with the currents. Corals feed by waving their stinging tentacles to snare baby fish and other tiny sea animals. The constant motion also extends outward from the reef, for several kinds of fish live in or near the reef. Small fish flit quickly back and forth, feeding on microscopic animal and plant life. Larger fish propel themselves around, oftentimes feeding on the smaller fish. Along the coastline, in rock pools and shallows, lobsters and crabs crawl about while waves splash against the shore. Overhead, gulls, terns, gannets, and other seabirds scan the shallow waters for something to eat while shorebirds scamper back and forth along the sandy stretches of beach.

All this represents only a small segment of nature's bountiful, bounding activities. Yet the influence upon humanity can be profound. As American dancer Isadora Duncan once said, "I was born by the sea and I have noticed that all the great events in my life have taken place by the sea. My first idea of movement, of the dance, certainly came from the rhythms of the waves."

Life, like nature, ought never to be still. Is there a natural motion that can so influence you, too?

I get in motion by getting out into the natural motion of life.

"We sang songs that carried in their melodies all the sounds of nature—the running of waters, the sighing of winds, and the calls of animals. Teach your children. . . ."

—AMERICAN INDIAN SAYING

CHILDREN'S NATURE

How can your child distinguish between the raucous call of a blue jay and the incessant *chip-chipping* of a cardinal while wearing headphones? Is the only sound of running water your child knows made by the water that gushes out of a faucet into a bathtub or from your backyard hose while you wash the car together? Can your child listen to the moans and stirs of the wind outside a bedroom window late at night and feel reassured rather than frightened?

Your child can never know nature until nature can truly be experienced. A fishing or camping trip or hike through the woods or up a mountain is a wonderful way to bring your child closer to nature, but if you allow this experience to include radios, headphones, comic books, battery-operated televisions, cellular car phones, or fast-food meals, then you're depriving your child of the magic that is part of the natural world.

American writer and lecturer Helen Keller once explained how she experienced the natural world without sight or the ability to hear. "Sometimes . . . I go rowing without the rudder," she wrote. "It is fun to try to steer by the scent of the watergrasses and lilies, and of bushes that grow on the shore." Let your child see nature, hear it, touch it, smell it, and taste it, and you allow your child to get in touch with the spirituality of nature. For as Gertrude Simmons Bonnin, a Dakota Sioux, remarked, "The voice of the Great Spirit is heard in the twittering of birds, the rippling of mighty waters, and the sweet breathing of flowers."

I allow my child to be touched by the experience of nature.

"The honey-bee's great ambition is to be rich, to lay up great stores, to possess the sweet of every flower that blooms. She is more than provident. Enough will not satisfy her; she must have all she can get by hook or by crook."

—AMERICAN WRITER AND NATURALIST JOHN BURROUGHS

LIVING WITHIN YOUR MEANS

When you read stories of billionaires who seem to own half the world but are filing for bankruptcy, do you shake your head in bewilderment, wondering how one person can accumulate so much wealth and so many possessions and yet not be able to pay a single bill? Do you then think, "If I had that kind of money, I'd never have any financial problems. I'd manage the money wisely."

But are you living in debt yourself, mismanaging your own money, as you accumulate more and more possessions, enjoy vacations that are well beyond your budget, and purchase extravagant gifts? Are you unable to set reasonable financial limits on what you want so you can live comfortably and stress-free on what you need? Does your savings account reflect a small, but steady increase each month, or does it hover at a "dollars-and-cents" level or even sharply decrease from time to time from emergency as well as nonemergency withdrawals?

Zen spiritualist Dogen tells this parable about living within your means. "When a fish swims, it swims on and on, and there is no end to the water. When a bird flies, it flies on and on, and there is no end to the sky. There was never a fish that swam out of the water, or a bird that flew out of the sky. When they need a little water or sky, they use just a little; when they need a lot, they use a lot. Thus they use all of it at every moment, and in every place they have perfect freedom."

I save and spend wisely in order to use what I need at the moment.

> *"Life is better than death, I believe, if only because it is less boring, and because it has fresh peaches in it."*
>
> —AMERICAN WRITER ALICE WALKER

VICTORY!

Author Joseph Conrad wrote a lengthy and intense novel, struggling repeatedly with the language. Because his native tongue was Polish, the task of working out precise English words and phrases in his story was very difficult. When he finally completed the book, he didn't write "The End." Instead, he scrawled a single word across the last page. It wasn't "finished" or "complete." Conrad wrote the word, "victory." And that eventually became the title of his novel, *Victory*.

A Chinese proverb states, "The man who moves a mountain begins by carrying away small stones." Imagine that the mountain is life; each moment you live involves carrying away small stones so you can feel a certain level of success, or victory, each day. Some of your victories will be major achievements—you earn a sought-after promotion, adopt a baby, or purchase your first home—while some may seem small and insignificant—you order new office furniture, sing your first lullaby to your baby, or install a closet door in your new home. But no matter what their size or how much closer such things bring you to moving your own mountain, each small stone is a victory. Without victory, there's no movement, there's no growth, and there's no progress.

Each victory in your life is like a birth. The aim of life is to be fully born, so you need to live in every minute of your life seeking victory. Stop looking for victory, and the novel of your life will never be complete, the mountain of your life will stand steadfast. Stop looking for victory, and you'll die before you've even been born.

I look for victory in everything I do.

"Man changes the conditions to suit the things. Nature changes the things to suit the conditions. She adapts the plant or animal to its environment."
—AMERICAN WRITER AND NATURALIST JOHN BURROUGHS

ADAPTABILITY

You can learn from an ordinary bamboo leaf that strength of the spirit is greater than physical strength—that softness can triumph over hardness and feebleness over power. In a snowstorm, the leaf will bend lower and lower under the weight of falling snow until it seems as if it will snap. But suddenly the snow will slip to the ground without the leaf having stirred, and the leaf returns to its original position, with no damage done. What this proves is that being flexible is always superior to being immovable; to control things, it's sometimes best to bend along with them.

This is what nature does every day. A rotting tree topples over in a windstorm, crashing to the forest floor. The homes of woodpeckers, chipmunks, and an owl may be destroyed, but the creatures simply relocate to another tree and continue on with their lives. The branches, leaves, and other fallen debris from the tree now prevent a small stream from flowing on its usual path, but the stream simply creates a twisting, turning detour around the blockage and then continues on.

Nature adapts itself to the environment and changes things to suit the conditions. But then man comes along, points to the forest, and says, "This is where I want to build. So it's gotta be leveled," thereby changing the conditions to suit the things.

I seek to change little in my environment and seek, instead, to adapt to it.

"The clouds are the children of the heavens, and when they play among the rocks they lift them to the region above."

—AMERICAN EXPLORER JOHN WESLEY POWELL

PLAYING THROUGH LIFE

Watch children at play, and what you'll see are games without rules, contests without scores, rapidly changing partnerships and teams, group participation in fantasizing and wild imaginings, laughter, smiles, and a sense of timelessness. Watch adults at play, however, and what you'll see are games with hard-and-fast rules, definitive scores and strong desires to win, obsessive loyalty in partnerships and teams, individuality in thinking, furrowed brows, frowns, and time constraints.

Shouldn't life be less stressful and more carefree? Shouldn't life be less like a factory assembly line and more like a playground filled with swings, jungle gyms, slides, and sandboxes? Shouldn't life be less like a corporate meeting and more like an excellent party—one you never want to leave, one that makes you want to linger?

Life ought to be a joyous celebration, filled with laughter and interesting conversation. Life ought to be a gathering together of people you find fascinating and whose company you enjoy. Life ought to be a festival of good things to eat and drink, with enticing pleasures of the palate to savor. Life ought to be fun and lighthearted, to bring out childish joy and play. Life ought to be an event that leaves you with marvelous memories.

The festival of life ought to teach you to look around you rather than straight ahead, to laugh at life's ironies, to kindle the fires of friendship, to encourage glad participation, and to be as carefree as a cloud in the sky.

Each day, I rush joyfully onto the playground of life.

"The country is both the philosopher's garden and his library, in which he reads and contemplates the power, wisdom, and goodness of God."
—ENGLISH RELIGIOUS REFORMER AND COLONIALIST
WILLIAM PENN

BROTHER ADAM, BENEDICTINE APIARIST

When Brother Adam, Benedictine monk and bee breeder, died in 1996 at the age of ninety-eight, he left behind a legacy that transformed beekeeping. His search for native strains of bees took him to the remotest deserts and highest mountains; a fellow apiarist once carried the then–ninety-year-old Brother Adam on a bamboo chair strapped to his back up Africa's highest mountain, the 19,340-foot Mt. Kilimanjaro, on a search for the area's Monticola bee; this journey was filmed for television. Brother Adam's crossbreeding work created the Buckfast Superbee, regarded by many as the healthiest and most prolific honey producer ever bred. In the 1990s, the U.S. Department of Agriculture imported queen bees that Brother Adam had bred to be resistant to acarine disease, which badly damaged honey production in the United States.

Traveling by car, on foot, or by donkey, his journeys before World War II in search of bees took him as far as the Sahara Desert. From 1950 to 1981, he searched for bees in the Mediterranean, the Middle East, and Africa. His body of work also includes books, now regarded as classics on the subject of beekeeping and breeding.

Brother Adam's bee research ended in 1992 when the monastery's new abbot insisted that the main function of the abbey's apiaries—which Brother Adam had supervised since 1919, when he was twenty-one—was honey production, not research. To the disappointment of bee breeders around the world, Brother Adam bowed to the will of his superior. Yet Brother Adam's legacy is remembered every day, in every honeycomb that's created and filled with the sweet nectar.

I recognize God's work in nature's growth.

"Like a fallen woman who sits alone in a dark room trying not to think of her past, the earth languished with reminiscence of spring and summer and waited in apathy for ineluctable winter."
—RUSSIAN PLAYWRIGHT AND STORY WRITER ANTON CHEKHOV

THE EEYORE ATTITUDE

Do you have the Eeyore Attitude? The Eeyore Attitude enables you to find something bad, something tragic, something hurtful, something impossible, something overwhelming, something unfair, and something wrong with every person and every thing. The Eeyore Attitude is like a garden that's sown with disgust, cultivated with complaint, enriched by pessimism, and harvested in hopelessness. The Eeyore Attitude gets in the way of things like wisdom and happiness and pretty much prevents any sort of real accomplishment in life. The Eeyore Attitude is, by its very nature, humorless and not much fun to experience.

When the day starts for the old gray donkey Eeyore and he's greeted by a cheery good morning from his friends Pooh and Piglet, his gloomy response is always, "Good morning—if it *is* a good morning. Which I doubt." Yet Pooh and Piglet never see the world this way. When Pooh starts his day, the first thing he wonders is what's for breakfast. When Piglet starts his day, he wonders what exciting thing is going to happen. Both Pooh and Piglet have noticeably different attitudes from Eeyore—an attitude of happy serenity. This attitude enables them to enjoy the simple things in life and spontaneously find joy and humor in everyone and everything.

Today, think about the attitude you wish to cultivate from now on. You can be a grumpy Eeyore or you can be a peaceful Pooh or Piglet. Which do you choose?

I consider life—and everything and everyone in it—to be very good.

"Deer, otter, foxes are messengers from another condition of life, another mentality, and bring us tidings of places where we don't go."
—AMERICAN WRITER EDWARD HOAGLAND

ANIMAL MENTALITY

Isna la-wica, or Lone Man, a nineteenth-century Teton Sioux, was proud of his name, which meant that he needed no one and nothing. When he was a young man, he went to a medicine man for advice concerning his future.

"I have not much to tell you," the medicine man began, "except to help you understand this earth on which you live. You think that, as Isna la-wica, you need only yourself—your strong muscles, your skills, your fine mind. But if a man is to succeed on the hunt or the warpath, he must not be governed by his inclination, but by an understanding of the ways of animals and of his natural surroundings, gained through close observation. The earth is large, Isna la-wica, and on it live many animals. The earth is under the protection of something which, at times, becomes visible to the eye."

A century later, Welsh hiker and writer Colin Fletcher reiterated the medicine man's words when he wrote, "All of us, I think, were conscious of that warm sense of privilege you get when you are lucky enough to watch, close up, as truly wild animals go about their quiet business."

There's much you can learn from the wild animals that reside near your home and that you may be privileged enough to see from time to time—a small herd of deer grazing at sunrise, a raccoon finishing his nightly rituals, a flock of Canadian geese resting before they wing their way south. You learn from them that in order to live and survive outdoors, you need the protection of natural surroundings as well as other living things for survival.

I feel lucky to be able to observe a truly wild animal.

"I had a vague feeling of perpetual warm sunny weather, when I used to be taken driving and notice the speckled shadows moving across the carriage, before it occurred to me that they were caused by the leaves overhead. (As soon as I discovered this, the scientific interest killed the impression, and I began speculating as to why the patches of light were always circular and so on.)"

—ENGLISH MATHEMATICIAN AND PHILOSOPHER
BERTRAND RUSSELL

EVERYDAY LEARNING

Do you remember when you would return home in the afternoon after school and one of the first questions your mother or father would ask you was, "What did you learn in school today?" Because you were young and there was so much you didn't know, every day offered something new to you— a new word to spell, a new math problem to solve, a new bit of history to learn, a new grammar rule, a new piece of scientific information, a new physical challenge, a new drawing to create.

Now that you're much older, do you feel that each day you have the opportunity to learn something new? Sometimes you may discover something new by reading the paper every morning. Sometimes tuning in to a cable news show or a public broadcasting station can reveal something you didn't know. Sometimes listening to the chatter of morning commuters can bring to light a topic you've never really explored.

If you want to learn more about the world you live in, you don't have to go back to school. There are lots of ways you can learn something new. Take a book out of the library or purchase a magazine on a subject you know little about. Go on a nature hike. Visit a museum. Take the time and make the effort to expand your knowledge base each day, and you'll learn something new every day.

What will I learn in the school of life today?

"What nature delivers to us is never stale. Because what nature creates has eternity in it."

—POLISH-BORN AMERICAN WRITER ISAAC BASHEVIS SINGER

A NEW AUTUMN

How long have you lived where you now reside or in a climate similar to your present locale? Since this is also the number of years that you have experienced summer's end and fall's return, chances are you're going to be bored with yet another passage into autumn. Or will you?

American writer May Sarton once observed in her journals, "The thud of the first apple falling never fails to startle the wits out of me; there has been no sound like it for a year." Over the years, does the fall foliage still present itself as a feast for your eyes? Is the chill of the morning still surprising? Does the sound of geese flying overhead in the familiar V still tug at your heart in indescribable ways? Are the tasks of fertilizing the lawn and harvesting the last vegetables before turning the garden still pleasurable? Does homemade applesauce or a home-baked apple pie still make your mouth water?

While some things that you experience year after year become old real fast, are often dreaded, and sometimes even cause stress, each segue into the fall season is rarely predictable or exactly the same. Last year's heavy winter snowfall and long spring rains may result in startlingly brilliant foliage this fall. An ideal balance of summer sunshine and moisture may result in particularly tasty apples. Proper fertilization and composting last fall may have created a bountiful harvest and lush lawn this summer. Every fall has its own personality and, because of this, continually presents itself each year in a brand-new way.

I greet this fall as I would an old friend who is returning home again.

"Watching the animals come and go, and feeling the land swell up to meet them and then feeling it grow still at their departure, I came to think of the migrations as breath, as the land breathing. In spring a great inhalation of light and animals. The long-bated breath of summer. And an exhalation that propelled them all south in the fall."

—AMERICAN WRITER AND NATURALIST BARRY LOPEZ

ANCESTRAL MIGRATIONS

Centuries ago, many of this country's earliest ancestors lived like the animals, migrating to a warmer, more forgiving climate in the fall in order to survive the winter, and then returning again for a spring and summer residence. Too, centuries ago, many immigrants came to America, fleeing the harsh and unforgiving political, economic, and social climates of their native countries for a more tolerant climate.

Writer Barry Lopez, who won the National Book Award for his best-selling *Arctic Dreams,* likens his own ancestry to the migrations of animals, even though his family has been in the Americas for nearly five centuries. His mother's English and German ancestors began farming on the Pennsylvania side of the Delaware River valley in the 1650s. A descendant of that group later moved to Virginia; his children moved into the Carolinas and eastern Alabama, where Lopez's mother was born on a plantation in 1914. Lopez's father's family, whose homeland was in northern Spain, were tobacco farmers in Cuba before they came to St. Louis and New York as tobacco merchants.

Lopez has made his own home in Oregon for twenty-four years. Although he understands the desire of his ancestors—and the ancestors of others—to migrate in order to find the right conditions, he believes in always having a place to call home.

I crave the stability of being able to put down roots in one place.

"I don't know what your destiny will be, but one thing I know: the only ones among you who will be really happy are those who will have sought and found how to serve."

—FRENCH MISSIONARY AND THEOLOGIAN ALBERT SCHWEITZER

LEARNING SELFLESSNESS

The renowned humanitarian Albert Schweitzer was, when a young man, as restless and dissatisfied with his life as many of today's youth. His first career was that of a musician; he was an organist and well-known interpreter of Bach. Then he switched careers and became a theologian, philosopher, and writer. But at the age of thirty, he returned to school and chose another career path—medicine.

Yet after years of school and medical training, Schweitzer made still another career move. He set off to help those who were less fortunate by becoming a jungle doctor. At the age of thirty-eight, he established a hospital on the Ogowe River in Gabon, French West Africa. But then he was interned as an enemy alien during World War I. At his release, he discovered his hospital in ruins—its buildings had collapsed from neglect—and he was fast approaching the age of fifty. Should he or shouldn't he return to a more comfortable life, back in "civilization"?

Schweitzer returned to the jungle and rebuilt the hospital, which he ran until his death at the age of ninety. In each of his several careers, he always achieved a level of renown that could have earned him enough money for a comfortable life surrounded by luxuries and recognition. Instead, he chose to exploit his talents in an African jungle and to use his gifted mind and giving soul to tend to the sick so each of his patients could feel the luxury of his care and the recognition of their importance to him as a human being.

I use my skills to serve others.

"Summer's lease hath all too short a date."
—ENGLISH PLAYWRIGHT AND POET WILLIAM SHAKESPEARE

THE END OF SUMMER

Even if you weren't aware of today's calendar date, you would probably still suspect that summer was nearly finished packing its bags and would soon be leaving. For autumn seems to have already arrived. The chill in the morning air; a fresh, crisp scent that drifts by you on stirring autumn winds; grass that drips with dew and rocks that glisten from a thick coating of moisture; fallen leaves that lie scattered about on the ground like toys strewn around a child's room; a low mist that hangs forlornly over the valley; wilting flowers and the last-of-the-season garden vegetables that look as if they belong on a supermarket bargain shelf; and an unusual surge of activity among living things are all signals that summer is rapidly coming to a close.

It may seem, as naturalist Henry David Thoreau once observed, "We had gone to bed in summer, and we awoke in autumn; for summer passes into autumn in some unimaginable point of time, like the turning of a leaf." You may lament the forthcoming passage from summer into autumn not so much for the loss of hours of evening light; the hot weather that beckoned you to enjoy the woods, beaches, and lakes; or the delicious pleasure of savoring ice-cream cones and foods cooked on the grill, but because you may have accomplished only a few of the many things you had wanted to do.

Yet while summer may be waning, there's another season about to be born—a season that's filled with its own particular pleasures. You can enjoy autumn as much as you did summer, and set goals for this season as well.

I look forward to enjoying autumn's pleasures.

"Success—to laugh often and much; to win the respect of intelligent people and the affection of children; to earn the appreciation of honest critics and endure the betrayal of false friends; to appreciate beauty; to find the best in others; to leave the world a bit better, whether by a healthy child, a garden patch or a redeemed social condition; to know even one life has breathed easier because you lived. This is to have succeeded."

—AMERICAN CLERGYMAN HARRY EMERSON FOSDICK

THE KEYS TO YOUR SUCCESS

Success means different things to different people. To some, it's a corner office and gold-embossed business cards. To others, it's a home in an exclusive neighborhood, with a fancy car parked in the driveway. And there are those who believe that success is helping others rather than helping themselves.

Africa-based English writer and aviator Beryl Markham once said, "I have had responsibilities and work, dangers and pleasures, good friends, and a world without walls to live in. . . . I sit there in the firelight and see them all." Imagine that you, too, are sitting before the warm glow of a crackling fire. As you peer into the flames, recall moments of your life that have brought you the feeling of success. What do you see? A personal victory? Great friends? A wonderful relationship with your parents? A risk you took? A passionate romance? A trip to a country you'd always dreamed of visiting?

Take a moment to reflect upon the things in your life that have instilled you with the feeling that you have been or are successful. Such things can be measurable—such as owning the home you've always wanted—or found within you—such as enjoying a beautiful sunrise. Such things are the keys to your success.

I recognize the successes in my life.

"SIT ON ME! I'M MADE FROM 240 MILK JUGS!"
—CONVERSION PRODUCTS INC. ADVERTISING SLOGAN

USEFUL RECYCLING

Do you ever wonder where all your recycling is going? One company—Conversion Products Inc., based in Maine—uses ground-up milk jugs that have been recycled into a kind of plastic lumber for the creation of durable "faux-wood" products. The products made from this plastic lumber look like wood but won't rot, splinter, or crack and are impervious to water, salt, oil, chemicals, and insects. Too, they don't have to be painted every year or stored at the end of the summer or during bad weather.

The company initially went into business selling recycled plastic benches, picnic tables, and trash receptacles to cities and towns for use in parks, golf courses, and zoos. But because it sometimes took municipalities months and even years to place a single order, the company ventured into mail-order home-and-garden products—and the business really took off. Flower boxes, planters, garden benches, footstools, and by far the most popular item—the plastic-wood Adirondack chair that sells for $225—have been eagerly purchased by environmentally sensitive consumers, who have been impressed that recycled materials can be turned into well-designed items that need minimal maintenance.

Susan Szensasy, editor of *Metropolis*, says that a competition for environmentally sound furniture was first held at the 1996 International Contemporary Furniture Fair. "This is a definite trend," she says. "It has to be if we're going to survive on Earth. But there's a lot of work ahead of us. And the consumer has to understand that recycled products are not synonymous with junk."

I support those who put recycled products to good use.

"We see as fine risings of the sun as ever Adam saw; and its risings are as much a miracle now as they were in his day—and, I think, a good deal more, because it is now part of the miracle, that for thousands and thousands of years he has come to his appointed time, without the variation of a millionth part of a second."

—AMERICAN STATESMAN AND ORATOR DANIEL WEBSTER

MORNING ATTITUDE

There's a parable about a monkey trainer who goes to his monkeys and tells them, "As regards your chestnuts, you are going to have three measures in the morning and four in the afternoon." Hearing this, they all become angry. So the trainer says, "All right, in that case I will give you four in the morning and three in the afternoon." This time they are satisfied. Although the two arrangements are the same in that the number of chestnuts does not change, in one case the animals are displeased and in the other they are satisfied.

So, too, it may be for you at the start of any day. Even though the sun rises day after day on cue, you awaken day after day at your appointed time, and ahead of you lies an amount of time each day that's equal to what every other living thing has, some days you may awaken displeased and other days you may awaken satisfied. If you continue to hold on to satisfaction, then the rest of your day will probably be satisfying. But if you start out displeased and remain that way, then the rest of the day will probably bring you further displeasure.

Can you begin this day in complete awe of the fact that you are privileged to witness another miraculous rising of the sun— the same sun that has set and risen unfailingly each day for centuries? Focus on the grandeur of this experience rather than the amount of chestnuts you may be given, and you can start the day satisfied.

I begin this day by looking at the "big picture."

"You cannot step twice into the same stream. For as you are stepping in, other and yet other waters flow on."

—GREEK PHILOSPHER HERACLITUS

ENDING STAGNATION

What's the difference between living a life that embraces change and living a life that leads to stagnation?

- A life of change causes you continually to measure yourself against yourself and encourages you to ask, "What can I do better?"; a life of stagnation causes you to measure yourself against others and ask, "How am I better?"
- A life of change accepts taking paths that sometimes result in minor inconveniences, mild discomforts, or even major exertions prior to reaching a destination; a life of stagnation encourages you to drop out at even mild distress for no other reason than a weak will.
- A life of change realizes that victory is something that can only be attained by making an effort; a life of stagnation refuses to try anything unless success is assured.
- A life of change finishes every goal set, even the smallest ones; a life of stagnation refuses to set goals.
- A life of change seeks to do something in a way that's never been done before; a life of stagnation accepts that something has never been done before in a certain way and therefore doesn't do it.
- A life of change leads to the promise of greater change; a life of stagnation leads nowhere.
- A life of change has flowing waters that cleanse, refresh, and revitalize; a life of stagnation is just a muddy puddle.

Do I live a life of stagnation or change?

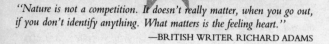

"Nature is not a competition. It doesn't really matter, when you go out, if you don't identify anything. What matters is the feeling heart."
—BRITISH WRITER RICHARD ADAMS

PULLING TOGETHER

Not too long ago, American runners were considered to be racing's elite, adept at setting and breaking course and world records as well as winning races. But gradually runners from other countries—particularly Kenya—started to outpace Americans in some of the most prestigious races. For example, German female runner Uta Pippig has won the coveted Boston Marathon for three consecutive years; Kenyan men have dominated the male Boston Marathon field for years.

It didn't take the American runners long to start to voice their complaints about medals and prize money being taken out of their hands, particularly in races run on American soil; in response, some races offered separate awards for American runners. But rather than complain, other runners studied both American and Kenyan racing strategies and soon discovered an important distinction. The Americans, observers noted, usually ran and trained alone and then raced for themselves; the Kenyans, on the other hand, usually ran and trained as a team and then raced as a team, oftentimes choosing a "pacer," whose function in that particular race was to keep the *team*, as well as "the winner," at a winning pace, long before the race was over. Kenyan teammates took turns as pacers as well as winners; the goal was simply for a Kenyan to win, for then the whole team won.

Just as the Kenyan runners know there is no "I" in team, so, too, do you need to realize that there is no "I" in nature. Each living thing functions for the good of all.

I pull together with others for group success.

"When I dance, I dance; when I sleep, I sleep; yes, and when I walk alone in a beautiful orchard, if my thoughts drift to far-off matters for some part of the time, for some other part I lead them back again to the walk, the orchard, to the sweetness of this solitude, to myself."

—FRENCH ESSAYIST MICHEL DE MONTAIGNE

LIVING IN THE MOMENT

One morning after breakfast a man asked Buddha for a moment of his time so he might seek advice about his life. Buddha invited him into his chambers and then listened patiently as the man rambled on and on for several minutes about a variety of different issues that he deemed troubling. Finally, Buddha held up his hand, and the man promptly stopped talking, eager to hear what Buddha had to say.

"Did you eat your breakfast?" asked Buddha.

The man nodded.

"Did you wash your breakfast bowl?" asked Buddha.

The man nodded again, and then opened his mouth to speak.

Buddha spoke before the man could. "And did you dry your bowl?" the wise man asked.

"Yes, yes," the man responded in frustration. "Now can you tell me what I should do about all the things I talked to you about?"

"You have your answer," Buddha replied, and then showed the man out.

Days later, the man finally realized the wisdom of Buddha's advice. In his questions, Buddha was reminding the man to stay focused in the present—to be fully and completely conscious of the moment, for that was what truly mattered.

I am conscious of each moment and so am fully alive in each moment.

"It is a remarkably pleasant occupation, to lie on one's back in a forest and look upwards! It seems that you are looking into a bottomless sea, that it is stretching out far and wide below you, that the trees are not rising from the earth but, as if they were the roots of enormous plants, are descending or falling steeply into those lucid, glassy waves. . . ."

—RUSSIAN WRITER IVAN TURGENEV

CHANGING YOUR PERSPECTIVE

When you look in the mirror, do you find yourself staring at lines and wrinkles, rolls and bulges, sags and spots, and other variations on your face and body that seem to have appeared overnight? You may be surprised, shocked, or even depressed when you look at photographs of your once youthful appearance and compare them to the "now" you. Too, you may relate to the words of the *Tao* about aging, which roughly translates to:

> *Lines on the face, tattoos of aging.*
> *Life is proved upon the body*
> *Like needle-jabs from a blind*
> *machine.*

Yet growing visibly older doesn't have to be so dismaying. What if you were to change your perspective on life's aging tattoos? Rather than think that life has taken its own creative liberties with you in marking up your body with evidence of aging, you can consider these words of French writer Victor Hugo: "When grace is joined with wrinkles, it is adorable. There is an unspeakable dawn in happy old age." Look upon life's tattoos as signs of wisdom, marks of maturity, evidence of great enjoyment and pleasure. Just as each tree contains rings that mark its passage of years, so, too, can each of your wrinkles be evidence of nature's measurement of your majestic progression in life's beautiful forest.

I show off my life tattoos with pride.

"Its mourners are few, perhaps, but the passing of the barn sign—there on the side of the road, a friend to man—is another symbol of the passing of an American era that was more rural, more tied to the land. . . ."

—WRITER DAVID M. SHRIBMAN

THE PASSING OF AN ERA

Do you remember the Mail Pouch barns, the ones painted for tobacco-industry profit and that today serve as a historical tribute to a time in America when tobacco was one of the country's earliest cultivated crops? Today, most of America views smoking as an annoying addiction rather than an enjoyable activity and devotes time and energy to kicking the habit rather than paying tribute to it.

But the disappearance of Mail Pouch barns—and all barn advertising, for that matter—signals as well that the country is, in many ways, no longer country. Cable television can reach into even the most remote and rugged rural areas; there's really no need for such advertising. The barn ads are fading out of existence, like the era they symbolized. So, too, are the long rows of planted fields and the grassy grazing acres fading away, along with the long stretches of winding country roads with cozy homes tucked into corners untouched by streetlights, where the night sky opened overhead like a museum planetarium.

American social scientist Jane Jacobs has observed, "It is no accident that we Americans, probably the world's champion sentimentalizers about nature, are at one and the same time probably the world's most voracious and disrespectful destroyers of wild and rural countryside." This weekend, take a ride to a nearby countryside. Fill your eyes with the natural beauty. Then offer a silent tribute to those who still live there, protecting the land for their—and your—enjoyment.

I appreciate the countryside and what it still stands for.

"It is interesting to contemplate a tangled bank, clothed with many plants of many kinds, with birds singing on the bushes, with various insects flitting about, and with worms crawling through the damp earth, and to reflect that these elaborately constructed forms, so different from each other, and dependent upon each other in so complex a manner, have all been produced by laws acting around us."

—ENGLISH NATURALIST AND WRITER CHARLES DARWIN

WORKING TOGETHER

When humorist Dave Barry volunteered to help his son Robert with a school science-fair project, both he and his son learned something not only about nature, but about themselves: "While Robert is drying [the papier-mâché ant the size of a mature raccoon], I get a flashlight and go outside to examine the experiment portion of our project, entitled 'Ants and Junk Food.' On our back fence we put up a banner that says 'Welcome Ants' . . . [with] potato chips, spicy beef jerky, Cheez Doodles, a doughnut and cream-filled cookies. Of course you veteran parents know what happened: the ants didn't show up. Nature has a strict rule against cooperating with science-fair projects." Yet in the process of helping his son on "our science project," father and the son were brought closer together and, at the same time, learned a little bit about the simple natural life around them.

This school year become more involved with your own children's school projects or volunteer to help children from single-parent or working-parent households in putting together special school projects. Offer support, knowledge, time, and attention to schoolchildren outside of the classroom, helping them to learn and grow from life's incredible natural experiences.

I become an after-school volunteer.

"You can grow intimate with almost any living thing, transfer to it your own emotion of tenderness, nostalgia, regret, so that often of a relationship one remembers the scene with the most affection. A particular line of hedge in a Midland country, a drift of leaves in a particular wood: it is only human to imagine that we receive back from these the feeling someone left with them."

—ENGLISH WRITER GRAHAM GREENE

BE A CANDLELIGHTER

If you've ever seen a candlelight ceremony, you know how powerful just one candle can be. Countless tapers can be lit from that one small flame until a room, large meeting hall, or even a darkened clearing in the woods is made brilliant with light.

Sometimes others may need your small flame from which they can light their own candles of hope, healing, and happiness. Maybe your aging parent needs your daily telephone call to ward off feelings of loneliness and isolation. Perhaps your partner needs reassurance that your love is steadfast. Maybe your pet needs time playing or walking with you outdoors. Or perhaps a friend needs your support in helping to make a tough decision.

Each day, you can give the gift of your "light" in small but meaningful ways to others. Offer encouragement to those who can use it, give support to those who are in need, provide strength to those who are weak, relate hope to those who are losing faith, and share your experience and knowledge with those who will listen. Be a candlelighter to others; let them light their candles from you. This gift of light can illuminate your world as well as theirs. By sharing the warm glow of loving feelings, nurturing acceptance, and laughter and lightness, others, too, can learn how to glow with the strength of an eternal flame.

I light the candles of others and keep them lit.

"*I was sitting in a birch wood one autumn, about the middle of September. . . . The leaves scarcely rustled above my head; by their very noise one could know what time of year it was. It was not the happy, laughing tremolo of spring, not the soft murmuration and long-winded talkativeness of summer, not the shy and chill babblings of late autumn, but a hardly audible dreamy chattering.*"

—RUSSIAN WRITER IVAN TURGENEV

NATURAL MEDITATION

More and more people are meditating while out in nature to make themselves feel better, to gain a sense of control in their lives, to feel spiritually connected, to enhance relaxation and sleep, to restore clear thinking, to refresh weary muscles, to diminish tension, and to raise self-worth.

There are many different ways to meditate while out in nature. One technique you can use while sitting still at the top of a mountain, on a rock or log in a forest, or by the seashore is called gazing. Find and then focus on an object that's in the distance—a cloud in the sky, leaves on a tree, or a sailboat. Take three deep abdominal breaths, gradually relaxing your muscles with each slow exhalation. When you feel comfortably settled, gaze at the object you've chosen while continuing to breathe easily, keeping your eyes and body relaxed. Notice everything about the object—its texture, shape, color, size, movement. Trace the edge of the object with your eyes as you take in all the minute details that you might not ordinarily notice. If you become distracted, simply return your gaze to the object.

Practice this "natural" meditation technique on a regular basis so you can learn how to still your restlessness and respond to life in a more relaxed way.

I meditate for stillness and inner peace.

"If the world were merely seductive, that would be easy. If it were merely challenging, that would be no problem. But I arise in the morning torn between a desire to improve (or save) the world and a desire to enjoy (or savor) the world. This makes it hard to plan the day."

—WRITER E. B. WHITE

A SENSE OF NATURE

When rancher and nature writer Gretel Ehrlich went to Wyoming to make a film while her partner in the project—and the man she loved—was dying, the rough beauty of the state helped pull her through the tragedy. The open spaces became a gentle, healing space to her.

How can you add such a "nature sense" to your life when you don't live in open country but in the heart of a bustling metropolis or suburban development? Foster this nature sense within yourself, within your heart and soul. Know that there's life around you that has no conditions or deadlines, no sure routes or routines, no peaks or goals, no desires or meaning beyond what lies at the surface. Know this life exists—this wildness and freedom amid all the chaos of "civilized" living—and you can then seek it from time to time, through connections to seemingly unconnected things.

American naturalist and explorer William Beebe once wrote, "If . . . I went to the end of the street, climbed down into a rowboat, and started out, the limits of possibility would encircle the whole globe . . . there is actually open water between my little pier and the edge of the Antarctic barrier . . . the Amazon-drained eastern slopes of the Andes, the arctic foam churned up by swimming polar bears. . . . The garbage-strewn tide swirling around the unlovely piles off my Sixty-seventh Street pier takes on a meaning and a dignity which it never had before."

I sense nature in many areas of my day-to-day life.

"Soon the child's clear eye is clouded over by ideas and opinions, precon-
ceptions and abstractions. Simple free being becomes encrusted with the
burdensome armor of the ego. Not until years later does an instinct come
that a vital sense of mystery has been withdrawn. The sun glints through
the pines, and the heart is pierced in a moment of beauty and strange pain,
like a memory of paradise. After that day . . . we become seekers."

—WRITER PETER MATTHIESSEN

PLEASURE OR PAIN?

Do you experience the world only as a source of pleasure
or pain? You may experience periods in your life that seem
to be one roller-coaster ride after another. Sometimes you're
riding high, experiencing thrills, adventures, risks, emotional
surges of delight, fulfilling relationships, and a strong spiritual
connection; other times you're riding through the depths of
despair, filled with worry, anxiety, fear, boredom, hopelessness,
and loneliness. Every positive emotion, you learn, has its negative side—love can result in pain, success can turn into a great
loss, expectations can be dashed, hopes can be shattered, doubt
can infiltrate even the most upbeat moods, relationships can
turn sour.

But when you're able to withdraw temporarily from participating in the events of your life, you can see that between the
two extremes of pleasure and pain are levels of different emotions—gentle, rolling rides with less drastic twists and turns.
Look outside yourself, and you'll recognize that there's much
more to this world than your own little space with your own
little issues. There's a whole world around you that's teeming
with wonders and mysteries, intense beauty, passionate movement, history, and heritage. Focus on this world; seek the stability of its pleasures.

I experience the pleasures of the world around me.

"Ah, the waning days of summer . . . Summer is when we somehow are pulled, almost atavistically, out of our climate-controlled routines back into a face-to-face encounter with the elements. . . . We approach the fall with a new awareness of the environment. . . . Wistfully, we recall that faraway 'golden age' when humans lived in greater harmony with the environment. . . ."

—EDITOR MARK D. W. EDINGTON

GIVING BACK TO NATURE

One of the greatest ironies in today's discussions about the environment is the desire to go "back to nature" and what this concept implies. For no one can truly go back to nature; "that" particular nature no longer exists—America is no longer one massive primal forest, many rivers and lakes no longer move or are found in their original locations, acres of pastures have long since been buried under landfills. Nor can one truly exist in such wild nature the way humans once did, for the nature known to cave dwellers was much too brutal for weak, naked, starving bodies; shelters had to be sought, food killed, bodies clothed. Living out in nature meant death, not a wondrously meaningful experience.

In today's world, the reality is that staying warm sometimes means the earth must be ravaged for clean, efficient fuels; ten billion people in the world need to be fed from what is grown on available land; and industry, which almost single-handedly destroyed the natural world, now has the responsibility to clean it up.

Thus, going back to nature in its truest sense is not realistic in today's world. Living in a way that returns some of nature back to itself, however—restoring what has been dirtied, poisoned, or dug up—enables you to give back to nature.

I give back to nature some of what nature has given to me.

"The subtlest beauties in our life are unseen and unheard."
—LEBANESE POET, NOVELIST, ESSAYIST, AND ARTIST
KAHLIL GIBRAN

NATURAL ATTRACTIONS

Did you know that the bee orchid *(Ophrys speculum)* has so realistically mimicked the outline of a bee, the insect on which it depends for pollination, that bees will try to mate with it? This ensures the successful transfer of pollen from the flower to the bee, and thus the survival of the plant. Or that an orchid, which is found only in Madagascar, was initially discovered by Charles Darwin, who measured its nectar spur to be nearly eighteen inches and predicted that one day a moth would be discovered with a tongue of the same length—and fifty years later, the new moth species was suitably named *Praedicta*!

Whenever you think about your husband, wife, or life partner; your best friend or college roommate; a present employer or business partner; or your adopted child, do you ever marvel at the incredible forces that brought you together? Just as many of nature's living things have subtle beauties that attract one particular suitor or species of suitors while, at the same time, they repel others that would do the creatures harm or in which they have no interest, so, too, do you have subtle beauties that attract those who will love you, nurture you, share many of life's experiences with you, build your self-esteem, enrich your family's soul, and help you to survive.

An old Welsh proverb aptly states, "A seed hidden in the heart of an apple is an orchard invisible." So, too, do you have an "orchard invisible" within you. You have the potential, through natural attraction, to be placed on the same path, in the same space, and in the heart of special human beings who will make your life more beautiful.

I let my natural attraction draw a special person into my life.

"We need the tonic of wildness,—to wade sometimes in marshes where the bittern and the meadow-hen lurk, and hear the booming of the snipe; to smell the whispering sedge where only some wilder and more solitary fowl builds her nest, and the mink crawls with its belly close to the ground."
—AMERICAN WRITER AND NATURALIST HENRY DAVID THOREAU

THE TONIC OF WILDNESS

When she was sixteen years old, future nature writer Martha Reben (1911–1964) was diagnosed with an advanced case of tuberculosis. Because her mother had died of the same illness ten years earlier, Martha was promptly sent to various sanatoriums and, finally, to Saranac Lake in New York's Adirondack Mountains, a popular resort at the time for many of those who were afflicted with TB.

But after three bedridden years and three operations, Martha decided that she wasn't getting any better in the hospital environment and had had enough of doctors and medications. She read an advertisement in the local newspaper, taken out by a woodsman named Fred Rice who advocated the outdoors as a cure for TB, and responded to his call for a patient on whom to test his theory.

Rice took Martha twelve miles into the woods, to camp at the shores of Weller Pond. Through him, she learned how to sleep out in the open, to hunt—which she later gave up because she had "no heart for killing"—to fish, and to find her way through the forest with a compass. She spent summer seasons in the woods alone; each winter she returned to a small cabin on the outskirts of the village. Ten years later, doctors pronounced her free of TB.

Today, you, too, can use the "natural cure" for whatever afflicts your mind, body, or spirit.

I use the healing powers of nature to restore physical health and emotional well-being.

"First, I think peak-baggers are too focused on getting to the summit; they ignore the process of hiking, the experience. Also, I think it's dangerous. People get killed peak-bagging, because their desire to bag the peak causes them to go farther than they normally would."

—COMMENTS OF AN ANONYMOUS "THRU-HIKER"

LETTING GO OF A GOAL

Have you ever refused to revise or abandon a goal even when achieving it was not only impossible, but dangerous or unhealthy? Have you ever let working toward a goal so get in the way of other priorities that you knowingly did irreparable damage to a relationship, business, your finances, or another significant part of your life?

Too often the desire to achieve a goal can become so obsessive that you may find it hard to remember the steps you originally set for achieving your goal; during a temporary setback, you then find yourself unable to assess what your next step should be. Those people who are known as "peak-baggers"—mountain climbers whose goal is to reach a summit—often become a statistic or need to be rescued when they place their life in jeopardy during poor weather or climbing conditions. While it may be admirable to climb all the four-thousand-footers in New Hampshire's White Mountains, for instance, it's foolhardy not to turn back, even a few feet from a summit, and to risk losing life, limb, or even a few toes or fingers. Too, "thru-hikers"—those who hike thousands of continuous miles on a mountain-trail system such as the Appalachians—1,554 miles from Springer Mountain, Georgia, to Mt. Katahdin, Maine—know that living outside for up to six months can take a physical, emotional, and spiritual toll that needs to be constantly monitored.

I use my knowledge, energy, and resources to make smart decisions while achieving a goal.

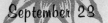

"Cut wood. Got birch bark. Picked berries, blue and cran."
—FROM THE DIARY OF F. CAMPBELL, SEPTEMBER 1948

LIVING SIMPLY

One of the most popular stage acts from the past involved one person attempting to do several activities at the same time—keeping plates spinning on the top of several poles without letting them fall while juggling balls, all the while making sure toy poodles were jumping through flaming hoops. Watching that one person frantically scurry from task to task was more fascinating than any one of the actions themselves.

Do you sometimes feel as if you're managing a similar stage routine as you constantly strive to juggle several activities throughout a day, such as working out on your exercise bike while talking on the phone while sorting through the day's mail while microwaving your dinner?

Sometimes the best way to live life is simply—by doing one thing at a time, savoring this activity, finishing it, and then doing another thing, savoring it, finishing it, and so on. The words of Buddha express this simple advice:

> *Sit*
> *Rest*
> *Work.*
> *Alone with yourself,*
> *Never weary.*
> *On the edge of the*
> *forest*
> *Live joyfully,*
> *Without desire.*

I do one thing at a time so I can savor it and do it well.

"I live alone in the country. I like it. The big kitchen in winter is full of potatoes and boots and sacks of seed. One can never be lonely in a room with a fifty-pound sack of sunflower seed. There it sits, large and comforting—a presence."

—AMERICAN FARMER AND WRITER JOSEPHINE JOHNSON

EASING LONELINESS

Loneliness can attack you like a disease. Physically, it can drain you like a potent strain of a flu, wearing you down to a point of exhaustion. Like a long bout with the flu, it can also drain you emotionally, eating away at your ability to think positively so you can heal yourself, as well as spiritually, eroding your faith that you'll soon feel better.

Not all living things are so uneasy with their own solitude; humans seem to be the species most afflicted with the inability to feel comfort while alone. Yet it's only in solitude that you can learn about yourself and how to handle what you share with all living things—your own eternity of aloneness.

One of the best antidotes to loneliness is to get outside yourself and into the world around you. Listen to the gentle sounds small streams make, as if they are taking you into their confidence and whispering great secrets to you. Look over a glorious field of wildflowers or climb high and take in the dramatic sight from a scenic vista, and let this magnificent vision fill your heart with gladness. Let the trees and the stones be powerful guides to your life by allowing them to teach you those things you can never learn from books. As English poet John Milton recommended, "In those vernal seasons of the year when the air is calm and pleasant, it were an injury and sullenness against nature not to go out, and see her riches, and partake in her rejoicing with heaven and earth."

I reach out and let nature in to ease my loneliness.

"Human beings possess such immense powers that few animals cause us to feel truly humble. A whale does, swimming beside you, as big as a reclining building, its eye carefully observing you. It could easily devastate you with a twitch, and yet it doesn't."

—AMERICAN WRITER DIANE ACKERMAN

MISUSING POWER

Back in the days of the "Wild West" every home had a gun, every stagecoach driver kept a rifle close at hand, every man walked around wearing a gun belt, and everybody knew to duck or run for cover at the first sound of gunfire. Living in such an environment was stressful; a man couldn't play a quick hand of poker while sipping a beer without using the mirror behind the bar to guard his back, and a woman couldn't hang out the laundry without wondering if danger lurked in the woods just outside the cabin clearing.

This is what it's like every day for creatures in the animal kingdom. It's a Wild West of hunter and hunted; the tiny field mouse awakens every morning hungry and needing to venture forth in a world where its enemies lurk behind trees, under bushes, and high in the sky. The field mouse's enemies have their own enemies, and these enemies have different enemies. Because of this, in the natural world, some creatures feel great and some feel small.

Yet when man walks through the woods, gun in hand, he feels neither great nor small—he feels invincible. His dogs can tree the most ferocious of bears, which he can then kill by twitching a finger. His snowmobiles, on which he relentlessly and mercilessly gives chase, can cause hearts to explode like balloons in the breasts of fleeing wolves. His traps can cause drowning or slow bleeding to death.

Yet what creature arms itself against man, hunts man, seeks to destroy man? Isn't it time to realize that the power man has over creatures needs to be controlled?

I respect the lives of all creatures.

"A human being should be able to change a diaper, plan an invasion, butcher a hog, conn a ship, design a building, write a sonnet, balance accounts, build a wall, set a bone, comfort the dying, take orders, give orders, cooperate, act alone, pitch manure, solve equations, analyze a new problem, program a computer, cook a tasty meal, fight efficiently, die gallantly. Specialization is for insects."

—WRITER ROBERT A. HEINLEIN

TIME FOR A CHANGE

Imagine today that you could do something you've never done before. Forget about the planning or training you'd need to do this, what it might cost, how it would fit into your current schedule, caretaking arrangements you'd need to make, what others might say, and numerous other considerations that, in the past, may have prevented you from pursuing this particular activity. Know that at this moment in time, you could do whatever you wanted to do. So what would you choose to do?

Too often you may take paths in your life you feel you should be on, which the majority of others are on, or which others have chosen for you. Yet it may not be too long before you discover that such paths don't really take you where you want to go, don't bring you fulfillment or enjoyment, or don't address your needs. So why stay on such paths when there are so many others to choose from? The beauty of being human lies in your ability to make such choices and to try out different things until you find what's right for you; most every other living thing, however, must respond to its instinctual drives and live within unchanging parameters, never varying its activities.

Today, resolve to explore at least one different path in your life. Make plans to pursue a dream, to learn a different skill, to break out of a set way of doing things, and to try something new.

I encourage diversity in my life.

"The creator created the Earth, our Mother Earth, and gave her many duties, among them to care for us, His people. He put things upon Mother Earth for the benefit of all. And as we travel around today we see that our Mother Earth is still doing her duty, and that we are very grateful."
—ONONDAGA CHIEF IRVING POWLESS, SR.

TREATING MOTHER EARTH WELL

A Chinese parable offers these distinctions in delivering apologies. If a man steps on a stranger's foot in the marketplace, then he quickly makes a polite apology and may also offer an explanation, such as, "This place is so terribly crowded." If an elder brother steps on his younger brother's foot, he quickly says, "Sorry!" and that is that. If a parent treads on his child's foot, nothing is said at all.

What this parable means is that the greatest politeness is free of all formality; perfect conduct, perfect wisdom, and perfect love, such as that between a parent and a child, result in perfect sincerity that needs no apology. So if you treat the planet Earth well for as long as you live upon it—if you care for it, remember that its resources are not only finite but also shared, keep it clean, and refrain from interference in all its matters, then you need never make any apologies to Earth. In turn, Earth will always treat you well. Yet step on Mother Earth's foot in your pursuit of self-satisfaction or financial gain in the marketplace of life, and she may not be so ready to accept your apology.

"In all your official acts," Cherokee Indian Dekawidah advised his people in 1720 with words of wisdom that hold true today, "self-interest shall be cast aside. You shall look and listen to the welfare of the whole people and have always in view, not only the present but the coming generations—the unborn of the future Nation."

I safeguard my future today by protecting Mother Earth.

"Even if something is left undone, everyone must take time to sit still and watch the leaves turn."

—AMERICAN WRITER ELIZABETH LAWRENCE

BALANCING YOUR LIFE

Will today be yet another day you let go by without doing something you want to do because you feel there are so many things you still have to take care of? Will you let an early-morning business meeting prevent you from taking a long walk in the woods with your dog or force you to skip your morning run? Will you let a pile of paperwork chain you to your desk at lunchtime instead of going outside and eating a bagged lunch with a coworker on a park bench? Will you let a long list of errands or chores keep you from playing catch with your child in the backyard this evening or tending to your garden?

If today was your last day on this planet, would you spend it in a meeting, at your desk, or running errands? Chances are such things would suddenly seem unimportant; being able to sit and watch the leaves turn would be far more rewarding. So why let such things take control of your life now?

A Zen proposition states that a good ox driver is one who knows how much load the ox can carry and so keeps the ox from being overloaded. So, too, you must know your way and state of mind so you don't carry too much. Becoming too absorbed in any area of your life can take time and attention from other areas and make your entire life unbalanced. To change this, imagine placing each activity in your life on a scale and weighing the amount of focus you give it. Decide to give less time and attention to those activities that weigh a lot and more to those that weigh little.

I redistribute my time and attention to bring balance into my life.

"An old Indian teaching was that it was wrong to tear loose from its place on the earth anything that may be growing there. It may be cut off, but it should not be uprooted. The grass and trees have spirits."

—19TH-CENTURY CHEYENNE WARRIOR WOODEN LEG

PROTECTING PROUD TREES

You never realize how important a tree can be to you until it is lost forever. A once close-knit group of people who lived in a suburban neighborhood discovered this one year when an older neighbor who had recently lost his wife decided to devote his energy to growing prize tomatoes. So he hired a tree company to cut down two healthy trees in his yard that were blocking the sunlight he felt would make his tomatoes grow better.

As the chain saws roared and branches cracked and fell to the ground with sickening thuds, the man's neighbors rushed out of their homes and apartments, frantically pleading with him to stop the trees from being felled. Their protests were ignored. The man's closest friend stormed back to his own house and slammed the door. One woman spent several minutes on the telephone with a lawyer to find out if she could legally do anything to save the trees. Two elderly sisters watched in horrified silence, linked together arm in arm, as tears streamed down their faces.

Weeks after the tree company had done its work, the man's neighbors still refused to talk to him. The man labored every day in his garden, sweating profusely. Often he would pull a handkerchief from his back pocket, look up at the relentless sun that now baked the earth, mop his brow, and mutter, "Hot! I never see such hot! Why did I ever do such a stupid thing?"

It's up to you to protect those thriving, proud trees that provide you with shade and offer natural barriers between you and your neighbors.

I preserve surrounding, healthy trees.

"I believe that only one person in a thousand knows the trick of really living in the present. Most of us spend 59 minutes an hour living in the past, with regret for lost joys, or shame for things badly done (both utterly useless and weakening)—or in the future which we either long for or dread. Yet the past is gone beyond prayer. . . . There is only one world, the world pressing against you at this minute. There is only one minute in which you are alive, this minute—here and now."

—BRITISH WRITER STORM JAMESON

HERE AND NOW

Do you always see each day as a new beginning—one that's fresh and clean and full of possibilities for the future—or do you sometimes begin a day by looking back at the previous day or another time from the recent or distant past and think instead about all the things you could have or should have done differently?

Beginning a day with thoughts about a day or a time gone by is like writing on a chalkboard that hasn't been washed since the start of a school year. Your new message is going to be hard to distinguish among all the other faded messages on the dusty surface. Chalky, ghostly images of minutes, hours, and days gone by make it hard to focus on the activities of the present or to even look ahead and see into your future—whether that future is one minute from now or one year from now.

Here's the best way to start today with the same freshness, newness, and cleanliness it offers you. "This is what you shall do," wrote American poet Walt Whitman. "Love the earth and sun and the animals, despise riches, give alms to everyone that asks, stand up for the stupid and crazy, devote your income and labor to others, hate tyrants, argue not concerning God. . . ."

I treat each day as a unique time of fresh starts and new beginnings.

"Life is frequently more worth living because of a blackbird's song, a yellow elm tree in October, or some other natural phenomenon which does not cost money and does not have what the editors of the Left-wing newspapers call a class angle."

—ENGLISH WRITER GEORGE ORWELL

SLOWING DOWN, NATURALLY

Fall impels bears to hibernate, frogs to burrow deep into the mud at the bottom of ponds, birds to wing south, and trees to decelerate their growth with a final burst of glorious color. Fall induces most creatures to either shut down, slow down, or leave their spring and summer homes in preparation for the cold, dark end of the year.

Do you find that you, too, shut down, slow down, and want to leave? With the approach of colder weather, family holidays, and a time change that causes darkness to advance, you may find yourself feeling lethargic and a bit disinterested in life. Yet it's only natural that you, too, are experiencing a slowing down similar to nature's, for you're part of nature's cycles of ebb and flow, high energy and dormancy, renewal and decline.

At times like this, staying in touch with nature can help you to feel better. Rather than focus on your problems or stresses, you can look outside your window and see the changing colors of nature in the trees—some still boast bright reds, oranges, and yellows, while others display colors that are muted or browned. You can watch the leaves cascade to the ground like feathers from a torn down pillow. You can listen to the songs of the birds and rustle of the wind as it stirs up the fallen leaves. At this time of year, there's really so much more to focus on than early darkness, each day's duties, the problems of the world, preholiday pressures, and other stresses.

I am part of the natural phenomena of nature.

> *"Sunshine is delicious, rain is refreshing, wind braces us up, snow is exhilarating; there's really no such thing as bad weather, only different kinds of good weather."*
>
> —ENGLISH ART CRITIC AND WRITER JOHN RUSKIN

THE NECESSITY OF CHANGE

Just as seasons change, tides turn, temperatures fluctuate, animals shed summer coats for winter ones, and fruits ripen on trees, so, too, do things in your life change. Nothing ever stays the same; the natural evolution of time takes away some things and brings back other things in their place.

As disruptive as any change may be to you—even one you may actively seek, such as going back to school or getting married—and as difficult as some changes may be to get used to, such as the ending of a relationship or even a new hairstyle, there are never any bad changes. For change is a necessary part of life, as necessary as the shift each year from summer into fall. American theologian Tyron Edwards once described natural change in terms of its physical, emotional, and spiritual significance: "The leaves in autumn do not change color from the blighting touch of frost, but from the process of natural decay. They fall when the fruit is ripened, and their work is done. And their splendid coloring is but their graceful and beautiful surrender of life when they have finished their summer offering of service to God and man."

Without change, there would be no sunrise or sunset—no times of fresh beginnings and no moments of peace and closure. Change is as vital to your life as the ever-unpredictable weather that greets you each day. Each bit of weather is like a dose of good medicine delivered to the planet; something that heals, that soothes, that cleanses, that caresses—that reassures you that all is well, for all is changing.

I embrace change as a necessary part of life.

"All through my life I never did believe in human measurement. Numbers, time, inches, feet. All are just ploys for cutting nature down to size. I know the grand scheme of the world is beyond our brains to fathom, so I don't try, just let it in. I don't believe in numbering God's creatures."

—AMERICAN WRITER LOUISE ERDRICH

THE MEANING OF TIME

Do you know that on average during each second of a day, according to writer Barry Evans, five humans are born and two die, the sun radiates thirteen million times the annual U.S. energy consumption, eight million blood cells in a normal, healthy human body expire, and light travels three quarters of the distance from the moon to the Earth? Do you also know that the universe is fifteen billion years old, but your time spent in this universe will amount for approximately two or three billion *seconds*!

Do you marvel at such facts and figures, or could you care less about them, relating more to these words of English poet Lord Byron: "When one subtracts from life infancy (which is vegetation), sleep, eating and swilling—buttoning and unbuttoning—how much remains of a downright existence?—the summer of a dormouse."

Perhaps, then, it's best to think of each second, minute, hour, week, month, and each new year of your life on your day of birth—not in terms of years but in terms of the most special gifts you can receive. Another year of your life *is* a gift. Although you may lie about your true age, avoid discussion of how old you are, or even cringe at the realization of how many years you've already lived, each year of your life is a gift.

I enjoy the gift of time each year on my birthday.

"When I shot any kind of bird, when I killed, I saw that its life went out with its blood. This taught me for what purpose I am here. I came into this world to die. My body is only to hold a spirit life. Should my blood be sprinkled, I want no wounds from behind. Death should come fronting me."

—MID-19TH CENTURY NEZ PERCÉ CHIEF TOOHOOLHOOLZOTE

KEEPING DEATH IN MIND

Do you believe, as Toohoolhoolzote did, that your purpose in life is to die and so, bearing this eventual end in mind, seek to live each day in ways that enable you to uphold the spirit life within you for as long as you've been given, appreciating all of life through this inner spirit? If you do, then you understand the words of Oglala Sioux holy man Black Elk, who said, "Hear me, four quarters of the world—a relative I am! Give me the strength to walk the soft earth, a relative to all that is! Give me the eyes to see and the strength to understand, that I may be like you. With your power only I can face the winds."

Or do you believe that your time on earth is to be spent differently, to achieve, to do, to go places, to meet different people, to be all you can be, without thinking there will ever be an end? Then you can better relate to the words of English writer George Eliot, who wrote in a letter to a friend, "The years seem to rush by now, and I think of death as a fast approaching end of a journey—double and treble reasons for loving as well as working while it is day."

As your journey in life speeds ahead, decide whether you want to speed along, too, watching the scenery as it blurs by you, or if you want to live in ways that enable you to make some meaningful stops along the way as you venture forth to greet death face-to-face.

I desire to make my life worthwhile for as long as I can.

"I'm astounded by people who want to 'know' the universe when it's hard enough to find your way around Chinatown."
—ACTOR, WRITER, AND FILM DIRECTOR WOODY ALLEN

PROMOTING INVENTIONS

While much has been written and said about the problems in the developing world, and there's a kind of fashionable jargon used in relation to it, familiarizing yourself with such things doesn't make you capable of understanding how the long-term survival of mankind as well as many species of living things on this planet are being jeopardized. And just because Western nations seem to have all the technological know-how and the economic theories about such things doesn't mean they have all the answers or are ready to actively seek solutions. A prime example of this involves the world's energy needs versus the impact such needs are having on the environment. Prototypes of electric cars proved to be both energy-efficient and workable decades ago, yet gas-guzzling vehicles continue to be mass-produced, the earth continues to be raped for its oil, and at least one oil-tanker spill occurs every year in some valuable waterway, choking the life out of aquatic creatures, destroying the livelihood of small-business owners, and robbing taxpayers of dollars that could be put to better use in areas other than a massive cleanup. Yet too few consumers know about the viability of electric cars because politicians, corporations, and oil-producing nations don't want to create a consumer demand that will deprive them of valuable votes, take away their profits, or leave them with little bargaining power to acquire arms, technology, and other goods for trade.

Today, learn what options exist for making life better naturally, and then strive to give such options greater currency. Write a letter to the editor, contact your representative in Washington, or form a community awareness group.

I push for the use of environmentally sound inventions.

"The sea has been called deceitful and treacherous, but there lies in this trait only the character of a great natural power, which renews its strength, and, without reference to joy or sorrow, follows eternal laws which are imposed by a higher power."

—GERMAN PHILOLOGIST AND STATESMAN
KARL WILHELM VON HUMBOLDT

WHAT DO YOU BELIEVE?

A belief is something you hold on to because you think it's true. So a person suffering from claustrophobia who walks into a party may immediately think, "This room is too small" or "There are far too many people here," and the person's body may respond in kind to the stimulus the mind is creating—the feeling of fear.

Your beliefs about some natural things can have the same kind of power over you. For example, because ticks frequent woods and fields and carry diseases dangerous to both man and animal, you may believe the woods and fields are dirty and infested with all sorts of creepy, crawling things that can harm you rather than valuable spaces that provide shelter for beautiful creatures and offer tremendous wild growth. Because boats capsize, people drown, giant waves wash out villages and erode shorelines, and sharks can make vicious attacks on swimmers, you may believe the ocean is treacherous rather than a powerful, life-sustaining force. Because you've been told or read that wolves take domestic stock from farms and ranches and possibly even pose a danger to humans, you may view wolves as horrible creatures that should be shot, trapped, or poisoned rather than gentle, intelligent animals that prune deer and moose populations and pose no threat.

If you let such limiting beliefs about nature dominate how you live with and respond to the environment, then you'll never be able to see nature as your nurturing companion in life.

I believe those things that tell the truth about nature.

"If I were to name the three most precious resources of life, I should say books, friends, and nature. . . . Nature we have always with us, an inexhaustible storehouse of that which moves the heart, appeals to the mind, and fires the imagination,—health to the body, a stimulus to the intellect, and joy to the soul."

—AMERICAN WRITER AND NATURALIST JOHN BURROUGHS

NATURE'S LESSONS

Nature is as much a social entity as it is a physical one; in addition to the resources it provides for itself—for self-preservation—nature plays an important role in the daily life of human society—for our enjoyment, use, and sometimes, abuse. Nature is the starting point of all living things as well as their sustainer. Nature, therefore, is essential to humankind; referring to nature as "Mother Nature" is apt, for nature is humankind's nurturing protector.

In today's society, however, Mother Nature has been left with many empty nests. For, as most people grow older, they come to believe that nature isn't "where it's at." Where it's at, they discover, is in the city, in front of the computer, in the living room watching television, on the telephone, in a morning or evening commute, in a project, in the stresses of day-to-day living—in sum, in countless other pursuits, problems, and pastimes.

Nature has many valuable lessons to teach you—lessons of stability and tranquillity, creation and imagination, beauty and harmony, growth and faith. They are lessons that can never be learned from books, from experts, or from the media. They are lessons that can only be learned from the fields, the sky, the woods, the riverbank, the seashore, the animals, and the earth. By seeking the natural elements in your everyday life, you can strengthen your relationship with nature.

I learn from and live with nature.

"That man's best works should be bungling imitations of Nature's infinite perfection, matters not much; but that he should make himself an imitation, this is the fact which Nature moans over, and deprecates beseechingly. Be spontaneous, be truthful, be free, and thus be individuals! is the song she sings through warbling birds, and whispering pines, and roaring waves, and screeching winds."

—U.S. ABOLITIONIST, WRITER, AND EDITOR LYDIA M. CHILD

BECOMING YOURSELF

At the age of seventy, author May Sarton wrote, "I am more myself than ever before." Yet finding this self is not always easy. Too often you may spend years defining yourself in relationship to other people, other places, other things. You're someone's wife or husband, another person's life partner, someone's child, or a child's parent. You're a student at a particular college or university or a resident of a community. You're an assistant to, a manager of, an owner of, a chairman of, a collector of, or a participant in.

In so defining yourself, you certainly answer the question of who you are through what roles you fulfill. But you don't even touch upon who you are by uncovering what's in your heart and soul. British author D. H. Lawrence once remarked, "The human being is a most curious creature. He thinks he has got one soul, and he has got dozens." What this means is that there's much more to you than meets the eye—the eyes of others, certainly, and more importantly, your own eyes. Finding out who you are is an exercise in letting go of what you've always thought or expected of yourself and then looking in the mirror and seeing not the person you've tried to be or to most resemble, but the person you really are. Self-discovery is about discovering as well as recovering your individuality.

I set sail today on a voyage of self-discovery to learn all I can about myself.

"A bird does not sing because it has an answer—it sings because it has a song."

—CHINESE PROVERB

FINDING A SIMPLE SOLUTION

Have you ever thought back to a time in your life when you experienced a tough time—a baffling problem, a major change, an important exam—and, at this later time, reflected on the experience and realized that the lesson to be learned from it was really so simple and obvious that you wonder why you hadn't known how to figure it out at the time? Yet sometimes the simplest solution can be the most elusive. It's like trying to outsmart a squirrel trying to steal food from your bird feeders. As your wallet shrinks with the purchase of new and improved baffles, repellents, and "squirrel-proof" feeders and as your blood pressure rises at the sight of the squirrel's latest assault, deterring the animal is no longer the goal but an obsession that gets more and more complicated with each passing day. Yet the simplest solution proves the most elusive: you could simply fill the feeders for the birds and spread seed and nuts on the ground for the squirrel; by feeding both species—which you're doing anyway—you'll be saving time, money, and aggravation.

So many things in your life may be made more complex when you strive to solve a problem or fulfill a desire in only one way or try too hard to find the answer right away. Often many different solutions and options are available to help you. Some are discovered after a great deal of thinking, some by trial and error, some through your own foolishness or stubbornness, and some as a result of mistakes or wrong turns. But most are found by simply living each day in your own way.

I remember to seek simple solutions to my problems.

> *"Everything belonging to the spider is admirable."*
> —AMERICAN THEOLOGIAN JONATHAN EDWARDS

FRIEND OR FOE?

The spider, like many of nature's small living things, has earned itself a bad name since it began crawling around on the earth 400 million years ago. To most people, the spider is an odious, frightening little creature—the stuff of horror films and the only reason for the existence of arachnophobia—that everyone hastens to crush underfoot or squish to death in a tissue. There may be many good reasons to be so terrified of spiders and, thus, so murderous. Consider their menacing appearance—how they silently and sinisterly stalk toward you on numerous legs covered with tiny hairs—the sheer numbers that inhabit your basement, and the eerie, goosebumpy feeling you may have when your skin contacts an unseen web strand.

Yet for every spider killed for no reason other than fear or hate, another of the most dominant predators of any terrestrial ecosystem is lost. "Modern arachnologists . . . say spiders consume many times the number of insects eaten by birds," writes Des Kennedy in his book *Nature's Outcasts*. "In the control of pest insects the much-maligned spider may in fact be humankind's most important ally. Some have gone so far as to speculate that human habitation of many regions of earth is only made possible by the countless billions of spiders also living there."

Even though nature gives life to many small creatures that you may hate or fear, killing them won't ease such feelings. Learning about the good these creatures do, their harmlessness, and some of their fascinating behaviors, however, may help you to understand and appreciate them more.

I seek to learn more about those creatures I fear more than I understand.

"I had naively assumed that, the digging done, I could step back and let my pond take care of itself. Not so. Digging this hole, I took on a responsibility—sharing, for better or worse, in the life and death of a pond. No longer a spectator standing on the shore, I'm now in deep."

—WRITER MICHAEL POLLEN

WORKING FOR NATURE

When Michael Pollen hired excavators to create a backyard pond one October day, he was amazed at how quickly the pond filled with water and life began to teem in and around it. In March, algae began to drift through the water. By the end of the month, the song of the spring peepers came from the pond, soon joined by a chorus of bullfrogs. In May, backswimmers sought meals of insect larvae and whirligig beetles zoomed across the surface. Water striders, aquatic plants, cattails, and waterfowl used the pond during warm months, while the tracks of foxes, wild turkeys, deer, raccoons, woodchucks, and various species of birds were visible in the winter snow.

Elated at the success of his pond, Pollen was "happy now to let nature take its course, pleased to have had a hand in the making of a thriving new ecosystem." He brought a jar of its water to a local biology teacher to gain a deeper knowledge of the life his pond was sustaining. But as the teacher viewed the water, he informed Pollen that his man-made pond would not remain a pond for very long. Left untended, the algae and weeds would continue to grow, die, and then settle to the bottom. This would make the water shallower, which, in turn, would let more light into the bottom of the pond, so the weeds would redouble. The pond would eventually turn into a swamp, then a wet spot, and then its original state—woodland—unless Pollen began a rigorous program of pond maintenance.

I am responsible for maintaining the integrity of the nature in my own backyard.

"You must not hurt anybody or do harm to anyone. You must not fight but do right always."

—PAIUTE PROPHET WOVOKA

COMPASSIONATE LIVING

The son of a visionary named Tavibo, Wovoka spread a message of hope and salvation to the Plains-region Indians when he implored them in the late 1880s to gather together for many days to pray, chant, and dance in large, open-air circles. Do this, Wovoka preached, and the old world will return, the landscape will look as it did before the white man, buffalo will thicken the plains, and whites will disappear.

But Wovoka's message of nonviolence was downplayed and, instead, fears about his talk of a world free of white man led to a call for military help. Along Wounded Knee on the Pine Ridge Reservation, 7th Cavalry troops rounded up a band of Hunkpapa Sioux suspected of potential trouble, composed mostly of women and children. The Sioux were herded into a tight group, surrounded by five hundred soldiers, and later, when a weapon accidentally discharged, were fired upon. Within an hour, two hundred Indians trying to defend themselves with stones, sticks, or bare hands were dead or dying. A few who escaped were rounded up and then killed, but one hundred fled and eventually froze to death in the hills.

While the Wounded Knee massacre is a tragic symbol of violence designed to dominate, it's also dramatic evidence about how misunderstandings can escalate. To live peacefully with other people and living things on this planet, you need insight and careful judgment. Unless you've known someone else's pain or burden, you can never know how you might react in the same circumstances. Only compassion and understanding can lead you to the truth.

I refuse to judge any other living thing until I have walked two moons in his moccasins.

"There are waves of planting. We plant a million elm trees. . . . Then a million dogwoods. When one of these species gets a bad disease, so many trees die it looks like a judgment from God."

—ARBORIST, WRITER, AND DIRECTOR OF THE BOTANIC
GARDENS AT SMITH COLLEGE, KIM TRIPP

BRANCHING OUT

Fall is the time of year when New Englanders are most aware of trees and shrubs, looking up to them for color and thinking about planting for next year's garden. But in a northeastern region where typically over four thousand kinds of specimens can survive the ever-changing climatic conditions, probably only forty shrubs and trees make up 90 percent of the landscape plantings. This is often because people buy what looks pretty at nurseries during the "spring fever" months of April and May. This favors early bloomers such as lilacs, forsythias, and Bradford pears but virtually eliminates those trees or shrubs known for their fall berries or foliage. This shortchanges home owners as well by creating monotonous landscapes composed of the same stuff everyone else has planted.

Why not create the diversity you have within your own family community to the landscape "community" you plant in your yard? Your family community is probably made up of a variety of lifestyles, backgrounds, cultures, ethnicities, religions, and so on. Such things make your family rich, colorful, and strong; each supports the other. Creating a garden with similar diversity will help ensure that some plants will survive climate changes, surges in plant diseases and pests, as well as provide you with a rewarding tapestry of colors, textures, and fragrances that can be enjoyed throughout the year.

I plant a living community of diversity in my yard.

"It comes quietly as mist in the night, but doesn't vanish as the sun rises. It remains, stronger day after day. It spreads, leaf to leaf, branch to branch, tree to tree. It climbs from the valley to the hilltop. Soon it will possess the countryside. . . . We sum it all up in two words: The Color."

—WRITER HAL BORLAND

FALL'S ATTRACTIVENESS

The enticing smell of freshly brewed coffee wafting through your kitchen in the morning or invading your nostrils when you open the door to your favorite coffee shop on the way to work signals its presence, guides you toward it, and implores you to take a sip. Too, the mouthwatering aroma of cookies baking in your oven can invade your senses so completely and urgently that you barely give the cookies time to cool on a wire rack before you take your first bite. The delicious smells you associate with a variety of favorite foods and drinks can immediately capture your interest and lure you toward them, encouraging you to lift pot lids, run a finger through a bowl, or crack open the oven door to sneak a peak.

Rutgers University biologist Edmund W. Stiles has theorized that fall's brilliant colors serve a similar purpose for migrating birds that are moving through new territory. Unfamiliar as the birds are with the food sources available to them along the way, the contrast of colored leaves against a mostly green forest background alerts them to the presence of food. Stiles coined a term for such plants that turn color early and, coincidentally, also have ripe fruit. These "foliar fruit flags" attract such fruit-eating migratory birds as American robins, cedar waxwings, eastern bluebirds, veeries, and wood thrushes, to name a few, which, in turn, help to perpetuate the food source by eating the fruit and then dispersing the seeds through digestive systems while the seeds are still viable.

I give in to nature's delicious colors and smells.

"Days have gone by. It must be October, mid-October I think, because the leaves are flying fast. The great maples are skeletons against the sky. . . . Pansy, now the nights are cold, sometimes comes to sleep with me. . . . The only time I weep is when she is there, purring beside me. I . . . can hardly bear the sweetness of that little rough tongue licking my hand."

—POET AND DIARIST MAY SARTON

PET PARTNERSHIPS

At the moment you're reading this page, thousands of pets are providing comfort and companionship to their owners and, in many cases, performing duties such as helping people to safely cross a street, reminding those who are sick to take their medication, retrieving money from automated teller machines, and even saving lives. Any kind of pet can be a lifesaver—a man with sleep apnea has a pet iguana that sleeps on his chest and wakes him whenever he stops breathing. Too, any pet can be a life enhancer, improving the quality of a person's life.

Aspen, a golden retriever that bears the name of trees that are strong and sturdy, regularly visits Mike, an active young man with severe brain damage suffered in an accident, through the Golden Retrievers' Pet Partners program. By playing catch with Mike, Aspen helps him meet specific therapeutic goals, which include increasing his range of motion, walking more sturdily, and improving his speech. Nancy, an outpatient receiving cancer treatments, looks forward to her visits from pet partner Koko, a playful and cuddly Burmese cat. And Finn, a large German shepherd, visits a class of children with developmental disabilities twice a week, where he helps provide motivation in reading, speech, math, and motor skills; one little girl uses Finn as a backrest while she reads books to him about animals.

I adopt or support the adoption of a pet partner from an animal shelter or humane society.

"Late on the third day, at the very moment when, at sunset, we were making our way through a herd of hippopotamuses, there flashed upon my mind, unforeseen and unsought, the phrase, 'Reverence for life.'"

—FRENCH PHILOSOPHER, CLERGYMAN, AND MEDICAL
MISSIONARY ALBERT SCHWEITZER

REVERENCE FOR LIFE

Along some roads in Germany, traffic signs and flashing lights have been installed not to alert drivers to watch their speed or to be aware of roadwork, but to drive cautiously through approaching salamander crossing sites. Salamander protection systems abound in Germany; the country takes the survival of its salamander species seriously. In fact, in some locations fences have been erected to herd the salamanders into an underground tunnel that then leads them safely under the road to their spawning pools.

Why all this fuss over the lowly salamander? Because the amphibians keep the insect population under control by laying eggs in vernal pools—breeding grounds for aquatic insects—so larvae can feed on the insects until they're mature enough to leave the pool. Without the larvae, the insects would have no predator.

But why go to such great lengths to ensure the salamanders' safety during once-a-year mating migrations? Because nature teaches that humankind is always part of a future—a future that only humans possess the power to shape in a negative as well as a positive way. Nature teaches that all living things are bound too tightly together to let any one species be sacrificed or ignored. In order for life to be sustained, you must have reverence for this life—for all of life—as the book of Job advises, "But ask now the beasts, and they shall teach thee; and the fowls of the air, and they shall tell thee: Or speak to the earth, and it shall teach thee: and the fishes of the sea shall declare unto thee."

I protect the fragility of nature.

"It is far from easy to determine whether [Nature] has proved to man a kind parent or a merciless stepmother."

—ROMAN SCHOLAR PLINY THE ELDER

NATURAL DISASTERS

There comes a time in every horror film when you know something bad is going to happen. Even though every action, character interaction, and line of dialogue in the movie has directed you to this moment of tension and terror, even though you know it's only a movie, and even though you know you could get up from your seat and walk out of the theater, you remain still, eyes riveted to the screen, heart pounding, palms sweating, holding your breath and waiting for the expected event to explode into view.

You may feel that same kind of trembling fear and anxiety when nature is about to unleash some of her terrible furies. Thunderstorms, floods, hurricanes, earthquakes, volcanoes, tidal waves, tornadoes, and countless other natural happenings can be horrific examples of an incredible power that can easily control mankind—a far superior force with a devastating and destructive capability no movie special effect could ever replicate. English naturalist and scientist Charles Darwin once described the lasting impact of one of nature's most riveting temper flares. "A bad earthquake," he wrote, "at once destroys our oldest associations: the earth, the very emblem of solidity, had moved beneath our feet like a thin crust over a fluid;—one second of time has created in the mind a strange idea of insecurity, which hours of reflection would not have produced."

And yet it's one of nature's dark ironies that the most horrific expressions of strength can also be the most beautiful—powerful, poetic portraits of nature's dominance over humanity.

I respect nature's power and the beauty of this power.

"To write honestly and with conviction anything about the migration of birds, one should oneself have migrated. Somehow or other we should dehumanize ourselves, feel the feel of feathers on our body and wind in our wings, and finally know what it is to leave abundance and safety and daylight and yield to a compelling instinct, age-old, seeming at the time quite devoid of reason and object."

—AMERICAN NATURALIST AND EXPLORER WILLIAM BEEBE

DETACHMENT

Can you imagine what it would be like if you not only had to move every year, but either had to find an unoccupied living space before bad weather set in or had to build your own shelter from whatever scrap materials you could find? Can you imagine how difficult it would be to have to hunt or forage for your food every day, from sunup to sundown? Can you imagine having to rely upon your outer covering to provide you with warmth and protection from the elements? Can you imagine how unsettling it might be to live in fear for your life each day, never knowing when you might become another living creature's next meal? Can you imagine having no painkillers to anesthetize your pain, no doctors to treat your wounds and injuries, and no bandages or ointments to stop your bleeding?

French author and philosopher Voltaire once pointed out that "Animals have a prodigious advantage over us: they foresee neither evils nor death." Because of this, animals—as well as all living things—know how to be detached from the things human beings are quite attached to. All living things accept the fluidity of life and its changeability; they know how to adapt because they must adapt. Can you let go of the obsessive human need for attachment to people, places, and things and instead focus on your connection to the universe outside you?

I detach from possessions and instead attach to knowing and understanding life's ever-changing panorama.

"Nature is not only what is visible to the eye—it shows the inner images of the soul—the images on the back side of the eyes."
—NORWEGIAN PAINTER AND PRINTMAKER EDVARD MUNCH

NATURAL INFLUENCES

One day, on the famous "bullet train" from Kyoto to Tokyo, a commotion occurred among the passengers. They all rushed to one side of the train just in time to see thick clouds suddenly part, revealing the beauty and majesty of Mt. Fuji. Passengers exclaimed and took pictures until, just as suddenly, the clouds once again hid the mountain from view. But the incident changed the atmosphere on the train for the rest of the ride. People who had been strangers or who had shied away from human contact were now chatting like close friends. Those who had been sleeping now opened their eyes and marveled at the green lushness of the rice fields they were passing. Many commented on the beauty that had touched them and, miraculously, united them for a brief time. What had happened was that each person on the train had been given the opportunity to be influenced by nature; from this, they gained a new appreciation not only for the old, familiar sight that whizzed by each day, but for their fellow "passengers in life"— those people with whom they shared the same train every day but had not taken the time to know.

You, too, can let the clouds that cover familiar sights lift so you can appreciate their beauty and significance to your life. Maybe you've neglected to pay attention to your partner; take time now to truly look at him or her. Perhaps you haven't noticed how the trees in your yard look; are they different from the last time you noticed them? Maybe you've forgotten to take in a glorious sunset or a beautiful sunrise; resolve to do so. Push away the clouds in your life, and you'll be surprised at what new things you'll discover on your "old" horizons!

I allow myself to be influenced in positive ways by nature.

"A rock has being or spirit, although we may not understand it."
—PUEBLO INDIAN WRITER LESLIE MARMON SILKO

SPIRITUAL ROCK

As you enter Baxter State Park in Maine and view the majestic monolith that rises up for a mile out of the forest, from each approach Mt. Katahdin has a completely different look. From one view, it's a huge igneous wall—hard, cold, and seemingly insurmountable; from another, it's a luscious, long green ridge that seems to rise gently to several negotiable peaks. Hunt Trail, also known as the final five miles of the Appalachian Trail, leads hikers past the glorious, ninety-foot Katahdin Stream Falls, which roar through a rocky chasm. The Knife-Edge Trail is a narrow glacial pass that looks like the spiny back of a prehistoric creature; mountain-sized cliffs pose monstrously challenging travel, especially when the winds roar through. Baxter Peak, the 5,240-foot summit—allows commanding views in clear weather.

But it has been said that the rocks of Mt. Katahdin hold the spirits of ancestors; one climber who was repeatedly pushed back from the peak due to high winds and icy rain attributed his failure to a candy wrapper he had left behind that he felt had angered the gods. So he hiked back to his lunch spot, retrieved the wrapper, and went on to reach a summit that was bathed in sunlight and becalmed.

The very rocks themselves—and their ancestral spirits—owe their protective existence to Maine Governor Percival Baxter, who spent most of his adult life acquiring land to create the unique 314-square-mile sanctuary that bears his name. He made Mt. Katahdin its centerpiece because "The works of men are short-lived. Monuments decay, buildings crumble and wealth vanishes. But Katahdin in its massive grandeur will forever remain the mountain of the people of Maine."

I respect the life within rocks that have existed, steadfast and immobile, for centuries.

"If only hunters, anglers, and environmentalists would stop taking potshots at each other, they'd be an invincible force for wildlands protection."
—HUNTER, FISHERMAN, ENVIRONMENTALIST, AND WRITER
TED WILLIAMS

BENEFICIAL ALLIANCES

Do you know that hunters and anglers have had a long history of protecting and restoring fish, wildlife, and habitats in the United States? America's 92-million-acre wildlife refuge system was started by the nation's most well-known hunter, President Theodore Roosevelt. Duck hunter J. N. "Ding" Darling, a Pulitzer Prize–winning political cartoonist for *The Des Moines Register,* allied with fellow waterfowlers in 1934 to push through Congress a law requiring duck and goose hunters to purchase a federal permit in the form of a stamp; since that day, duck-stamp money has gone to national wildlife refuges. To raise money for wildlife management, throughout the years hunters and anglers have successfully lobbied for excise taxes on fishing tackle and ammunition. Today, they are even joining with other nature lovers to push for new excise taxes on an even wider range of outdoor products—such as backpacks, tents, birdseed, and field guides—in order to provide an additional $350 million a year for ecosystem management.

Ironically, hunters have also saved game and many species that are now classified as nongame from commercial market hunting, such as shooting wolves from aircraft, and joined with environmentalists to ban aerial wolf-hunting permanently. Today, thanks to alliances forged between hunters, anglers, and environmentalists, the populations of white-tailed deer, elk, antelope, and wild turkeys have soared and ecosystems are returning to health.

I challenge those who hunt without a license and applaud those who join in environmental causes.

"Lord make us mindful of the little things that grow and blossom in these days to make the world beautiful for us."

—WRITER AND EDUCATOR W.E.B. DU BOIS

DAILY PRAYERS

When do you make a conscious contact with a Higher Power through prayer? Most people pray only when they're faced with an emotional or physical difficulty so they can make what's difficult a bit easier to bear. But can't you also pray as a way of giving thanks, as a way of recognizing the blessings that are all around you, or even as a way of "checking in" every day, when you don't need but rather want to communicate with your Higher Power?

Author Rumer Godden once wrote, "There is an Indian belief that everyone is a house of four rooms: a physical, a mental, an emotional and a spiritual room. Most of us tend to live in one room most of the time, but unless we go into every room every day, even if only to keep it aired, we are not complete." At this moment, whether you need your Higher Power or not, you can open the door to your spiritual room and keep it open in order to maintain an ongoing spiritual dialogue.

There are many ways to welcome your Higher Power into your "house." You can remind yourself each day to live by the words of Salish Indian Mourning Dove, who said, "Everything on this earth has a purpose, every disease an herb to cure it, and every person a mission. This is the Indian theory of existence." You may choose to create your own prayer—one that brings you spiritual guidance and wisdom. Or you may simply ask your Higher Power each morning to make you mindful of the beautiful, natural living things around you. Make such communication a part of your daily routine, and you'll be rewarded by a profound and more intimate relationship with your Higher Power.

I find time every day to pray.

"Surely there is something in the unruffled calm of nature that overawes our little anxieties and doubts: the sight of the deep-blue sky, and the clustering stars above, seem to impart a quiet to the mind."
—AMERICAN THEOLOGIAN JONATHAN EDWARDS

QUIETING YOUR MIND

Centuries ago in China, Chi Hsing Tzu, a famous trainer of fighting cocks for King Hsuan, was commanded to train a new bird for combat. One day the king asked Chi Hsing Tzu if the bird was ready.

"Not yet," said the trainer. "He is full of fire. He is ready to pick a fight with every other bird."

"But surely that is the sign of a good fighter," the king countered.

"Not so," the trainer replied.

Several days later, the king asked if the bird was ready to fight.

"Not yet," said the trainer. "He flares up when he hears another bird crow."

"But surely that is the sign of a good fighter," the king countered.

"Not so," the trainer replied.

A few days later still, the king asked if the bird was now ready to fight.

"Not yet," said the trainer. "He still gets that angry look and ruffles his feathers."

"But surely that is the sign of a good fighter," the king countered.

"Not so," the trainer replied.

Yet another week later, the trainer asked to see the king. "Now he is ready," he said. "When another bird crows, his eye does not even flicker. He stands immobile like a block of wood. He is a mature fighter. He is sure of himself. Other birds will take one look at him and run."

The words and actions of others never ruffle my feathers.

"How the sun silently mounts in the broad, clear sky, on his day's journey! How the warm beams bathe all, and come streaming kissingly and almost hot on my face."

—AMERICAN POET WALT WHITMAN

LIGHTENING YOUR MOODS

Research has shown that exposure to full-spectrum light— light that contains all the wavelengths of sunlight—positively influences mental as well as physical health. Not getting enough of this type of light can have a profoundly negative effect on mental outlook, moods, and overall well-being. For example, inhabitants of northern countries who are deprived of sunlight for months at a time have extremely high rates of suicide and alcoholism. Too, now that the season is changing and daylight hours are shrinking, you may be spending more time indoors and sorely missing the brightness that once greeted you each morning and stayed with you long into the evening.

How do you react to light? Does sunshine make you feel happy? Do your days seem to go better when they're bright and sunny? Do you feel despondent on cloudy days and worse after a series of gray, rainy days? Are you dreading the upcoming months of darkness that lie ahead of you in the late fall and early winter, especially when you know that soon you'll be forced out of bed for work in the morning while it's still dark, and return at night to a dark house?

Today, get into the habit of spending at least a half hour a day outdoors in natural daylight, even on cloudy days or when you don't feel like it. If rain forces you indoors, work, read, or watch television near a window. Use light as your natural mood elevator.

To lift my mood, I make it a goal to get outside for a few minutes every day.

"A nature lover is a person who, when treed by a bear, enjoys the view."
—ANONYMOUS

LOVING NATURE

How do you define a nature lover? Is a nature lover someone who jumps out of bed bright and early on a weekend morning to creep around the woods, binoculars in hand, while identifying every bird seen and every birdcall heard? Is a nature lover a perfect emulator of Henry David Thoreau, someone who has spent most of the summer "out there" in the wilderness camping and whose goal in life is to be able to live year-round in the woods with no electricity and no plumbing? Is a nature lover someone who constantly canvasses the neighborhood, gathering signatures on a variety of petitions that protect the rights of animals and who is captured on camera for the evening news flinging red paint at women who are wearing coats made from animal furs?

Too often you may equate being a nature lover with being a bit "nutty"—needing to live, eat, and breathe nature almost to an obsession in order to qualify as someone who truly cares for and appreciates it. Yet loving nature can be as simple as enjoying the feelings nature brings you. When you allow yourself, for even a short time, to be a part of the quiet world of nature—perhaps by looking up at the autumn night sky when you're putting out the trash or maybe by watching a squirrel make its crazy, circular ascent of a tree, an acorn in its mouth, on your way to work—your heart can be filled with a joy that's equal to the joy you feel when you're doing something you love or when you're spending time with someone you love. Being a nature lover means enjoying nature and allowing it, from time to time, to become part of your inner self.

I am a nature lover and love nature every day.

"Those to whom the trees, the birds, the wildflowers represent only 'locked-up dollars' have never known or really seen these things."
—AMERICAN NATURE WRITER EDWIN WAY TEALE

PROTECTING NATURE

In 1854, Suquamish leader Chief Seattle delivered a speech to the commissioner of Indian affairs for the Washington Territory. "The Great Chief in Washington sends word that he wishes to buy our land," he began. "We will consider your offer. For we know that if we do not sell, the white man may come with guns and take our land." Then Chief Seattle spoke eloquently and emotionally about what the land meant to "the red man," its sacredness to his people. "This shining water that moves in the streams and rivers is not just water but the blood of our ancestors . . . you must remember that it is sacred and that each ghostly reflection in the clear water of the lakes tells of events and memories in the life of the people. The water's murmur is the voice of my father's father . . . you must remember, and teach your children, that the rivers are our brothers and yours, and you must henceforth give the rivers the kindness you would give any brother."

History has recorded Chief Seattle's words; as well, history has recorded how the white man fell short of living up to the chief's trusting words, words that were based on the promise of protection not only to a people, but also to the nature that the people considered sacred. White man came along and altered the flow of streams, blasted into walls of rocks, burned acres of pasture, and leveled forests; Indians held the land sacred and felt it should in no way be altered, praying instead for rain, for example, rather than diverting a river from its natural course.

Will your appetite for living devour the earth, or will you savor life in ways that protect and preserve it?

I know the beauty of nature and so wish to protect it.

"My mother thought it would make us feel better to know animals had no souls and thus their deaths were not to be taken seriously. But it didn't help and when I think of some of the animals I have known, I wonder. The only really 'soulful' eyes in the world belong to the dog or cat who sits on your lap or at your feet commiserating when you cry."
—AMERICAN COLUMNIST AND WRITER LIZ SMITH

THE IMMORTAL SOULS OF ANIMALS

In the early 1900s, French novelist, critic, poet, and playwright Anatole France wrote a story about a missionary who was shipwrecked on an island. The missionary, whose eyes were nearly swollen shut after his ordeal in the sea, exuberantly baptized the babbling inhabitants of the island in his gratitude for saving his life, not realizing that they were really penguins. The missionary's action caused a great controversy in heaven. So God assembled clerics and doctors for consultation on how to deal with the matter, while St. Augustine participated in a great debate and concluded that the penguins must be sent to hell when they died. The wise St. Catherine of Alexandria was then consulted; she advised granting the penguins an immortal soul, but of a very small size. In the end, however, God turned the penguins into men who would "commit sins they would not have committed as penguins."

More and more, those who study animals and observe their behaviors find that the animals have an intense empathy with man and even other animals outside their species, exhibiting such empathy in ways that suggest they're capable of a deep, soul-felt understanding. They feel concern for an animal or human in trouble even when they can't do anything for it, and thus show man how, in all of creation, faith has been instilled in both man and beast.

I seek to understand the souls of animals.

"All they could see was sky, water, birds, light and confluence. It was the whole morning world."

—AMERICAN WRITER EUDORA WELTY

PERSPECTIVES ON PROBLEM SOLVING

While on a business trip or vacation, have you ever become lost in a new city or felt overwhelmed while trying to negotiate the complexity of such congested areas? When you're surrounded by tall buildings, jostled about on crowded sidewalks while attempting to read a street map, or more and more confused dealing with one-way streets and traffic rotaries, the city may seem like an endless maze, an area of haphazard building construction and placement.

Yet if you were to view an aerial photograph of the same city, what you'd see would be an impressive display of orderliness and forethought in planning. Suddenly there are no confusing twists and turns but neat blocks; the placement of buildings makes perfect sense.

When you feel similarly lost in your life or muddled by a particular circumstance, viewing things from a different perspective can help you feel that your life is in order and that any troubling puzzle or problem can be resolved. American writer Joyce Carol Oates suggests that instead of looking at the human world around you, look instead at the natural world above you. "Contemplate the sky," she suggests, "it's there to be contemplated. A mild shock to see it so blank, blue, a thin airy ghostly blue, no clouds to disguise its emptiness."

When you, too, can view your life, your home, yourself, and your circumstances from a distance, you can see the boundlessness rather than the limitations, the new rather than the old, the way out rather than no way at all.

I remember that a view from outside me can clear my head.

"There was a time in our culture, not long ago, when the essential role of men and women was to nurture and protect each other, to be the caretakers of life and earth."
—JOAN MCINTYRE, FOUNDER OF PROJECT JONAH, TO STOP THE SLAUGHTER OF WHALES

A STRONG FAMILY COMMUNITY

A little over one hundred years ago, a small band of Italians left Roseto Val Fortore, a village in the foothills of the Apennines, and journeyed to America. They longed to achieve a better life in Pennsylvania; they named their village Roseto and recreated the strong community of their Italian heritage.

Most of the residents of Roseto lived in three-generational households. They centered their lives around family. They even built their houses so close together that neighbors could easily chat with one another as they sat on rocking chairs on their front porches.

In the 1960s, with interest level high in communal-style living, researchers who studied the close-knit community of generations realized that while Roseto shared the same water supply and many other services with nearby communities, the town had only 40 percent as many deaths from heart attacks. "At first," Judy Foreman writes in her article on Roseto, "researchers thought the Rosetans might carry some special, protective genes. But this was not the case, for Rosetans who moved away—even to the nearby village of Bangor—lost whatever magic the town possessed against heart disease."

The seeming anomaly was dubbed the "Roseto Effect," but the "magic" was simple: by maintaining close, strong family ties; by passing down family traditions from generation to generation; and by living in an atmosphere of familial and familiar love, support, and acceptance, the people lived longer, healthier lives.

I create a close-knit family community.

"Given the proper incentive, no mountain, it seems, is too high to climb, no current too swift to swim."

—NATIVE AMERICAN WRITER GRACE STEELE WOODWARD

PERSEVERANCE

To get the most out of life, you need to put effort into it. You've probably heard that advice stated in a variety of ways before; what it all boils down to is, you don't get something for nothing. In order to attain what you want, you have to expend energy, not just in one or two efforts but repeatedly.

Nature teaches you that such perseverance has its rewards, but only if you're willing and able to give a full, complete effort. Take, for example, the food-gathering habits of a particular population of crows that nests on an island near the coast of British Columbia. The crows gather whelks at low tide and then drop them in particularly rocky areas to break the shell. But since only about one in four drops breaks the shell right away, many shells have to be picked up and dropped over and over again. Unless disturbed during this time, the crows persist in the retrieval-and-drop process until the shell finally breaks; sometimes it takes as many as twenty drops before the shells crack and the soft parts can be eaten.

How many times have you exhibited similar perseverance in your life, choosing to do something over and over again until you finally earned your anticipated reward? Never giving up, despite the odds or obstacles, is not only a test of belief in yourself and what you can do, but also a sign of how you approach life. It may be far easier to give up after one, two, or only a few tries. But such an action can shape the attitude you then bring into every situation of your life—an attitude that can spell the difference between success and defeat.

I persevere until I succeed.

"At sea nothing happens to the sea. Nothing happens to the sky. The sun comes up from the east and goes down to the west. The moon grows from a sickle to an arc lamp, and comes later and later until she is lost in the light as other things are lost in the darkness. After the typhoon, the flying-fish glitter in the sunshine like birds. It's amazing how they get along, all things considered."

—ENGLISH PLAYWRIGHT AND CRITIC GEORGE BERNARD SHAW

MAKING AN IMPACT

Do you often begin your day by asking yourself, "What impact can I make today?" Certainly this is a legitimate and important question to pose; making an impact is important. Unless you make an impact, you don't get noticed. If you don't get noticed, you don't earn rewards. If you don't earn rewards, you don't get to attain and maintain your lifestyle. So you must make an impact today.

But does your quest for your daily impact always have to be driven by dollar signs and material achievements? Can't it also be driven by a quest for new experiences—experiences that educate, broaden horizons, allow meaningful escape from the "rat race," heal mind, body, and soul, and enrapture through the enjoyment of nature?

Rather than begining today questioning what impact you can make on the world, why not ask, "What impact can I let the world make on me?" What new experience would you like to enjoy today? Whether your choice of new experience involves something as elaborate as a sail-around-the-world adventure, as rugged as a weeklong hike along the Appalachian Trail, as mind expanding as learning about an ocean creature, or as pampering as a retreat to a spa, let the experience make an impact on your personal enjoyment of life.

I seek fulfillment from a natural life experience.

"The flow of the river is ceaseless and its water is never the same."
—JAPANESE WRITER AND BUDDHIST HERMIT KAMO NO CHOMEI

GOING WITH THE FLOW

Have you ever tried to swim against a current or undertow? Even if the safety of shore is only yards away, the force of the current or undertow may be so strong that even an Olympic swimmer couldn't overcome the tremendous pull of the water. In such a case, the best plan of action is to relax and go with the flow of the current; you'll gradually be able to ease your way to shore, even if you're some distance from where you really want to be.

Have you ever watched a bird in flight on a windy day? At first, it struggles to maintain its desired course as it's buffeted around in the sky. But then the bird smoothly glides a bit higher and tries to regain its course, hoping to discover a favorable air current or a decrease in wind velocity that will enable it to fly in the desired direction.

Do you go through each day as willing and capable of altering your travel on the "river of life" when the course you'd like to follow isn't always available, may not be easy to travel upon, or isn't flowing at the pace you'd like? Today, use the words "go with the flow" as a reminder to stop struggling against the current of life when it's not what you want it to be. Some things are going to happen that will be totally out of your control. Try to force changes in people, places, or things, and soon your energy will be depleted and your peace of mind disrupted. So resolve to go with the flow. Accept circumstances—both in yourself and in others—without trying to force an outcome or get your way. Relax, take a deep breath, and simply go where life takes you today.

I accept today's pace and go with the flow of my life.

"Whom shall one take with him when he goes a-courting Nature? That is always a vital question. There are persons who will stand between you and that which you seek: they obtrude themselves; they monopolize your attention; they blunt your sense of the shy, half-revealed intelligences about you. I want for companion a dog or a boy, or a person who has the virtues of dogs and boys,—transparency, good-nature, curiosity, open sense, and a nameless quality that is akin to trees and growths and the inarticulate forces of nature."

—AMERICAN WRITER AND NATURALIST JOHN BURROUGHS

FRIENDSHIPS

Imagine what the natural world would be like if members of different species were "friends" with one another. You might see a raccoon and a deer sampling tree bark together, a puma and a wolf racing each other, a bear and a moose chatting by the river's edge, a rabbit taking a chipmunk on a tour of its home. But such friendly gestures would be based on commonalities the different species share with one another. What would happen when the raccoon wanted the deer's help in building a dam, when the puma wanted to race the wolf up a tree, when the bear wanted some food the moose didn't want to share, or when the chipmunk wanted to invite the rabbit to tour its own home?

Some people are your friends because you share many things in common—childhood experiences, educational background, hobbies, sports, and so on. Some people are your friends because they share one particular interest with you—employment at the same company, for instance. And some people are your friends because they're different from you, and, through these differences, enrich your life.

Choose your friends wisely, put the effort into strengthening friendships that are meaningful to you, and be a good friend yourself.

I value the friendships that add value to my life.

"The natural world is dynamic. From the expanding universe to the hair on a baby's head, nothing is the same from now to the next moment."
—AMERICAN WRITER AND NATURALIST HELEN HOOVER

A WORLD OF CHANGE

The biggest change Helen Hoover (1910–1984) and her artist husband Adrian made in their lives was their renunciation of city life in 1954 and move to a cabin on a Minnesota lake forty-five miles from town on a one-way road, where they spent their first nine years without a car. They were often considered "genuine" pioneers because they so appreciated the natural beauty around them that "When Ade and I had the opportunity of receiving electric power and telephone service at the cost of felling a swath through our old trees, we decided in favor of the trees."

Helen wrote about their wild life in the North Woods, chronicling their progress from greenhorns to seasoned woodspeople in a series of books that her husband illustrated. Each book detailed "worlds of changes" they experienced together, such as one that occurred one winter when Walter the weasel came to beg food of them. "Gradually we gained mutual confidence," Helen wrote, "until he took meat from my bare hand with care and daintiness." From that point on, Helen observed Walter as he relocated from the deep woods onto their property, creating storehouses and shelters under stumps, outbuildings, boulders, and brush piles near their cabin. When Walter's life became filled with deadly peril because his larger cousin and archenemy, the fisher, tried to take his claim from him, the wounded Walter held firm to his territory, healing his wounds and expertly hiding from the fisher until he left. Walter and a life in the wild woods taught Helen and her husband that in nature all is flux; nothing stays still.

I welcome the changes in my life, symbols of the changes in nature's wildness.

"Your feet shall be as swift as forked lightning; your arm shall be as the thunderbolt, and your soul fearless."

—CHEROKEE INDIAN METHOATASKE

WILDERNESS SURVIVAL

Do you have faith in yourself that, if you had to, you could survive "out in the wild" for a period of time? There have certainly been many incredible stories about human survival in the wild—people have clung to buoys in stormy seas for several hours after their boat capsized, others survived plane crashes in remote areas and lived for long periods of time prior to being rescued, hikers have become lost and disoriented in the woods and ended up being found safe and sound days—and subzero temperatures and blizzards—later.

Sometimes people have purposely placed themselves in dangerous survival situations by scaling mountains, diving deep into oceans, crossing deserts, voyaging to remote islands, and rocketing into outer space. Pole expedition leader Sir Ernest Shackleton quickly formed the group that accompanied him in his tortuous foray into the frigid elements with the following notice: "Men wanted for hazardous journey, small wages, bitter cold, darkness—constant danger, safe return doubtful—honor and recognition in case of success."

For years, humankind has endured and survived incredible things; for years humankind has accepted dangerous missions and outings involving great risks that tested the limits of human endurance. Do you trust that you could survive as well as others have if you were thrust into a situation where you would be called upon to test your limits, your strength, your endurance, your knowledge, and your courage in handling the challenges of the wilderness?

I trust my capabilities, my strengths, and my stamina.

"Animals were once, for all of us, teachers. They instructed us in ways of being and perceiving that extended our imaginations, that were models for additional possibilities."

—AMERICAN WRITER AND WHALE EXPERT JOAN MCINTYRE

MODEL ZOOS

How do animals act and why? While much has been written about animal behavior, the best instructors in such behaviors are the animals themselves. But since living out in the wild for years in order to establish a trusting relationship for such observation is unlikely, the best option available to you and your family members is a zoo or aquarium that has earned an accreditation from the American Association of Zoological Parks and Aquariums (AAZPA), which recognizes those zoos that most nearly replicate animals' natural habitat and resources and strictly enforce humane practices.

An AAZPA-approved zoo might provide its beavers with aspen branches; you can then see the zoo beavers work furiously to build a lodge. Video cameras might be set up in dens dug by foxes, offering a fascinating glimpse into domestic life that's impossible to see in the wild. Raised walkways might allow you to peer into the construction of a bird's nest in the aviary. Posts might be provided in exhibits so zebras can rub their hides and lions and tigers can rake their claws. Feeding techniques that capitalize on the different ways animals satisfy their hunger in the wild might afford a firsthand glimpse of things you've only read about—a bear digging out honey from a "hive" in a log, chimps fishing out food stuffed into "termite mounds" with sticks, wild cats hauling down "live prey" in the form of meat suspended from a string.

I write to the Humane Society, 2100 L Street NW, Washington, DC 20037, to find out what zoos near me are receiving high marks.

"The goal of life is living in agreement with Nature."
—GREEK STOIC PHILOSOPHER ZENO

BENEFICIAL GOAL SETTING

Which do you think is worse: not reaching a goal that you've worked hard to attain, or not having any goal to reach? You might think that having no goals is better than falling short of a desired goal; without the need to reach a goal, you won't feel the stress or pressure to succeed and you certainly won't fail. Too, you may think that American society is far too goal-oriented, so having no goals will let you enjoy life more and remove the constant need to compete with yourself and others.

But what exactly is a goal? A goal is simply a change you wish to bring about in any area of your life so you can improve its overall quality. Most goals begin with a desire that springs from a dream: a vision of how you could be, how things could be, or how you could be in tandem with the things in your life. So why not begin today to live in agreement with nature—to take time to seek the natural elements in your everyday life, to strengthen your relationship with nature, and to think about the valuable lessons nature can teach you.

Writer Benjamin E. Mays once opined, "It must be borne in mind that the tragedy of life doesn't lie in not reaching your goal. The tragedy lies in having no goal to reach. It isn't a calamity to die with dreams unfulfilled, but it is a calamity not to dream. It is not a disgrace not to reach the stars, but it is a disgrace to have no stars to reach for." So what's worse is to have nothing to look forward to, nothing to strive for, nothing to reach, nothing to attain. Life is much more interesting when you can create new visions of what your life can be like and what you can be like when you achieve a goal.

I envision a better life through a goal of natural living.

"When, as a very small child, I was playing with a horsetail that had been growing as a weed in one of our flower-beds, dismantling it section by section like a constructional toy, I remember how my father told me it was one of the oldest plants on earth, and I experienced a curious confusion of time. I was holding the oldest plant in my hand, and so I, too, was old."
—ENGLISH ARCHAEOLOGIST AND WRITER JACQUETTA HAWKES

GROWING YOUNGER

There's no secret of youth more powerful than that of learning. You're only as old as the information that swirls through you; new knowledge, new skills, and new ways of looking at the world can keep the mind as well as the body fresh and vibrant, full of life.

Greek philosopher and moralist Diogenes Laertius once advised, "Let no one be slow to seek wisdom when he is young nor weary of the search thereof when he is grown old. For no age is too early or too late for the health of the soul." Go out into nature, and you'll enter a world that has ancient teachings to impart as well as fresh new ideas to share. In the heart of Manhattan, for instance, you can see that workmen who are drilling into the ground for new construction are invading rock that's two billion years old. "Look at it as it crops out here and there in Central Park," urged American naturalist and explorer William Beebe, "quiet, gray, patient. . . ." Or go to any beach and recall the words of American biologist and writer Rachel Carson, who observed that "When we go down to the low-tide line, we enter a world that is as old as the earth itself . . . [an] endlessly varied stream of living things that has surged through time and space to occupy the earth." What in youth you merely enjoyed in your interactions with nature, in age you can learn from and better understand in ways that'll keep you young, appreciative, and lively.

The fountain of youth is ever-growing knowledge of the natural world.

> *"Sometimes I go about in pity for myself, and all the while*
> *A great wind is bearing me across the sky."*
>
> —OJIBWA SAYING

ELIMINATING SELF-PITY

There's a story told about a visitor from the West who traveled a great distance to the East to consult with a wise Zen master about her inability to feel good about herself and her life. When the Master greeted her, she immediately began to talk about her life. The Master silently prepared and poured tea for himself as the woman rambled on and on. Then the Master began to pour tea for the woman. The woman held out her cup and continued to talk as the Master poured. Then she gasped and suddenly stopped her monologue in mid-sentence. For the Master had already filled her cup but was continuing to pour the tea, which was now overflowing the cup and spilling out onto the floor.

"Stop!" the woman shouted, but the Master continued to pour.

"Why do you continue to pour after the cup is full?" she demanded.

The Master then stopped pouring the tea. "To show you," he replied, "that you are like this cup: so full of yourself, so full of the things that do not work out for you, and so full of all the minutiae of your life that nothing can go into you—the cup—in the present. You cannot experience true happiness until you have emptied your cup."

Think of how much good and fulfillment you could have in the present if you could only let go of self-pity. What's past is past, what's done is done, what's over is over. It's that simple. But there's so much more that's yet to come.

I see my journey in life as one in which emptiness is fulfilled rather than filled.

> "The purpose of a fish trap is to catch
> fish, and when the fish are caught,
> the trap is forgotten.
> The purpose of a rabbit snare is to
> catch rabbits. When the rabbits are
> caught, the snare is forgotten."
>
> —TAOIST WRITER CHUANG-TZU

UNFAIR FASHION

Centuries ago, people coveted the loose, feathery plumes of the ostrich. The symmetrical plumes were once considered a symbol of justice in Egypt. Romans used the feathers for the "Mohawk" decoration on the helmets of soldiers. Tribal Africans used ostrich feathers in their ceremonial costumes.

But it was the use of ostrich feathers in plumed hats, first worn by fashionable European women in the 1500s, that eventually resulted in the greatest destruction to the ostrich population. For when American fashion designers resurrected plumed-hat fashion in the 1800s, ostrich plumes became South Africa's fourth largest export, after gold, diamonds, and wool.

Then the market for ostrich feathers plummeted in 1914, when open-topped automobiles came into vogue and top speeds of nearly twenty miles per hour lifted the feathers airborne for the first time—for ostrich are flightless birds. Tight-fitting bonnets then became all the rage, but the damage had already been done. Ostrich had been hunted to extinction in former habitats in Asia and the Middle East; destruction of their habitats continued to limit the number living in the wild to fewer than 200,000 in the entire world.

Today, only five of the nine original ostrich species still exist. And feathers are still provided to the fashion industry from African ostrich that are bred on ranches in Africa and the United States.

I refrain from wearing fashion that uses animal parts.

"We were taught to believe that the Great Spirit sees and hears everything, and that he never forgets; that hereafter he will give every man a spirit-home according to his deserts. . . . This I believe, and all my people believe the same."

—NEZ PERCÉ CHIEF HINMATON YALATKIT

RETURNING TO NATURE

Four people who had died on Earth stood at the gate to the Great Spirit's heaven. The first person, a former CEO of a manufacturing corporation, was asked by the Gate Angel, "And how did you notice nature while you were on earth?" The person answered, "Well, I discovered that oceans are deep and can hide radioactive materials. But then a lot of money must be spent on cleanup." The Gate Angel replied, "Good. You may enter." The next person stepped forward. "And how did you notice nature while you were on earth?" asked the angel. The person answered, "I operated an exotic pet business, selling captured creatures for great sums of money, until I was caught. I lost my business, but paid my debt by working in an animal shelter." The Gate Angel replied, "Good. You may enter." The third person stepped forward. "And how did you notice nature while you were on earth?" asked the angel. "I set the woods on fire during a hot summer," the person began, "and destroyed hundreds of acres of trees, then worked in the gardens at a minimum-security prison." The Gate Angel replied, "Good. You may enter."

Then fourth person stepped forward. "How can you let such people into heaven? I've done nothing to nature—I haven't sailed the seas or heard the cry of an exotic bird or set foot in a forest. I'm more deserving of a place in heaven."

"Not so," replied the Gate Angel. "Heaven is for those who return to nature, not those who desert nature as you did in your time on earth."

I return to nature through nature's open door.

"Human beings are set apart from the animals. We have a spiritual self, a physical self and a conscience. Therefore, we can make choices and are responsible for the choices we make. We may choose order and peace, or confusion and chaos."

—CIVIL RIGHTS ACTIVIST ROSA PARKS

SAFEGUARDING FREEDOM

Rosa Parks was born in the South, fifty years after slavery, at a time when racial segregation was legally enforced. Her grandparents told her what it was like to be brought up as slave children; she knew firsthand of Ku Klux Klan activity in her own community. Her parents and community raised her to always feel pride in herself, so she grew up determined to achieve the total freedom her grandparents and parents never really had—the freedom that was taught to her in history books, that was earned no matter what the sacrifice.

So when Rosa Parks refused to give up her seat on a city bus for a white person—when she stubbornly resisted being forced to the back of the bus with the other "colored people," she was standing up for her own freedom to choose. Yet her one simple, personal act helped to change the world for all African Americans; her struggle for her own freedom sparked others to struggle for theirs.

Rosa Parks once said, "To this day I believe we are here on earth to live, grow up and do what we can to make this world a better place for all people to enjoy freedom." The Reverend Jesse Jackson, president and founder of the National Rainbow Coalition, believes these freedoms today are bound to lie in environmental issues, for, he asks, "What is democracy, after all, if your air is too polluted to breathe? . . . We must now extend the right to breathe free to every nation and every individual, for the right to breathe free is the most basic human right of all."

I safeguard my freedom and the freedom of future generations.

"Perhaps middle age is, or should be, a period of shedding shells; the shell of ambition, the shell of material accumulations and possessions, the shell of the ego."

—AMERICAN POET, ESSAYIST, AND WRITER
ANNE MORROW LINDBERGH

MIDLIFE "MISSION"

American comedian Steven Wright, whose skewed vision of the world is both comically shrewd and absurd, once remarked, "I have a seashell collection; maybe you've seen it? I keep it scattered on beaches all over the world." To be able to possess something so large as a worldwide seashell collection—to have the most, more than anyone else—is the dream of youth. "When I grow up," the fantasy always begins, "I'm going to own the biggest house and the fastest cars and make more money than anyone else." Role models are millionaires from sports, music, movies, television. Rarely does a child dream of saving rain forests or making a lake swimmable; money-strapped activists, farmers, humanitarians, and naturalists are not likely candidates for role models.

But when you reach middle age, oftentimes those things that once seemed unimportant to you or had no significance in your life suddenly become all-important, profoundly meaningful. The fact that you can't take your child to the fishing hole your father once took you to because a suburban development now sits on top of it, the litter and broken glass that have become more than just an irritating eyesore in the woods where you like to walk but also a hazard to wildlife and pets, and the noxious fumes that clog your brain as you ride your bicycle through a city park next to bumper-to-bumper traffic may give you the impetus now to refocus your time, energy, and passion to new "midlife missions" that are more important, more vital, and more meaningful to your life and the lives of others.

I embark on a new midlife mission.

"A beaver does not, as legend would have it, know which direction the tree will fall when he cuts it, but counts on alacrity to make up for lack of engineering expertise."

—AMERICAN NATURE WRITER ANN ZWINGER

ZEST FOR LIFE

The beaver—the largest North American rodent—is a nocturnal animal that makes its home either by burrowing into a bank or, more commonly, by building an elaborate mud-and-stick lodge with a dam that regulates water level. With its sharp, chisellike incisors, the beaver can cut through a five-inch tree in three minutes. Researchers have often attributed evidence of thinking to beavers, known for being efficient engineers, for the animals could scarcely accomplish what they do without some awareness of the likely results of their activities, as seen in the way they inspect the dam on a daily basis to ensure that water level is maintained. When holes appear in their dams, the beavers immediately set to work plugging them with sticks and twigs that have been whittled down in such a way that they exactly fit the holes. Too, beavers have been able to surmount obstacles such as cylindrical fences—firmly anchored in the ground around trees and wired to branches above their reach—by piling a pyramid of branches and mud around the tree and then climbing up the pile to reach the unprotected trunk, which they then cut in their usual fashion.

And yet beavers are by no means perfectly efficient. They cut some trees halfway through and then abandon them. Others lean against neighboring trees as they begin to fall, and the beavers don't realize that cutting the supporting tree would yield double their supply. But they're enthusiastic creatures that demonstrate a spectacular zest for living.

I am as eager as a beaver in all the things I do.

"The glorious sun,—the centre and soul of our system,—the lamp that lights it—the fire that heats it,—the magnet that guides and controls it;— the fountain of color, which gives its azure to the sky, its verdure to the fields, its rainbow-hues to the gay world of flowers, and the purple light of love to the marble cheek of youth and beauty."
—SCOTTISH PHYSICIST SIR DAVID BREWSTER

A SUNNY VISUALIZATION

The reward for every morning of your life is the sun. Even though today may be cloudy, rainy, or snowy, daylight still greets you because the sun has once again appeared on your horizon. So no matter what activities lie ahead of you or what weather greets you, you can still start your day with a sunny disposition.

To do this, set aside a few minutes, before you rush out of the house or rouse still-slumbering children, to close your eyes and visualize walking down a pleasant, nature-filled path. Each step you take moves you closer to the warmth and brightness of the sun. Look around you as you walk. Breathe deeply. See lakes and mountains and hear the soothing sounds of a babbling brook; watch the rise and fall of gentle ocean waves that reflect a glorious sunrise; breathe deeply of the humid air in a tropical rain forest while being serenaded by an orchestra of jungle sounds. In the inner sanctuary you create in your mind, nothing is important—nothing except peace of mind and the hours ahead in which you can keep your mind filled with the warmth and light of the sun.

As you reach the end of your morning "nature walk," your body may feel as if it's filled with pleasant tingles. Your lips may be turned upward in a gentle smile. Now expand your lungs with a cleansing, deep breath. Say, "I appreciate this new day I've been given and will take something good from it." Then begin your day.

I begin my day warmed by the rays of inner sunshine.

"This brings rest to my heart. I feel like a leaf after a storm, when the wind is still."

—CHEROKEE INDIAN PETALASHARO

RESTORING HARMONY

What happens when the harmony of your world is disrupted? Imagine your life to be a still pond; suddenly a rock is tossed into the pond. Ripples extend out from the rock's point of entry, disturbing the surface of the water; over time, the pond's stillness will be restored.

So, too, it can be in your life. You may go along with the flow—the routines, the familiar people, the set way of doing things—when suddenly a "rock" is thrown into your still pond: your company begins a series of layoffs, new and noisy neighbors move next door, a parent suddenly falls ill and needs your care, your partner expresses dissatisfaction with the relationship, you become injured in an accident, you face an important career decision, an unexpected bill forces you to make some tough financial decisions. Because the harmony of your life has been disrupted, you may want to do something quickly to restore its balance. But quick reactions rather than well-thought-out actions not only affect that particular moment, but also on all the moments thereafter. So it's important first to bring your mind to stillness and restore harmony in your life before you take action or make any decisions.

American poet and philosopher George Santayana wrote, "In the concert of nature it is hard to keep in tune with oneself if one is out of tune with everything else." You must first still the ripples on the pond of your mind. Before doing anything, carefully consider not only the changes that are affecting your life, but also how each possible action will affect you, too.

I seek to restore harmony by taking the right actions.

"Perhaps nature is our best assurance of immortality."
—FIRST LADY AND WRITER ELEANOR ROOSEVELT

THE NATURE OF IMMORTALITY

To be able to live forever has, for centuries, sparked fruitless explorations, encouraged endless scientific experimentations, created a wide array of medicinal and cosmetic preparations, and inspired searches for countless other remedies, formulas, and regimens—all because living forever simply is not enough. Rather, the desire for immortality goes hand in hand with the desire for eternal youth, for what good is being able to live forever unless you can be physically active and mentally alert?

Today, it's not uncommon for people to live well into their seventies, eighties, and nineties in good health, with a sound mind and body. Over-sixty runners compete in marathons and race past runners who are far younger. Seniors participate in travel expeditions that provide them with unique physical challenges. Retirees sell their houses and set off in mobile homes to see the country's national parks and natural treasures. And retirement communities with the longest waiting lists boast of climates that encourage year-round participation in outdoor activities such as golf, mountain hiking, canoeing, and so on.

What those who live long, rewarding lives today have in common is their desire to get outdoors and stay outside in fresh air, sunshine, and beautiful surroundings, exercising their bodies and, in so doing, stimulating their minds and spirits. As Scottish-born American naturalist John Muir once commented, "Talk of immortality! After a whole day in the woods, we are already immortal. When is the end of such a day?"

I live a long life through my love of nature.

"If we do not go to church as much as did our fathers, we go to the woods much more, and are more inclined to make a temple of them than they were."

—AMERICAN WRITER AND NATURALIST JOHN BURROUGHS

NATURE'S TEMPLES

As homesteaders settled across the American West, one of the most prized possessions in every household was the Bible; in fact, it was often the book used to teach children to read and the one consulted when hard times hit. Too, one of the first buildings erected in nearly every community, after family homes and barns, was the church—a sanctuary where pioneer families could retreat from their daily hardships and regain their inner peace, a place where they could feel accepted and connected, a space where joyous and inspirational hymns could fill their hearts, a room in which they could feel closer to God.

Today, going to church may be a rarity for you—limited to religious celebrations and funerals—or may be part of the countless things you need to do in a week. Church may no longer be a place where you restore your inner energy, strengthen your trust and faith, or meet your spiritual needs; rather, such things may come to you during time you spend outdoors. An early-morning run that allows you the opportunity to glimpse the fading moon and stars as the sky gradually comes to light and life, a walk with your dog across a frost-covered field on a crisp morning, or weekends spent hiking through the woods may do more to restore your spiritual connection and help you regain your sense of inner peace than the most inspiring sermon, the most glorious hymn, or the most familiar religious ritual.

I worship in my heart and soul wherever I am.

"The multiple threats to the Earth are so complex that in most cases they seem beyond the reach of an average citizen's influence. Yet we can all launch a personal campaign to reduce consumption—though perhaps only after a change of mind-set, to overcome the fear of seeming poor, parsimonious or eccentric. This does not mean being deprived or uncomfortable. It simply means stopping to think, before each purchase, 'Do I really need this?'"

—IRISH AUTHOR AND ROUND-THE-WORLD BICYCLIST
DERVLA MURPHY

TAKING ACTION

For years, a small majority of people in America have been living and thinking in ways that prevent continued destruction of the planet. Through peaceful campaigns and protests, they've raised awareness about inhumane practices, encouraged more conservative consumption of natural resources, and offered viable alternatives for ways of living on the planet without diminishing comfort. Without such people, the environmental plight of the planet, the extinction and near-extinction of vital species, many devious and dangerous practices of businesses, corporation-supportive and consumer-insensitive congressional legislation, and inhumanities toward living creatures would never have been brought to light.

Now it's time for you to become a member of this small but ever-growing minority, not because you ought to, or because it's the right thing to do, or because environmental causes have become trendy, but so you don't continue to contribute on a daily basis to the destruction of the planet. Today, when a store clerk asks if you want paper or plastic—or, as one cartoon caption joked, "Choke a fish or kill a tree?"—refuse both and either carry your purchase unbagged or bring your own bags. It's time now to consider "Do I really need this?" in all that you do.

I show respect and attention to my planet in my actions.

> *"I live in the countryside of Skåne. . . . Crucial to this little paradise are the cows, who keep the meadows open by their grazing and provide the milk for farmers with no more than 100 to 200 acres of land. These cows are soon to disappear. Parliament has decided to slaughter 140,000 milking cows and divert 1 million acres of grain land to pinewood plantations."*
> —PER GAHRTON, MEMBER OF THE SWEDISH PARLIAMENT FOR THE GREEN PARTY

SCIENCE VERSUS NATURE

When a Swedish professor of molecular biology reported that cows are very inefficent "machines" that convert "a mere 0.004 percent of the solar energy they receive," Per Gahrton suggested, "So mankind really might circumvent nature altogether, living without cows . . . able to construct more efficient machines that can be fed with energy, water, carbon dioxide, nitrogen, and minerals, and deliver milk at the other end." The prospect, he determined, made him "mad with fear."

What things similarly make you mad with fear? Do you feel that you're the last romantic who yearns for the changing seasons? Do you wonder where the whiteness of the snow has gone? Are you concerned about the loss of forests, once full of birds? Do you often ask, "Where are the placid landscapes of my youth? Where are the flowers I used to gather near streams when I was a child?"

Despite scientific research that suggests otherwise, all things are necessary and vital in nature. Circumventing nature in ways that destroy it or that attempt inappropriate substitutes that disrupt natural harmony and destroy livelihoods isn't a sound solution. The "inefficient" black-and-white lowland cows on the meadows represent just one of the many critical refuges from industry's ultimate conquest over nature.

I protest any industry that impacts negatively on farmers and other small-business owners.

"As long as I retain my feeling and my passion for Nature, I can partly soften or subdue my other passions and resist or endure those of others."
—ENGLISH POET LORD BYRON

SOOTHING ANGER

Sometimes anger may be your first and only response to frustrating, trying, and disappointing times. Unfortunately, acting upon that anger without thinking—hastily saying things you may later regret, making shortsighted decisions that aren't what you really want, or slamming a door in someone's face—may do considerable damage. Sometimes a slammed door can't be opened again. Sometimes those you insult or snap at back off for much longer than you'd like. Sometimes a decision made in anger can't be undone—or may take considerable time and effort to undo. Sometimes you saw off the very limb on which you find yourself sitting.

Angry feelings don't always have to erupt in fiery volcanoes or even need to be expressed. More often than not, because much of your anger may result from situations you feel are out of your control or during times when you feel that you're out of control, your anger simply needs to be soothed. Discover effective ways to soothe your own anger, and you'll not only be able to avoid shameful, regretful results, but also develop greater self-respect, restraint, and inner strength.

The next time you're angry, why not go for a run through the woods, hike up a hill and sit quietly as you take in the view, or skip rocks on a pond. Let nature help you settle your anger and cool your temper so you'll be better able to step away from anger-producing situations and achieve a valuable, calming perspective.

I take the time to smooth my ruffled feathers.

". . . [Nature] is the one place where miracles not only happen, but happen all the time."

—AMERICAN NOVELIST THOMAS WOLFE

NATURE'S MIRACLES

Sometimes you may think that many of the inventions created by the human mind and imagination are miraculous—every day, airplanes fly thousands of people to cities around the world, traveling hundreds of miles in short periods of time; vaccines have effectively wiped out the threat of some terrible diseases, such as smallpox and tuberculosis; computers have evolved from massive receptacles for information storage to laptops that assimilate and exchange an amazing amount of information as well as talk to you and play games with you.

But as amazing as such creations are, remember that the natural world knew about flight long before man took to the skies, and that people will never be able to fly without external equipment and an external source of power. For aeons, animals have been successfully caring for and healing themselves; they can't, and don't need to, dial 911 in case of medical emergency. And all the knowledge that's stored within a computer must be accessed to be learned; animal babies know, almost from birth, what things are edible and what will kill them, which animals to fear, how to hunt and to fly, where and how to build a shelter, how to locate water, and how to care for their own young.

I see nature's miracles as being as wondrous as the miracles in the human world.

"Monotony is the law of nature. Look at the monotonous manner in which the sun rises."

—POLITICAL LEADER MAHATMA GANDHI

TRUSTING THE DARKNESS

Have you ever been startled out of a sound sleep in the middle of the night? Maybe you had a bad dream. Perhaps the cat knocked something over or the dog began to bark. Maybe a loud storm roused you. Or perhaps a problem invaded your subconscious thoughts and brought you to wakeful consciousness.

Whatever the reason, being wrenched out of a peaceful slumber can make you feel anxious and frightened. The fact that you're enveloped by darkness may not help either. "If only it was daylight!" you might say. "In the light of day, things always seem better." You may get up, make yourself a cup of tea, and read a book or watch television until you see the first light of dawn and hear the birds singing their gentle morning song. Then, and only then, do you feel at peace, calmed by the realization that nighttime is over, darkness is lifting, and the light of day will soon restore your feeling of safety and security in the world.

You may sometimes see your life as a similar movement between trust and fear, light and darkness. You may have been more trusting in the past than you are now. You may have felt more relaxed because the things you took for granted were always there—and now they aren't. You may have felt stronger, more sure of yourself and your place in the world; now you may feel confused.

One thing you can be sure of, however, is that the world, according to Roman scholar Pliny the Elder, "eternally revolves with indescribable velocity; each revolution occupying the space of twenty-four hours: the rising and setting of the sun have left this not doubtful." Trust that out of darkness will always come light.

The more I trust myself and my life, the more I can trust life.

"I am poor and naked, but I am chief of the nation. We do not want riches but we do want to train our children right. Riches would do us no good. We could not take them with us to the other world. We do not want riches. We want peace and love."

—19TH-CENTURY SIOUX CHIEF RED CLOUD

A TRUE THANKSGIVING

As you look forward to your upcoming Thanksgiving meal, to the friends and family who may be spending the day with you, and to time away from work, school, and other obligations, are you also thinking about the people who will experience Thanksgiving Day without a bountiful homecooked feast to quiet their rumbling stomachs, without friends and family with whom to share in the closeness of the day, and without a place to go in their hearts that doesn't feel spiritually empty?

There are many older people who live alone or in private-care facilities as well as homeless individuals whose Thanksgivings will be far less physically, emotionally, and spiritually fulfilling than yours. Why not extend the holiday to them? Gather the family together in a true spirit of thanksgiving and have everyone help prepare extra pies and platters of food and then deliver them to shut-ins or donate them to shelters that feed the homeless.

As well, think of the wildlife that may need your help in getting through the upcoming cold months. Hang and fill bird feeders and suet holders. Set aside some piles of brush and leaves for burrowing critters. Install a heater in your birdbath to provide fresh drinking water.

Thanksgiving Day is more than just a time in which you give thanks for all the blessings in your life. As well, it's a time for you to reach out and give to others—humans as well as wildlife.

I nourish my spirit and the spirit of others this Thanksgiving.

"Oh, give me a home where the buffalo roam, where the deer and the antelope play. . . . Where seldom is heard a discouraging word and the skies are not cloudy all day."

—ANONYMOUS

POLITICS OR PRESERVATION?

Siding with environmentalists in one of the nation's biggest wilderness battles, President Clinton, in the fall of 1996 declared 1.7 million acres of southern Utah's red-rock cliffs and canyons a national monument. Standing at the rim of the Grand Canyon, Clinton invoked a ninety-year-old law that allowed him to act without congressional approval to create the Grand Staircase-Escalante National Monument. He announced his decision near the spot where, in 1908, then-President Theodore Roosevelt used the same law to protect the Grand Canyon from development. "We are saying very simply," President Clinton announced, "our parents and grandparents saved the Grand Canyon for us. Today we will save the Grand Escalante Canyons and the Kaiparowits Plateaus of Utah for our children."

Clinton's action delighted environmentalists, who had lobbied hard for the protection of the area's natural arches and bridges, high cliffs of white, red, and yellow sandstone, and deep canyons from coal-mining interests. But not everyone was so enthused; Clinton received threats of political retaliation from the state of Utah, which has never supported a Democrat since Harry Truman. Too, a Dutch mining company that holds coal leases on the now-protected area was forced to cease mining operations and consider options to trade leases in the area for federal assets elsewhere.

But what ought to be more important—preservation of the land, or politics?

I look beyond party politics to actions that protect nature.

"We ought to think that we are one of the leaves of a tree, and the tree is all humanity. We cannot live without the others, without the tree."
—SPANISH VIOLONCELLIST, CONDUCTOR, AND COMPOSER
PABLO CASALS

BUILDING A COMMUNITY

Throughout history, individuals have chosen to live in communities so they could structure their lives according to their beliefs with other like-minded individuals. From St. Francis of Assisi and religious communities of the Middle Ages to Puritan and Quaker settlements; from communes of the 1960s to gay communities in San Francisco, Fire Island, Provincetown, and Key West; to New Age ventures and group collectives that follow a particular religious or political leader; and to retirement and "snowbird" communities, such separatism encourages people to believe that they're better off living with others who share their beliefs or lifestyle.

Yet harmony with humanity—like harmony in nature—means being able to be a separate individual or species as well as to connect with the diversity of many. It's easy to cooperate and to resolve conflicts in peaceful harmony when you're linked with others who think, feel, and act in similar ways. It becomes harder when you're faced with people who think, feel, and act differently.

You can create a community rich in diversity by thinking of friends, family members, and others as different trees in a forest. You each have your own set of needs, ways of growing, and individual appearance, yet you all can live in harmony and nourish and nurture one another despite these differences. Draw together those with whom you share a common bond and also those whose differences can teach you something about them, about yourself, and about the world.

I build a community for comfort as well as for learning.

"The swift is almost continually on the wing; and as it never settles on the ground, on trees, or roofs, would seldom find opportunity for amorous rites, was it not enabled to indulge them in the air."

—ENGLISH CLERGYMAN GILBERT WHITE

LET LOVE TAKE FLIGHT

Do you find that because of the frantic pace of daily living, divergent schedules, unresolved conflicts or resentments, fatigue, or lack of time and privacy you have little time to be amorous with your partner? Perhaps, then, it's time to add some heart-pounding excitement to your love life by learning from the courtship behaviors of America's oldest natural symbol— the bald eagle—whose high-flying, exhilarating antics give a new meaning to frolicking with a lifelong mate.

To reduce their aggression and synchronize their desires, amorous eagles fly together in three different, whirling, heart-stopping shows. The chase display is like watching two black kites connected by a string that are diving, looping, and erratically zigzagging in unseen winds across the sky. This flight truly replicates that of a roller coaster. One eagle rises to a great height, peaks, and then plummets to earth. Before hitting the ground, it flaps its wings and once again begins a steep ascent in a Red Baron–like barnstorming show designed to capture the attention of its mate. But the real thriller is the cartwheel display, in which the eagles soar high in the sky, lock their talons together, and then simply free-fall, spiraling down toward the earth in a great ball of feathers. Just as they are about to crash, they disengage and then fly away together, their high-pitched cries ringing in the air in a resounding declaration of their attraction and affection.

Can you and your mate soar as eagles tonight and display your love for one another?

I "fly" into my lover's arms to recapture our passion.

"God not only plays dice with the universe, but sometimes throws them where we can't see them."

—ENGLISH PHYSICIST STEPHEN HAWKING

INTERDEPENDENCIES

Sometimes nature's interdependencies can do more to restore order to the natural world than can man. Take, for instance, how Britain was able to bring back the large blue butterfly *Maculinea arion* from extinction in 1979. The butterfly was successfully reintroduced into the wild when scientists discovered a complex interdependence between two species. The large blue lays its eggs on wild thyme bushes. When the newborn caterpillar falls to the ground, it's picked up by one particular species of red ant, which believes the caterpillar is one of its own grubs. The ant drags the caterpillar to its nest, where it's kept safe while it gorges on the ants' grubs for nearly ten months before finally emerging as a butterfly. Because the large blue would be doomed without the intervention of the ant, naturalists are now trying to ensure that the habitats of the ants are not destroyed.

So, too, are you interdependent with nature in many ways. The dung from animals can be used as a rich, organic fertilizer; the crops that are then grown supply food for wildlife as well as farm animals. Trees that are not cut down keep a firm hold on the earth to prevent erosion as well as shed leaves that nourish the soil. Sheep provide an endless supply of wool for blankets, sweaters, and rugs. Bees produce honey and are responsible for valuable cross-pollination. Oceans, lakes, and rivers—if kept clean and flowing—offer to humanity some of the most enjoyable and popular playgrounds as well as life-giving sustenance to countless species.

I marvel at interdependencies that come from the creator.

"I am old, it is true; but not old enough to fail to see things as they are."
—CHEROKEE INDIAN WHITE SHIELD

TAKE OFF YOUR BLINDERS

There's much you can do to save the earth. Through the many roles you fulfill in your life—corporate employee, voter, citizen, parent, and consumer—you can make an impact upon company policy, laws that are enacted, the way your children learn about and treat the planet, and the things you purchase. But do you truly see what needs to be done, or do you choose to look away or feign ignorance in the face of the decimation of the planet—for example, in the candy wrapper that your child tosses on the ground and you choose to leave behind?

Horses that draw buggies around cities or that are ridden by mounted police on their patrols wear blinders to prevent them from seeing more than what lies ahead of them. But horses used for pleasure wear no blinders and can see all around them. When you live your life solely by seeing just what you want to see or what's comfortable for you to notice, then you go through life wearing blinders. The city horse that follows the same route every day would see a very different route if its blinders were removed. You, too, can experience a very different—and less nature-indifferent life—when you can take off the blinders and see that there's a whole world that needs your help.

How would you feel if all those things you took for granted—flowers and trees, birds and bees—were taken away from you without any warning? That's what can happen when you refuse to see. From this moment on, remember that the answers and solutions lie within you. Resolve to nurture nature instead of ignoring it.

I take off the blinders to see what I need to do to ensure a healthy future for my planet.

"When you lose the rhythm of the drumbeat of God, you are lost from the peace and rhythm of life."

—CHEYENNE PROVERB

"BURNING BOWL" CEREMONY

Traditions honoring the light and dark transitions of winter have been celebrated since the time when humans lived in this country in tribes. Wise tribal heads, who understood the need for spiritual renewal when the seasons changed and darkness came early, created rituals for encouraging the return of the sun, letting go of the mistakes of the past, and creating possibilities for the future.

In the glow of firelight, the tribe would gather in a circle around a blazing fire. Drums would beat steadily in the background. One at a time, members of the tribe would sing, chant, or speak of a wish for the future, a desire for the present, or a memory from the past. Then they would take an object created for the ceremony and toss it into the fire. The voices of the tribe would join in as the object burned while the speaker prayed. The one who prayed would ask what needed to be done to make a hope come true, what new strengths could be developed to let go of a past memory, and what could be done in the present to realize a desire. After all the members of the tribe had contributed their words, tossed their objects into the fire, and offered their silent prayers, the tribe would dance to the beat of the drums.

Even though you may not look forward to the approach of winter, you can think of ways in which this season brings good into your life. Keep the words of American painter Andrew Wyeth in mind: "I prefer winter and fall," he said, "when you feel the bone structure of the landscape—the loneliness of it—the dead feeling of winter. Something waits beneath it—the whole story doesn't show."

I focus my prayers on the good that comes out of winter.

"Winter is fury—and white silence. It can freeze a blade of grass with a glance. . . . Winter is the jealous season; it demands two distinct years for a single appearance. Mercilessly, it strips the orange and russet from autumn and looks defiantly ahead for spring to step onstage."

—AMERICAN JOURNALIST AND WRITER JIM BISHOP

KEEPING WINTER AT BAY

Winter's activities can sometimes subdue the spirit, cause unexplained feelings of melancholy and sadness, and create a view of life as an endless, storm-swept place of desolation. The upcoming holidays—when it seems that everyone is having such fun planning events, parties, and joyful gatherings—can be heart-wrenching if you're depressed, alone, or have recently lost a loved one. Couple these feelings with the reduced daylight hours during this season and the sad sounds of the wailing wind—once described by English novelist George Eliot as "nature's funeral cries for what has been and is not"—and each day can seem to fall upon your shoulders like heavy, wet snow.

There are things you can do to make this winter more enjoyable and less depressing than past winters. If your budget allows, regularly purchase fresh-cut flowers and place them around your home where you'll notice their bright colors and springlike smells—your bedroom or den, for instance. Grow herbs in an indoor garden and use them to enhance the flavor of the dishes you prepare. Pin posters and photographs that depict nature in spring and summer growth to your workplace bulletin board. Get outdoors as much as possible and for as long as you can so you'll enjoy being indoors more. Purchase an ant farm from a children's toy store and watch their daily-life activities. Adopt an animal from a local shelter. Discover those things in life that can bring you joy.

I bring joy, life, and growth into my home.

"Softness triumphs over hardness, feebleness over strength. What is more malleable is always superior over that which is immovable. This is the principle of controlling things by going along with them, of mastery through adaptation."

—SPIRITUALIST LAO-TZU

INNER STRENGTHS

The parable about the bet the wind made with the sun provides a good example of the difference between visible power and inner strength. The wind bet the sun that it could make a man who was walking along the road remove his jacket. The wind blew furiously at and around the man, frantic to prove itself right and win the bet. But the man only pulled his coat tighter around him. Then the sun took its turn. The sun gently beat its warm rays down on the man, and soon the man eagerly removed his coat.

Such is the difference between a power that strives to control and violently manipulate and a strength that gently cajoles. Try as it might, the wind—its effects so much more dramatic than the sun's—was incapable of getting the man to remove his jacket, while the sun, merely by gently caressing with its powerful warmth, easily triumphed over its blustery rival.

You may think that acting like you're a mountain of granite—immovable, steadfast, and uncompromising—means others will perceive you as strong. But remember that just a single, continuous, steady drip of water can eventually bore a hole into a mountain as easily as a drill, even though the water is fluid, changeable, and therefore seemingly weak. The strengths that lie within you are often not visible, but they can certainly make the greatest impact in your life.

I am stronger than I think I am; my strengths are within me.

"Life is a child playing around your feet, a tool you hold firmly in your grip, a bench you sit down upon in the evening, in your garden . . ."
—FRENCH DRAMATIST JEAN ANOUILH

LIVING MINUTE BY MINUTE

The cat that stretches out contentedly in the sun thinks of nothing more than the sheer enjoyment of the present moment. Moments later, the cat may begin to clean itself, become aware of its hunger, or set off on a hunt for mice. But until the moment when the cat stretches and rises from its glorious spot in the sun, it is free from anxiety and worry. The cat is one with the moment.

Can you, too, participate fully in such moments of pleasure, contentment, and happiness and enjoy them to their fullest? Or are you partially in the moment and partially out of it, your mind wondering what to do next or worrying over what has past?

If you're like most people, you probably spend fifty-nine minutes, fifty-nine seconds every hour living in the past with regret, shame, guilt, longing, or the desire to escape or in the future, which you may look forward to with anticipation or dread. Rare is the person who knows the trick of truly living in the present.

Writer Storm Jameson once penned, "There is only one world, the world pressing in on you at this minute. There is only one minute in which you are alive, *this minute*—here and now. The only way to live is by accepting each minute as an unrepeatable miracle. Which is exactly what it is—a miracle and unrepeatable."

Today, live each minute. Enjoy all the simple pleasures that you're blessed to experience. You'll never be able to be in the same minute—or experience the same miracles in that minute—again.

I live each miraculous minute to the fullest.

"I have always longed to be a part of the outward life, to be out there at the edge of things, to let the human taint wash away in emptiness and silence . . . to return to the town as a stranger."

—ENGLISH NATURE WRITER J. A. BAKER

SEEKING SOLITUDE

Can you imagine living on the earth at a time when a half day's walk—a matter of a few hours—took you far from civilization? Today a half day's walk takes you into another town; even a simple five-mile road race often winds its way through a few different communities from start to finish.

Getting away from it all—if "it all" means evidence of civilized life such as people, homes, businesses, radios, televisions, streetlights, mailboxes, sidewalks, barking dogs, power lines, and telephones—is next to impossible in this century. Tours and expeditions that brag about how deep into a canyon they go, or how isolated their island or mountain retreat is, guide you into nature with others, thereby countering, to some extent, your need to get away. Or they take you along well-worn paths that you know have been tramped down by countless others before you. Even part of the Outward Bound program in which you spend twenty-four hours in solitude, with only a journal and matches, has a sense of unreality about it, for others know your whereabouts and, after a night's sleep, will return for you.

Perhaps the truth is that in the world today, you can never be part of a life in which undiscovered, uncharted territories entice you away from humanity. Perhaps you'll always end up going where someone else has gone before or where someone will soon be. But when you can find those places and times of emptiness and silence, be sure to revel in them for as long as you can.

I refuse to give up my search for spaces of natural solitude.

"I shouldn't be surprised if it hailed a good deal tomorrow," Eeyore was saying. "Blizzards and whatnot. Being fine today doesn't Mean Anything. It has no sig—what's that word? Well, it has none of that. It's just a small piece of weather."

—ENGLISH POET AND NOVELIST A. A. MILNE

WINTER'S DEPENDABLE WEATHER

Each winter day presents you with "just a small piece of weather"—a temporary occurrence that has an impact on your life. Cold, bitter winds penetrate like needles through several layers of clothing, numb your skin, and blow you back indoors. Icy rains coat the ground with a slick polish that places surefootedness in jeopardy and forces you to walk like a penguin. Deep drifts of dry snow pile high on your walkways and driveway, bury your car, and enslave you with hours of back-breaking, shoulder-wrenching activity. "We get a little snow," writes American humorist Garrison Keillor, "then a few inches, then another inch or two, and sometimes we get a ton. The official snow gauge is a Sherwin-Williams paint can stuck to the table behind the town garage, with the famous Sherwin-Williams globe and red paint spilling over the Arctic icecap. When snow is up to the top of the world, then there is a ton of snow."

Yet why do you feel so overwhelmed and disheartened by each dose of winter weather? It's the same weather that has come your way this same time every year for the past however many years. Why are you surprised and even shocked at nature's natural winter actions—were you expecting balmy, tropical breezes and sunny, cloudless skies? If anything, winter weather is dependable. And isn't that one of the qualities you admire most in someone—dependability?

I see nature as a dependable friend rather than a heartless enemy.

"Pourchot is a big man. . . . He is well over six feet. . . . The muscles in his arms are strong from many hundreds of miles of paddling. This salmon, nonetheless, is dragging him up the beach. The fish leaps into the air, thrashes at the river surface, and makes charging runs of such thrust that Pourchot has no choice but to follow or break the line. He follows—fifty, seventy-five yards down the river with the salmon. The fish now changes plans and goes upstream. Pourchot follows. The struggle lasts thirty minutes, and the energy drawn away is almost half Pourchot's."

—AMERICAN WRITER AND NATURALIST JOHN McPHEE

WASTELESSNESS

In his book *Coming into the Country,* John McPhee wrote about what many consider to be the only remaining wilderness in the United States, in Alaska. He learned much about the Forest Eskimos, who live in five small villages on the Kobuk River, and how salmon are as valuable a commodity to them as the oil piped through the Trans-Alaska Pipeline. "We must have fish to live," the people say, and they use every part of the salmon in a way that you might never be able to comprehend even though you enjoy your lox, salmon pâté, or a grilled salmon steak or fillet. They eat the salmon eggs. They roast, smoke, fry, boil, and dry the flesh. They bury the fish heads in leaf-lined pits and leave them there for weeks; the resulting product is a cheeselike delicacy. Fermented salmon is placed on the neck and nose to treat colds and fevers. Salmon feed the sled dogs that the people depend upon for transportation; the dogs eat whole fish as well as the fins, intestines, and bones discarded by the people. One family might use as many as a thousand salmon a year, without wasting or discarding an ounce!

Can you begin to shop for and prepare your meals in such a way that you use all of what you buy, discarding and wasting nothing?

I cherish and value the food I eat.

"This moment, this being, is the thing. My life is all life in little. The moon, the planets, pass around my heart. The sun, now hidden by the round bulk of this earth, shines onto me, and in me as well. The gods and the angels both good and bad are like the hairs of my own head, seemingly numberless, and growing from within. I people the cosmos from myself, it seems, yet what am I? A puff of dust, or a brief coughing spell, with emptiness and silence to follow."

—WRITER ALEXANDER ELIOT

THE THREE FORCES OF LIFE

There are three forces that guide not only humans, but all living things: creation, or birth; destruction, or death; and maintenance, or the interval between creation and destruction, also known as life. Even though your life follows the forces sequentially—birth, life, and death—all three forces exist in the universe simultaneously. As someone or something is being created, someone or something else is being maintained and someone or something else is being destroyed. "This I understand," Italian writer Italo Svevo once penned, "Mother Nature is a maniac. That is to say, she has a mania for reproduction. She maintains life within an organism so long as there is hope of its reproducing itself. Then she kills it off, and does so in the most diverse ways because of her other mania of remaining mysterious."

Mystery or not, accept that these three forces are, in a nutshell, your life, and you can make the most of each moment of your life. How can you do this?

- Connect with and enjoy nature each day.
- Stay centered and focused even in the most stressful and chaotic situations.
- Be a child; enjoy fantasy and play.
- Remain open to new possibilities.
- Accept the changes that result from the progression of time.

I make the most of each of my life forces.

"The lights of the aurora moved and shifted over the horizon. . . . Great streamers of bluish white zigzagged like a tremendous trembling curtain from one end of the sky to the other. Streaks of yellow and orange and red shimmered along the flowing borders. Never for a moment were they still. . . ."

—AMERICAN TEACHER AND WRITER SIGURD OLSON

GETTING IN MOTION

Do you experience times in your life when you feel so run-down or blue that you just want to withdraw from all activity? Perhaps you plop down on the couch in front of the television and remain there for hours. Maybe you find talking to people so draining that you take the phone off the hook. Taking it easy or withdrawing from people every once in a while is a healthy way to recharge depleted energy. But when you can't get out of such doldrums, it's not just your body that suffers but your mind and spirit as well. Painter-inventor Leonardo da Vinci once said, "Iron rusts from disuse, water loses its purity from stagnation . . . even so does inaction sap the vigors of the mind." So the cure for lack of motivation, a foggy mind, and a disinterest in life is to get in motion!

Exercise keeps the muscles toned, moves the blood, and pumps oxygen to the brain for sharper concentration. You don't have to run a marathon, spend the day downhill or cross-country skiing, chop a pile of wood, or pump iron to get moving. Simply take a walk. Walk in the fields, in the woods, along a riverbank. Remember, "Nature ever flows; stands never still," as American poet and essayist Ralph Waldo Emerson observed. "Motion or change is her mode of existence." So, too, can it be yours. Let motion override low energy, and you'll soon get your rusty wheels turning!

I walk at least ten minutes every day.

"Each day in the old times in summer and in winter, we came down to the river to bathe. This strengthened and toughened our firm skin."

—CHEROKEE INDIAN CHIPAROPAI

FORGIVENESS

The fall and winter season are perfect times to reconnect with old friends and family members. Holidays provide the perfect excuses to send cheery cards and "catch-up" letters, to make telephone calls, and to extend invitations to others as well as to accept them. If you have any loose ends in your life, however—a family feud that rages on, resentment or anger toward a parent or an ex-partner, or guilt over a hurt you inflicted upon someone else—it may be difficult for you to initiate contact with some people. Something that has gone wrong that remains wrong can convince you there's nothing you can do to make things right.

But imagine what your life would be like if every time something went wrong—at the first sign of opposition—you fell down. You would become so bruised and battered that you would eventually grow too weak to rise. But if you can start today to refuse to fall down when something or someone challenges you, then you can learn how to stand tall, be strong, and overcome adversity and criticism.

This year, seize the opportunity to defuse an old hostility or make amends for a past transgression. Send a forgiveness card or letter to someone with whom you'd like to make a clean beginning or atone for the past. A simple greeting might be: "Sorry that we've lost touch. I'd like to forget whatever has gone on between us in the past and begin anew. If this isn't what you'd like, then please accept my blessings for good wishes, health, and happiness this season. If this is what you'd like, too, then I want you to know how much I look forward to hearing from you." Sometimes it takes extending a hand to be offered a hand.

I send a "forgiveness card" to someone I'd like back in my life.

"It probably doesn't matter if, while trying to be modest and eager watchers of life's many spectacles, we sometimes look clumsy or get dirty or ask stupid questions or reveal our ignorance or say the wrong thing or light up with wonder like the children we all are."

—AMERICAN WRITER AND NATURALIST DIANE ACKERMAN

LIVING EARTH ECSTATICALLY

Diane Ackerman describes herself as "an earth-ecstatic and a poet." An enthusiastic woman who has boundless energy, she has made expeditions from her home in Ithaca, New York, to the far reaches of the earth to write articles for *The New Yorker* about a wide range of living things—penguins, bats, whales, and crocodiles; traveled to a New Mexico cattle ranch to learn how to be a cowboy, an adventure that she described in *Twilight of the Tenderfoot;* and has learned how to fly a small plane from visits to a variety of airports, chronicled in *On Extended Wings.*

In addition to her prose and poetry collections, Diane has also written *A Natural History of the Senses,* a book that truly captures her enthusiasm for life. The book not only offers an exploration of the origin and evolution of the senses, but also delves into how each of the senses can be used to learn about and connect more intimately with the natural world. She writes, for instance, "In the Hall of Gems at the Museum of Natural History in New York, I once stood in front of a huge piece of sulfur so yellow I began to cry. . . . At the time, I called the emotion wonder and thought: Isn't it extraordinary to be alive on a planet where there are yellows such as this?" Because she feels that most people don't take the time to develop a sensual appreciation for life's natural wonders, her biggest concern is that "The sensory misers will inherit the earth, but first they will make it not worth living on."

I am ecstatic about the earth.

"The country lay bare and entirely leafless around him, and he thought that he had never seen so far and so intimately into the inside of things as on that winter day when Nature was deep in her annual slumber and seemed to have kicked her clothes off."

—ENGLISH WRITER KENNETH GRAHAME

RISKING INTIMACY

Not letting others know who you really are—your thoughts, your feelings, your dreams, your goals, your background, and your wants and needs—is like spending hours climbing up a mountain and then stopping just short of the summit. While being outdoors, breathing in the clean air, feeling the physical exertion of the climb, and ascending higher with each step are enjoyable, not being able to appreciate the view from the top deprives you of truly being able to experience the climb.

While risking full openness, through emotional intimacy, and intense closeness, through physical intimacy, isn't always easy—letting close friends give you a hug, for example, or spending time just snuggling with your life partner—the discomfort and pain of not letting anyone close to your heart can far outweigh potential areas of discomfort. The pain of alienation can diminish you as you lose your sense of attachment to others.

Intimacy, however, is a gift. It can help you discover ways in which you're like others, foster greater trust and honesty in your relationships, help you to develop faith, and nurture healthy personal growth. Think about why you may be keeping intimacy at bay with a friend, family member, or loved one. Then consider these words of American writer, poet, and naturalist Annie Dillard: "I startled a weasel who startled me, and we exchanged a long glance. . . . Our eyes locked, and someone threw away the key."

I risk intimacy and so experience life more meaningfully.

> *"I had no idea nature made so much noise."*
> —AMERICAN WRITER RICHARD POWERS

NATURE'S "SURROUND-SOUNDS"

Take a walk in the woods on an early winter morning and you'll find that even with an insulating blanket of fresh snow, the woods are far from silent. Listen to the wailing, whooshing sounds made by the chilling wind as it stirs the pine boughs and shakes snow from them. Hear the *snap-snap-snap* sounds made by the bare, shivering, ice-coated tree branches as they chatter against each other in the wind. Listen to the groans and moans and then sometimes the sharp, rifle-shot reports that reverberate from the expansion and contraction of ice on a lake. Hear the howl of a far-off wolf or the cry of the owl in the predawn hours.

Or go for a winter morning walk on a beach. Listen to the waves roar as they race to the shore, like dozens of young athletes rushing onto a playing field for the championship game with their biggest rivals. Then hear the waves crash upon the beach, making sounds described by Irish writer James Joyce as "a fourworded wavespeech: *seesoo, hrss, rsseeiss, ooos.* Vehement breath of waters amid seasnakes, rearing horses, rocks. In cups of rocks it slops: *flop, slop, slap*: bounded in barrels. And, spent, its speech ceases. It flows purling, wisely flowing, floating foampool, flower unfurling."

Or simply listen to the sounds outside your bedroom window. You might hear the woodpecker, with its incessant, head-banging drilling; the raucous call of blue jays; the chattering complaints of squirrels. The sounds of nature can at times be soothing and at other times quite deafening—filled with grunts, drummings, squeaks, roars, clatters, bangs, and deep moans.

I appreciate the silences as well as the noises offered to me by nature.

December 12

> *"To those who have not yet learned the secret of true happiness, begin now to study the little things in your own door yard."*
>
> —AMERICAN BOTANIST GEORGE WASHINGTON CARVER

SENSES OF THE SEASON

Are childhood memories triggered for you at this time of year? The smell of freshly baked bread that invades your senses from the bakery near work may remind you of the times you sat on a stool in your grandmother's kitchen, helping her sift the flour for her special holiday bread. You may remember how you watched her strong hands knead the dough, then later marveled at how delicious baking bread made the whole kitchen smell and what it was like to eat a slice of steaming-hot and moist bread. Or whenever you breathe in the scent of freshly cut pine as you pass by Christmas-tree-and-wreath stands, you may remember your father's workshop in the basement—filled with the smells of clean, fresh wood shavings—and how he would listen to the football games on the radio while hammering, sanding, and staining.

Too, the sight of your childhood home as you turn into the driveway, the scent of your mother's perfume and the soft caress of the collar of her jacket as you embrace, the sound of a fire crackling in the fireplace, the taste of sugar cookies warm from the oven may return you to a time in your life when the holidays were filled with childhood glee and delightful discoveries.

Make this upcoming holiday season a time when you appreciate the people, places, and things in your life that have made you feel warm and comforted. Even though you may live far from home or a beloved relative will no longer share the holiday with you, remember that your happy memories are always near at hand—as close as your own back door—for they live forever in your heart.

I close my eyes and sense wonderful memories from the past.

"Remember that you are this universe and this universe is you."
—NATIVE AMERICAN (CREEK) WRITER JOY HARJO

LIVING IS NOW

Many learned people from all professions have, over the years, pondered the meaning of life. French writer André Gide once said, quite simply, "Life eludes logic." Former California governor Jerry Brown determined that "Life just is. You have to flow with it. Give yourself to the moment. Let it happen." Writer Kurt Vonnegut decided, "Life happens too fast for you to ever think about it. If you could just persuade people of this, but they insist on amassing information." Theologian Elbert Hubbard advised that "The best way to prepare for life is to begin to live." Philosopher Kierkegaard opined, "Life is not a problem to be solved but a reality to be experienced." Filmmaker Federico Fellini said, "There is no end. There is no beginning. There is only the infinite passion of life." And writer Havelock Ellis mused, "Dreams are real while they last. Can we say more of life?"

But perhaps French writer Albert Camus gave the best advice when he surmised, "If there is a sin against life, it consists perhaps not so much in despairing of life as in hoping for another life and in eluding the implacable grandeur of this life." Polish-born French chemist Marie Curie echoed this sentiment by saying, "All my life through, the new sights of Nature made me rejoice like a child." In reality, the only meaning to life that needs to concern you is the moment-by-moment existence you go through. It's the breath you take at this second, the blink of your eyes as you read this page, the finger that absentmindedly scratches your nose, and the thoughts that float through the corridors of your mind. There is no secret to life or to living. Life is now. Living is now.

I live totally in the present moment so I can appreciate each moment.

"Don't carry a lantern in moonlight."

—JAPANESE PROVERB

AN INNER GLOW

Have you ever met people who seem to have a glow about them—a brightness, an ability to illuminate even the darkest times? Not only does it seem as if they themselves are lit up like a Christmas tree, all cheery and bright, but it's as if they light up everything and everyone who comes in contact with them. Pets as well as wild animals gravitate toward them, instantly tamed. Their outdoor gardens flourish, houseplants thrive, and "sick" plants they take in are "cured." They hike up and down rugged mountain trails with boundless energy. Their telephone is always ringing, and people often visit, drawn to them like bees to flowers.

You can develop a similar light within you. All this requires is a shift in attitude from what you consider to be important in your daily life—petty arguments, silly conflicts, or financial worries, for example, which can dim the light within you—to what you consider to be important in you. Focus on how you can best connect with the people, places, and things around you in positive ways. Like a landscaper who must prune bushes and trees to keep them healthy and strong, you need to cut off those things that take valuable nourishment away from you. You then grow luminous each day by keeping your life light, open, and free. As American writer and naturalist Henry David Thoreau once wrote, "Once it chanced that I stood at the very abutment of a rainbow's arch, which filled the lower stratum of the atmosphere, tinging the grass and leaves around, and dazzling me as if I looked through colored crystal. It was a lake of rainbow light, in which, for a short while, I lived like a dolphin."

I nurture the glow within me.

"The garden could serve as a metaphor for the whole school. Outside its wire fence: cracked sidewalks, smashed beer bottles, the emblems and detritus of an urban slum. Inside: plants, flowers, vegetables, pathways—all orderly and thriving."

—*BOSTON GLOBE* WRITER FRED KAPLAN

A GARDEN OF LEARNING

The Harriet Tubman Elementary School, located in one of the worst urban neighborhoods in Newark, New Jersey, is an "island of excellence," as it was once described by a national education panel. Even though the public school's four hundred or so students are mainly poor and black and live within three blocks of the school, which qualifies them as the socioeconomic group most likely to score poorly on national tests, many Harriet Tubman students regularly score above their grade level in math, writing, and reading.

On the outside, the school looks different from other buildings around it. No windows are broken. There's no litter, no graffiti. Inside, each class has a teacher and a paid teacher's assistant. A local physician who was impressed by the school comes each spring to teach a once-a-week anatomy class. A first-grade class is studying an intricate plastic model of the human body; sixth graders are constructing electromagnets. And all students participate in the "living laboratory"—an abandoned lot the school acquired from the city's Adopt-a-Lot program that the students converted into a vegetable garden. With the help of college agricultural students and neighbors who allow use of hoses for watering, students tend the garden and then pick ripe vegetables to take home and eat. "We don't accept poverty as an excuse for not learning," comments principal Delores Ollie. "We don't accept any excuses for not learning. . . . I'm trying to nurture leaders."

I nurture the garden of learning in local school systems.

"And that was another gap between us. Between all men and all insects. We humans, saddled for a lifetime with virtually the same body, naturally find it difficult to imagine a life in which you can, at a single stroke, outside a fairy tale, just by splitting your skin and stepping out, change into something utterly different."

—WELSH HIKER AND WRITER COLIN FLETCHER

OPENING YOUR HEART

Just as there are differences between you and living things in the natural world, so are their differences between you and other people with whom you share this planet. Some of these people are more fortunate than you—capable of making financial, emotional, physical, and spiritual changes in their lives—but many are less fortunate, unable to make changes, and so could benefit from your help.

Every day hungry and homeless men, women, and children wander streets and alleys searching Dumpsters for scraps, lining up outside crowded shelters and soup kitchens for a once-a-day meal, or panhandling. Every day an elderly person living on a limited budget is shut in and therefore shut out of the ebb and flow of life. Every day adults as well as children battle debilitating and life-threatening diseases and injuries. Every day a disabled person faces numerous challenges.

You can provide welcome change for at least one person on this planet today. Share your abundance with those who may go to bed hungry tonight by donating a bag of groceries to a local food pantry. Deliver a meal to or have coffee with a shut-in. Raise money from pledge sheets and participate in road races and walks to benefit research needed to fight diseases. Provide financial support for a disabled person's companion dog or wheelchair, read to someone who's blind, or volunteer carpooling services to those who are unable to get around on their own.

I open my heart and give to others.

"While we exist as human beings, we are like tourists on holiday. If we play havoc and cause disturbance, our visit is meaningless. If during our short stay—100 years at most—we live peacefully, help others and, at the very least, refrain from harming or upsetting them, our visit is worthwhile."
—TIBETAN BUDDIST SPIRITUAL LEADER THE DALAI LAMA

SAVING YOUR EARTH

Nobody can make you "save the Earth" against your wishes. You can leave all the lights on in your house twenty-four hours a day, drive a gas-guzzling car, waste food, refuse to recycle, leave trash behind at the beach and in the woods, kill for sport, and illegally dispose of hazardous materials. But doing any or all of these things—or supporting such behaviors in others—slowly destroys the planet.

Just as you can destroy the planet, so, too, can you save it. You can play an integral role, through the collective ability of the human race, to do good things for future generations and the rest of life on Earth. To do so, you need to take personal responsibility—personal responsibility that's as much about future generations as it is about those with whom you share your short tenancy here. The beliefs of some cultures already embody such an ideal. The Hopi Indians, for example, believe that the interests of the seventh generation should play as significant a role as the interests of those people in the present generation, who are making daily decisions about the quality of their lives.

What personal responsibility boils down to, then, is the umbilical link not only between you and your children, but to all of humankind, all living things, and all of nature's picturesque and open places that compose Earth's natural heritage.

I strive to live as earth-consciously as possible.

> *"Is it politically reprehensible, while we are all groaning, under the shackles of the capitalist system, to point out that life is frequently more worth living because of a blackbird's song, a yellow elm tree in October, or some other natural phenomenon which does not cost money . . . ?"*
> —ENGLISH WRITER GEORGE ORWELL

ACHIEVING GREATNESS

There once was a little boy who always wanted the biggest of everything because he thought the biggest was the greatest. One day he was invited to dinner at a friend's house. He took the biggest piece of meat, but it was tough and gristly. He took the biggest baked potato, but it was uncooked in the middle. He grabbed the biggest piece of chocolate cake, but it was bitter and stale. The moral of the story: The biggest isn't always the greatest.

But the boy was too young and stubborn to accept such a truth. He always expected the biggest box under the Christmas tree, even though the box invariably contained something he thought wasn't the greatest, such as a shirt or a sweater. He went to college and chose his major based on the biggest paycheck he could earn, but later discovered that his salary wasn't the greatest. He bought the biggest house, but found the house too hard to heat in the winter and too difficult to cool in the summer.

Then, one morning as he lay snuggled under the biggest pile of blankets, he noticed a tiny bird perched on the balcony railing, its feathers fluffed up to protect itself against the bitter wind. The man left his warm bed, carefully opened the balcony door, stepped onto the snow-covered balcony in bare feet, and coaxed the tiny bird onto his palm. Then he returned to the room, closed the door, gently cradled the bird in his hands, and blew his warm breath upon it. And it was on that day that the man achieved greatness, for he had made the biggest difference.

I know that greatness is achieved through deeds and not debts.

"It's funny how dogs and cats know the inside of folks better than other folks do, isn't it?"

—AMERICAN CHILDREN'S WRITER AND NOVELIST
ELEANOR H. PORTER

ANIMAL CONNECTIONS

At this moment dogs and cats are bringing joy, friendship, healing, laughter, comfort, and love into the hearts and homes of millions of people. For nearly twenty years, an organization known as the Delta Society has supported studies to learn just how such companion animals so dramatically affect the health and well-being of their owners through the ability to create powerful and meaningful human-animal bonds.

Yet centuries ago, Native American people understood the significant connection not only between people and animals, but also between animals and natural phenomena. What is thought of today as Devils Tower National Monument in Wyoming, for instance, was, according to Indian lore, the place where two Indian children climbed to escape from a giant bear. To get at the children, the bear clawed the rocks, thereby creating the ragged, grooved surface seen today. As the children tried to leap higher, away from the reach of the bear, they flew up into the sky, where they burst into the stars now scattered about the night sky.

Pawnee Indian Eagle Chief once explained the great importance animals have in the lives of people. "In the beginning of all things," he said, "wisdom and knowledge were with the animals, for Tirawa, the One Above, did not speak directly to man. He sent certain animals to tell men that he showed himself through the beasts, and that from them, and from the stars and the sun and the moon should man learn."

I learn much from the love I give to and receive from an animal.

"The family—that dear octopus from whose tentacles we never quite escape, nor, in our innermost hearts, ever quite wish to."
—ENGLISH WRITER AND PLAYWRIGHT DODIE SMITH

FAMILY MATTERS

Holidays focus on families. Because of this, it may be hard to escape old hurts or unhappy memories when you return to your childhood home or interact with your parents. It may be hard not to feel as if you're an unhappy child all over again, and you may spend your holiday trying once more to get the love, attention, support, validation, or apologies you may not have gotten from your mother and father when you were growing up. In effect, you may want your parents now to finally make you happy and to give you the happiness you believe they deprived you of in childhood.

But not only can't you expect someone to give you happiness, you also can't change your childhood. What you can strive to do now as an adult, however, is to reconnect with your parents today, to create a good relationship now—and possibly in the future. Belgian philosopher Raoul Vaneigem once advised how to live life more meaningfully in the present: "Our task is not to rediscover nature but to remake it." So, too, can you remake your relationship with your parents in order to become a happier son or daughter.

Today, you need to keep in mind that your relationship is no longer parent to child—it has been remade into adult to adult. So instead of making demands on your parents, expect less from them. Rather than carry old grudges and hurts with you when you go home for the holidays or your parents come to visit you, take a moment to think about all the things you appreciate about your parents—the little things they've done for you or kind or considerate words they've said to you.

I am happy with my parents of today.

"It is the general belief of the Indians that after a man dies his spirit is somewhere on the earth or in the sky, we do not know exactly where, but we are sure that his spirit still lives."

—SIOUX INDIAN CHASED-BY-BEARS

LIFE EVERLASTING

Holidays can sometimes be painful reminders of the loved ones you've lost. A parent, grandparent, child, husband or wife, best friend, or even a pet may no longer be with you this season; an empty, hollow space is carved in your heart.

But what if today you were to imagine a place on the earth, in the sky, or at the ocean where your loved one would want to be? Maybe you picture your dog running free in the woods, nose pointed excitedly to the ground, hot on the trail of a wonderful scent. Perhaps you see your grandfather fishing on his favorite lake, sitting in his rowboat as an early-morning mist rises over the water and the cry of the loons provides him with soothing background music. Maybe you see your mother tending to her rose garden on a sunny summer day, her hands delicately working through the blooms. Perhaps you think about your best friend realizing a dream to rocket from planet to planet in outer space.

When you can think in such ways, you never really lose anyone in your life, for you're always able to see the living world as full of the spirits of friends, relatives, and lovers. You can still hear their voices in the murmuring of mountain springs, the whispering in the wind through the pines, the cries of the eagle and the hawk, the trills of the songbirds, the shouts of the jungle animals. You can still see their smiles in sparkling waves. You can still feel their touch in the warm caress of the sun on your body; their kisses can be felt once again whenever you look up at the sky and feel the gentle rain or wet snowflakes upon your lips.

I trust in the spiritual afterlife of loved ones.

"Never make your home in a place. Make a home for yourself inside your own head. You'll find what you need to furnish it—memory, friends you can trust, love of learning, and other such things. That way it will go with you wherever you journey."

—AMERICAN WRITER TAD WILLIAMS

"HOME IS WHERE THE HEART IS"

As much as you may love your home, if you had to lose it or leave it, you can still create a home elsewhere. Even if a home is shared with other family members, even if a home is just you and your pets, or even if a home is a bed, half of a room, and a shared bathroom in a dormitory or crowded barracks, you can still call such locales home. For home is a feeling deep within you; four walls, a roof, windows, and a couple of doors are just the physical space of where you live, not the essential components that comfort and connect you with the world.

There can be much truth in the saying "Home is where the heart is," for wherever your heart is, that can also be where your home is. Too, there's much truth in the saying as it applies to the nesting, home-building world of wild, living things. For young kangaroos, opossums, and other marsupials, home is simply a pouch. Other species raise their young and seek shelter on the ground, in the ground, in water, on branches, in tree trunks, on the sides of cliffs in abandoned nests of other animals, in natural cavities and rock crevices, in homes built from scratch—or even in your own home. American nature writer John Hay once remarked, "I cannot forever keep out the woodpecker that mistakes my house for a dead tree." Nor can you keep out the squirrels, chimney-nesting birds, the skunk under your shed, or the mouse that forms a cozy nest in your bag of birdseed.

Home is a feeling of comfort within me that I can take everywhere.

"Here, man is no longer the center of the world, only a witness, but a witness who is also a partner in the silent life of nature, bound by secret affinities to the trees."

—SWEDISH DIPLOMAT AND HUMANITARIAN
DAG HAMMARSKJÖLD

JOY TO THE WORLD!

At this time of year, it may be hard for you to see beyond your problems and pressures, tensions and stresses, and concerns and worries to notice the beauty of seasonal decorations, both artificial and natural. Go for a walk or take a drive around the neighborhood with friends and family in the evening and enjoy the festive home decorations. In the morning, after a stormy night, go outside and look at how the freshly fallen snow has created interesting shapes on trees and shrubs; too, look on the ground for evidence of earlier visits made by wild animals, and try to identify as many prints as you can. Go for a hike in the woods and collect fresh pine boughs, pinecones, and other woodsy items to create a forest-festive natural centerpiece and fill your home with the natural smells of the trees. Decorate your Christmas tree with store-bought ornaments as well as natural decorations that you and others have collected over the years—seashells, small rocks wrapped in a bright ribbon, acorns, bird feathers, autumn leaves, driftwood, or even a bird's nest.

Take time to get out of your own head for a few moments—a head that's swimming with details about meal preparations, flight arrivals and transportation needs, guest-room preparations, and last-minute gift wrapping and shopping. Enjoy the colors, music, smells, and sights—the "true" joys—of the world.

I celebrate this holiday season by expanding my limited picture to include all the joys of the world.

"Now, when there are billions of people, and not so many trees, it is sustaining to imagine what it might be like to open one's flowers on a spring afternoon, or to stand silently, making food out of sunlight, for a thousand years. It gives proportion to the world."
—AMERICAN WRITER DAVID RAINS WALLACE

EXPRESSIONS OF GRATITUDE

Perhaps the most wondrous gift you could give and receive today is that of gratitude—gratitude for the people in your life, gratitude for the health you've been given, gratitude for the experiences you've gone through, gratitude for the emotions you've been able to feel, gratitude for all the wonders of the world you've been able to see, and gratitude for your humanity toward others.

Perhaps the most wondrous gift you can give today to another person is one that's given from your heart, not your wallet, and from your time, not your haste. The best gift you can give is to show your gratitude for all you've been given in very simple ways by giving back in return in some way. Organize your neighbors in gathering up household goods for a community donation to a worthwhile charity. Provide a home, food, or payment for medical treatment for a rescued animal or one in a shelter. Go for a nature walk with someone who feels down. Order fresh flowers to be delivered to a shut-in. Send for brochures and newsletters from local environmental groups to become better informed about the well-being of nature in your area.

You can also express such gratitude to others. As Cherokee Indian Parra-Wa-Samen once said to a dear friend, "My heart is filled with joy when I see you here, as the brooks fill with water when the snow melts in spring. . . ."

I give a gratitude gift from my heart today.

"Have we greatly missed the things that make Christmas Day in civilization? Other loved human beings, Christmas carols, wonderful food? I suppose so, but I think that this lack is more than made up for by the deep contentment of our healthy minds and bodies, by our closeness to and awareness of the earth, and of each other."

—AMERICAN NATURALIST AND WRITER
THEODORA STANWELL-FLETCHER

"CHRISTMAS IN DRIFTWOOD VALLEY"

Award-winning nature writer Theodora Stanwell-Fletcher and her husband had "a taste for the loneliness and realism of out-of-the-way places and peoples." From August 1937 to January 1939 and again from February to September 1941, they lived in Driftwood Valley, an unexplored wilderness in north-central British Columbia. Theodora's journal of their experiences won the John Burroughs Medal for nature writing and includes details of one Christmas day at their wilderness home.

"This morning I was the first one out of bed," Theodora wrote. "It was still dark outside; dawn had not yet begun although it was long past eight. The windows were so densely frosted that it seemed as if daylight, even if it were there, could never penetrate the cabin." The thermometer that hung above their dining-room table registered twenty-five below. By the time dawn was approaching, she and her husband had scraped two peepholes in the frost on the panes and "we stood quiet to watch the winter sunrise. The radiant peaks of the Driftwoods, cut like white icing into pinnacles and rims against the green-apple sky, were brushed with pink, that, even as we watched, spread down and down and turned to gold. . . . The snow-bowed trees of the south and west shores were hung with diamonds. . . . No Christmas trees decorated by human hands were ever so exquisite as the frosted trees of this northern forest."

I marvel at the Christmas morning dawning outside my home.

"I am enjoying to the full that period of reflection which is the happiest conclusion to a life of action."

—AMERICAN WRITER WILLA CATHER

TAKING A STAND

What legacy would you like to leave to younger generations? You can start work today to shift environmental policies so the world moves in directions that don't neglect the needs of the planet—now and in the future. In doing so, you can continue to make your life worthwhile, remain active, make waves in the world around you, and be a contributing, caring, and creative member of the natural society.

One organization that represents environmental interests on an international scale is Friends of the Earth International. Founded in 1971 as a network for the exchange of information and for the funding of environmental campaigns such as global warming and marine issues, Friends of the Earth includes twenty-one industrialized nations, sixteen developing nations, and six Eastern European countries, comprising nearly a million members. Issues of concern to Friends of the Earth include tropical rain forests, the ozone layer, destructive dam construction, global warming, and marine concerns. Members are bound together by one common cause: the conservation, restoration, and rational use of the Earth's resources.

Now is the time to take and make stands. Whether you chain yourself to logging equipment to save a stand of century-old trees, provide classroom materials for raising children's awareness of nature, or sign petitions to stop aerial hunting of wolves, make your life on Earth truly active and meaningful.

I participate in the preservation and protection of the environment such as with FoEI, P.O. BOX 19199, 1000 GD Amsterdam, the Netherlands.

"Scuba diving in the Bahamas some years ago, I became aware of two things for the first time: that we carry the ocean within us; that our veins mirror the tides. . . . I was so moved my eyes teared underwater, and I mixed my saltiness with the ocean's."

—NATURALIST AND WRITER DIANE ACKERMAN

THE NOVELTY OF NATURE

Have you ever watched a gerbil on its exercise wheel? Day in and day out, the gerbil probably logs hundreds of miles of activity, but it never experiences a change of scenery or comes in contact with anything new.

American writer A. P. Herbert once noted, "Imagine how little good music there would be if, for example, a conductor refused to play Beethoven's Fifth Symphony on the grounds that his audience may have heard it before." In life, you need to stop seeing or doing the same thing over and over again; you need to do something simply because you've never done it before or reexperience in a whole new way something you've done or seen countless times before.

Even though you've already heard the birds sing, seen the sun rise and set, tasted a wild herb, or looked out over the fields, begin today to see such things in a whole new light. Even though nature doesn't proceed by leaps and bounds or make dramatic shifts and changes, it does have a certain free margin—even a vagueness—about it that allows for mystery, surprise, enjoyment, and sentiment. There are no instant replays in nature, so you must continually be alert and observant; too, there are no repeat performances, which means there's very little monotony. Be a gerbil in all your "civilized" endeavors if you so desire, but in natural pursuits, be a wanderer and wonderer.

I always find something new and exciting in nature.

"The crow came close on this cold morning. A great crow, with a neck so large and sleek one imagined it might feel to touch like stroking the sleek black arch of a horse's neck. It watched the world, and I watched its eyes and tried very hard to imagine looking out from inside that shining head, imagine what it was thinking, feeling, its cells moving about in an orderly fashion as mine moved. But nothing came to me—or I went nowhere— so locked are we in our own frames, so locked we cannot even imagine the limitations of a crow."

—AMERICAN WRITER AND NATURALIST JOSEPHINE JOHNSON

ANIMAL FEELINGS

Does an animal think? Does an animal make choices? Does an animal feel?

Anna Sewell, the author of the children's classic *Black Beauty,* once wrote, "We call them dumb animals, and so they are, for they cannot tell us how they feel, but they do not suffer less because they have no words." The rabbit that's being pursued by the fox races for its life out of instinct, for example, but surely it also feels fear, for why else would it flee? Too, the cow that loses a stillborn calf may look around the barnyard for another calf because of its maternal instinct, but surely it also feels the loss as well as needs the comforting presence of a young life.

Lois Crisler, who filmed wolves and raised a litter of wolf pups taken from its parents in the wild, was witness to many "feeling" wolf behaviors, most notably how one wolf responded when one of Lois's dogs wandered off on a daily walk. "The wolf with us ran to me, cried up to my face, then standing beside me looked searchingly around, call-howling again and again. When the dog sauntered into view the wolf bounded to him and kissed him, overjoyed." And when one dog got his nose full of porcupine quills, "the wolf Alatna hovered anxious-eyed around his face, whimpering when the dog cried in trying to tramp the quills out."

I respect the fact that all living things have feelings.

"I have been in Sorrow's kitchen and licked out all the pots. Then I have stood on the peaky mountain wrapped in rainbows, with a harp and a sword in my hands."

—AMERICAN WRITER, FOLKLORIST, AND CULTURAL
ANTHROPOLOGIST ZORA NEALE HURSTON

SHOWING YOUR TEARS

You know that it would be so much easier to get over your sorrow so you can regain your strength to face life's challenges if you had someone with whom you could share your tears, who would hold you tightly for as long as you needed to sob, to whom you could say all the things you need to say to clear your mind of the sad feelings. But too many people reject sadness because they want, instead, to see happiness. Such people want to see the world as one big universal grin, for a smile poses no threat and requires no need for meaningful discussion or a caring exchange. Tears, however, signal an emotional need that requires time, attention, and caring.

While a smile can be beautiful and can certainly be restored, it really says little about what a person truly feels inside. Tears, on the other hand, say much about a person. The Minquass Indians have a proverb: "The soul would have no rainbow if the eyes had no tears." Tears are not only your way of opening your heart to your own feelings, but a way of opening yourself up to others. So it's important that you express this emotion. Share your sadness with another. Ask for help and for a hug if you need it. There will be some people in your life who will have the ears to listen, the arms to hold you, and the time to care for you. They can be there for you, but only if you choose to open the windows of your soul to them.

I show and share my tears with a trusted friend or family member.

"He had learned this: Nothing that lived, nothing that walked or crawled or flew or swam or slithered or oozed—nothing, not one thing on God's earth wanted to die. No matter what people thought or said about chickens or fish or cattle—they all wanted to live."

—AMERICAN CHILDREN'S WRITER GARY PAULSEN

WISE ANIMAL PROTECTION

For a wild animal to live, something else has to die. It's simply a law of nature that identifies some creatures as predators and some as prey. Yet too often the most vocal animal-rights activists are those who believe that no living thing should ever be hunted, trapped, or destroyed.

Today, there's a wealth of encouraging evidence that shows how such beliefs have resulted in surging populations of nearly extinct wild species. Yet, as well, there's frightening proof that without sufficient natural as well as human predation, over-protection is causing certain species of wild animals to die horrible deaths through starvation. Overpopulation crowds habitats, shrinks territories, and ravages food sources.

In nature, populations flourish and decline depending on the availability of sustenance. What needs to be of great concern, particularly during the long winter months, is whether being a "true" animal-rights activist means understanding the need for culling populations in order to create healthy, non-stressed animals or whether the best animal-rights activists are those who so vehemently cling to the belief that inhumane effects are felt on countless wild animals. Protecting animal rights means ensuring safe, healthy environments that can adequately provide for an entire population.

I support an animal's right to live with adequate food sources.

"*If I had my life to live over again, I'd dare to make more mistakes next time. I'd relax. I would limber up. I would be sillier than I have been this trip. I would take fewer things seriously. I would take more chances. I would take more trips. I would climb more mountains and swim more rivers. I would eat more ice cream and less beans. I would perhaps have more troubles, but I'd have fewer imaginary ones.*"

—AMERICAN WRITER NADINE STAIR

TRAVELING INTO TOMORROW

The first step in your journey toward growing closer to the natural environment begins with words from the *Tao:* "A journey of a thousand miles starts with a single step." Each step in such a journey brings you closer to the strength and courage you need to face the challenges, changes, and risks presented when you allow yourself to experience the outdoors in ways you may have never allowed yourself to before. Each step brings you greater awareness and heightened sensitivity so you can truly enjoy nature's sensual pleasures and appreciate her breathtaking beauties. Each step brings you closer to the wisdom and maturity you need in order to benefit from the lessons constantly being offered in nature's living classrooms.

The journey toward growing closer to nature is different for everyone—where you go is not necessarily where others will also go; what you do is not always what others will enjoy doing; what you get out of an experience is not always what others get. And yet your journey is always one of progress—of looking ahead.

From this moment on, learn to be strong, yet yielding. Be open to all things, yet let nothing disrupt your center. Be compassionate and kind. Seek harmony with nature and within yourself. Let nature's peaceful way of life fill the days of your life.

I travel into nature to enrich my life.

Source Credits

Anderson, Lorraine, ed. *Sisters of the Earth*. New York: Vintage Books, 1991.

Berger, Terry, ed. *Garden Proverbs*. Philadelphia: Running Press, 1994.

Bergon, Frank, ed. *The Wilderness Reader*. Reno, Nevada: University of Nevada Press, 1980.

Evans, Barry. *Everyday Wonders*. Chicago: Contemporary Books, 1993.

Hughes, Holly, ed. *Meditations on Earth*. Philadelphia: Running Press, 1994.

Murray, John A., ed. *American Nature Writing 1996*. San Francisco: Sierra Club Books, 1996.

Native American Wisdom. Philadelphia: Running Press, 1994.

Readings from the Hurricane Island Outward Bound School. Hurricane Island Outward Bound, Rockland, ME, May 1991.

Songs of the Earth. Philadelphia: Running Press, 1995.